GREECE

Richard Sterling
Georgia Dacakis
Kate Reeves

WORLD FOOD Greece 1
1st edition – February 2002

Published by Lonely Planet Publications Pty Ltd ABN 36 005 607 983

Lonely Planet Offices
Australia Locked Bag 1, Footscray, Victoria 3011
USA 150 Linden Street, Oakland CA 94607
UK 10a Spring Place, London NW5 3BH
France 1 rue du Dahomey, 75011 Paris

Publishing manager Peter D'Onghia
Series editor Lyndal Hall
Series design & layout Brendan Dempsey
Editor Patrick Witton
Mapping Natasha Velleley
Photography Alan Benson

Photography
Many images in this guide are available for licensing from
Lonely Planet Images. email: lpi@lonelyplanet.com.au

Front cover – Kalamata olives
Back cover – Another busy street in Paros town, Cyclades

ISBN 1 86450 113 8

Printed by
The Bookmaker International Ltd
Printed in China

MAP KEY

○ Place to Eat & Drink		Freeway	✪	National Capital
Mall/Market		Primary Road	○	Town
Building		Secondary Road	🏛	Museum
Campus		Tertiary Road	✝	Church
Park, Garden		Lane	☪	Mosque
Sports Ground		Steps	🏰	Fortress
International Border		Wall	⚔	Ruins
		Railway, Station	🐾	Zoo

About the Authors

Richard Sterling is known as the Indiana Jones of Gastronomy for his willingness to go anywhere and court any danger for the sake of a good meal. His other books include *The Fire Never Dies*; *Dining with Headhunters*; *The Fearless Diner*; and the award winning *Travelers' Tales: A Taste of the Road*. He has been honoured by the James Beard Foundation for his food writing, and by Lowell Thomas awards for his travel literature. His lifestyle column 'Maitre d'' appears monthly in *San Francisco* magazine. Though he lives in Berkeley, California, he is very often politically incorrect.

Richard wishes to thank: Mrs Evie Voutsina for her secret knowledge of things ancient and new; Clio Tarazi for her soulful insight; the Athens chapter of the Hash House Harriers for the beer; Pamela Washington for the fun; Martha Hatzopolous for the company; and the divine Miss Eleni Dinopap for the dance.

Georgia Dacakis leads a double life. By day a university lecturer in speech pathology, by night a restaurateur of two Melbourne uptown restaurants – Cafe K, a Mediterranean bistro, and Kri Kri, a Greek mezethopoleion. Her love affair with Greek food is fuelled by annual field trips to the Greek mainland, the islands and her beloved Crete.

Kate Reeves is a Melbourne writer. Greek in her last life she plans to be Greek in the next – being reincarnated as an ancient poetess or as the fisherman/cook/owner of a hypothetical beach taverna in the Dodacanese.

John Burke studied Latin and ancient, medieval and modern Greek in Melbourne and Thessaloniki and lectured at the University of Melbourne. He translated the official Greek grammar book and examines translators and interpreters. He now researches Byzantine chronicles while working as a web publisher and database consultant. Computational linguistics is still a hobby. Editing Greek gratifies an obsessive streak. So does cooking. But his three children can't be wrong: they think wife Ersie is the better cook (she's also a writer of history books). So John mostly sticks to growing the herbs and vegetables but indulges wantonly in the dinner conversation.

About the Photographer

Alan Benson is a food and lifestyle photographer. Born in Manchester, he trained as a chef in London and now lives in Australia. He is a regular contributor to *Australian Gourmet Traveller*, among other publications.

Alan wishes to thank: Anne Kokotos from Semeli Winery for her invaluable help, and my assistants, Alex McCowan and my sister Joanne Benson, for their great help, good humour and map reading skills.

From the Publisher

This first edition of *World Food Greece* was edited by Patrick Witton and designed by Brendan Dempsey of Lonely Planet's Melbourne office with assistance from Wendy Wright. Natasha Velleley mapped, Katharine Day and Joanne Newell proofed, Lyndal Hall coordinated production and indexed. Thanks to Lonely Planet Images for coordinating the supply of photographs, and for captioning, cataloguing and pre-press work. Peter D'Onghia, manager, dealt with big picture issues, thereby releasing the team to work their magic.

WARNING & REQUEST

Things change – prices go up, schedules change, good places go bad and bad places go bankrupt – nothing stays the same. So, if you find things better or worse, recently opened or long since closed, please tell us and help make the next edition even more accurate and useful. We genuinely value all the feedback we receive. A well-travelled team reads and acknowledges every letter, postcard and email and ensures that every morsel of information finds its way to the appropriate authors, editors and cartographers for verification.

Everyone who writes to us will find their name listed in the next edition of the appropriate guidebook. They will also receive the latest issue of *Planet Talk*, our quarterly printed newsletter, or *Comet*, our monthly email newsletter. Subscriptions to both newsletters are free. The very best contributions will be rewarded with a free guidebook. We may edit, reproduce and incorporate your comments in all Lonely Planet products, such as guidebooks, Web sites and digital products, so let us know if you don't want your comments reproduced or your name acknowledged.

Send all correspondence to the Lonely Planet office closest to you:

Australia Locked Bag 1, Footscray, Victoria 3011
USA 150 Linden St, Oakland, CA 94607
UK 10a Spring Place, London NW5 3BH
France 1 rue du Dahomey, 75011 Paris

Or email us at: **talk2us@lonelyplanet.com.au**

For news, views and updates see our Web site: **www.lonelyplanet.com**

contents

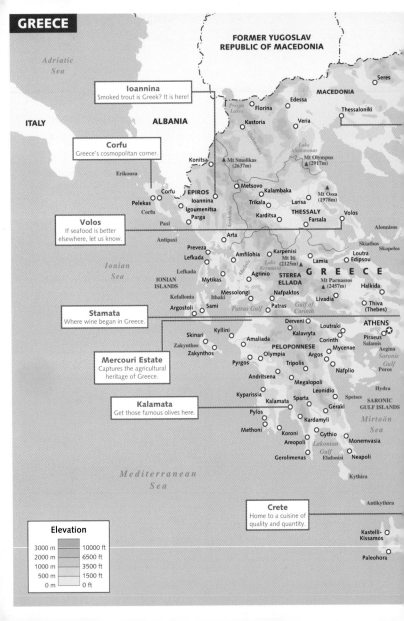

GREECE

FORMER YUGOSLAV REPUBLIC OF MACEDONIA

Adriatic Sea

ITALY

ALBANIA

MACEDONIA

Seres

Florina
Edessa
Thessaloniki
Kastoria
Veria

Ioannina
Smoked trout is Greek? It is here!

Presma Lakes

Corfu
Greece's cosmopolitan corner.

Konitsa
▲ Mt Smolikas (2637m)

Lake Alokmonas
Mt Olympus ▲ (2917m)

Erikousa

Corfu
Metsovo
Kalambaka
▲ Mt Ossa (1978m)

Pelekas
EPIROS
Ioannina
Trikala
Larisa

Corfu
Igoumenitsa
Karditsa
THESSALY

Paxi
Parga
Farsala
Volos

Volos
If seafood is better elsewhere, let us know.

Antipaxi

Arta
Alonnisos

Ionian Sea

Preveza
Amfilohia
Karpenisi
Mt Iti (2125m)
Skiathos
Skopelos

Lefkada
Lake Kremasta
Lamia
Loutra Edipsou

Lefkada
Agrinio
G R E E C E

IONIAN ISLANDS
Mytikas
Messolongi
Nafpaktos
STEREA ELLADA
Mt Parnassos ▲ (2457m)
Halkida

Kefallonia
Ithaki
Livadia

Argostoli
Sami
Patras Gulf
Patras
Gulf of Corinth
Thiva (Thebes)

Stamata
Where wine began in Greece.

Derveni
Loutraki
ATHENS

Kyllini
Kalavryta
Piraeus
Salamis

Skinari
Amaliada
Corinth
Mycenae
Aegina

Zakynthos
Olympia
PELOPONNESE
Argos
Saronic Gulf
Poros

Zakynthos
Pyrgos
Tripolis
Nafplio

Mercouri Estate
Captures the agricultural heritage of Greece.

Andritsena
Megalopoli
Leonidio
Hydra

Kyparissia
Sparta
Spetses
SARONIC GULF ISLANDS

Kalamata
Get those famous olives here.

Kalamata
Geraki

Pylos
Kardamyli
Mirtöön Sea

Methoni
Koroni
Gythio

Areopoli
Lakonian Gulf
Monemvasia

Gerolimenas
Elafonisi
Neapoli

Mediterranean Sea

Kythira

Crete
Home to a cuisine of quality and quantity.

Antikythira

Kastelli-Kissamos

Paleohora

Elevation

3000 m	10000 ft
2000 m	6500 ft
1000 m	3500 ft
500 m	1500 ft
0 m	0 ft

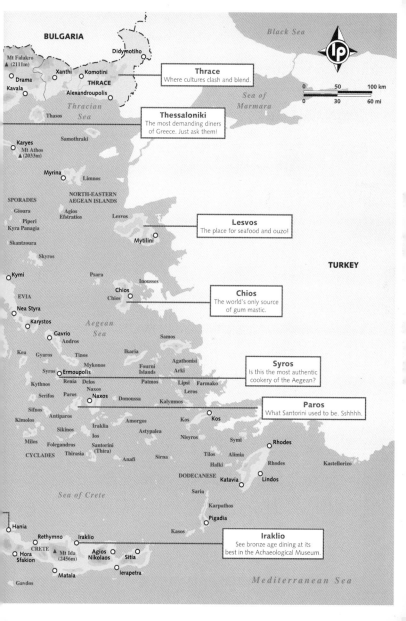

BULGARIA

Mt Falakro
▲ (2111m)

Drama

Xanthi Komotini

Kavala **THRACE**

Alexandroupolis

Didymotiho

Black Sea

Thrace
Where cultures clash and blend.

Sea of Marmara

0   50   100 km
0   30   60 mi

Thessaloniki
The most demanding diners of Greece. Just ask them!

Thracian Sea

Thasos

Samothraki

Karyes
Mt Athos
▲ (2033m)

Myrina

Limnos

NORTH-EASTERN AEGEAN ISLANDS

SPORADES

Gioura

Agios
Efstratios

Piperi

Kyra Panagia

Skantzoura

Skyros

Lesvos

Lesvos
The place for seafood and ouzo!

Mytilini

TURKEY

Kymi

Psara

Inousses

EVIA

Chios

Chios

Chios
The world's only source of gum mastic.

Nea Styra

Karystos

Aegean Sea

Gavrio

Andros

Samos

Kea

Gyaros

Tinos

Ikaria

Mykonos

Syros Ermoupolis

Fourni
Islands

Agathonisi

Arki

Syros
Is this the most authentic cookery of the Aegean?

Kythnos

Renia Delos

Patmos

Lipsi Farmako

Serifos

Paros

Naxos

Leros

Naxos

Donoussa

Kalymnos

Sifnos

Antiparos

Amorgos

Kos

Kos

Paros
What Santorini used to be. Sshhhh.

Kimolos

Sikinos

Iraklia

Astypalea

Milos

Folegandros

Ios

Nisyros

Symi

Rhodes

CYCLADES

Thirasia

Santorini
(Thira)

Anafi

Sirna

Tilos

Alimia

Rhodes

Halki

Rhodes

Kastellorizo

DODECANESE

Katavia

Lindos

Saria

Sea of Crete

Karpathos

Pigadia

Hania

Kasos

Iraklio
See bronze age dining at its best in the Achaeological Museum.

Rethymno

Iraklio

Agios
Nikolaos

Sitia

CRETE ▲ Mt Ida
(2456m)

Hora
Sfakion

Ierapetra

Gavdos

Matala

Mediterranean Sea

The cuisine of Greece is western history right in your mouth. It is a cuisine created by people who have long known the greater world and its gifts, but equally its hardships. And so it is a cuisine whose practitioners have learned to extract the last ounce of nutrition, as well as the last iota of pleasure, from every ingredient. Greek cuisine will give you sensory memories to savour forever. You'll marvel at the bread and wonder why they don't make it like that at home. You'll quaff wine straight from the barrel, eat cheese that was milk only that morning and enjoy sweets made from recipes that are over a thousand years old. You'll feast on a garden of tasty vegetables and you'll extend your capacity for olive oil (lucky it tastes so good). And every day, everywhere in Greece you'll encounter **mezedhes**, the small dishes taken as snacks or, if there are enough, a full meal. Mezedhes are not just food, they are where Greek gustatory verve and kitchen panache are displayed. This is where food is fun, colourful and whimsical. Mezedhes are a twinkle in the cook's eye, a smile on the diner's lips. They are the way the Greeks make love to your tummy.

Yet Greek cookery is unpretentious. Food will not be tarted up and made to look cute, grand, rare or costly. There is no over reliance on sauces, no confusion of tastes. You can be sure that whatever you order it will taste of what it is. Plus olive oil. The basis of Greek cuisine is the Holy Trinity of grain, olive and wine. These will be served at every meal, as they have been since antiquity. Apollo had three granddaughters: Spermo (Grain), Elais (Olive) and Oeno (Wine). These three are still the Greek equivalent of the kitchen gods. And deity continues to play a mighty role in the Greek kitchen, and the kitchen plays a mighty role in Greek life, as you shall see in this book. The Greeks imbibe the spirit at every meal. The menu is informed by the religious calendar. Ancient Greeks dined with nymphs and sprites; their contemporaries dine with saints. The bread of the table is also the bread of life and the heavens. The Greek word **plastis** means both rolling pin and Creator of the Universe. God as patissier, baker of all that is.

If the pot boils, friendship lives – Greek proverb

the **culture** of
greek cuisine

Greek cuisine is Mediterranean soul food, comfort food, good in the
mouth and good in the belly. It is uncomplicated, undemanding yet
very giving. It is the culmination of 3500 years of experience in the
kitchen as well as untold years of want and poverty. It is the food of
a nation that has long reached out to the world, as well as the food
of a community isolated by a harsh climate and terrain.

Greek cuisine is worldly and homely, sacred and profane. We can say that Greece is the largest Christian community in the eastern Mediterranean. If you travel this part of the world you'll find many commonalities at the table. Bread and olives are constants, as are sweets made with honey and nuts. The music sounds familiar and the coffee is just as chewy. This is because the whole of the eastern Mediterranean is of a piece. It always was. Conquerors come and go, but the common crops remain.

Bronze frying pan, National Archeological Museum, Athens

History

In a glass case in the national archaeological museum in Athens sits a bronze frying pan. It is about nine inches across, an inch deep, and the handle is a representation of the god Apollo. It is a beautiful piece of craftsmanship, the work of a great artificer. And how revealing this simple instrument is. When we think of meals taken by ancient Greeks our imaginations are informed by renaissance paintings and Hollywood movies. We think of grapes and figs, cheese and bread, wine, water, perhaps a New Testament grilled fish or a Homeric roast. Picnic fare. But consider what the Greek householder of 500 BC might have had for breakfast with this simple technology of a frying pan and a charcoal fire. It could have been a mushroom omelette with chunks of cheese, a thing popular even today. It could have been accompanied by a dish of curds, fruit juice, sausages, a cup of herb tea. This same pan could have yielded a dinner of fried fish, with a sauce enlivened with capers and spring onions. A salad or dish of wild greens might round out the meal, with bread of course. And the diner would have said grace, thanking Apollo for the gift.

The world's oldest surviving work of gastronomy is The Deipnosophists (Banquet of the Wise), by Athenaeus (circa AD 200). What is remarkable about this tome is that it draws on a time before the golden age of Pericles. In the work the author quotes numerous writers who had been dead for centuries. Greeks have always been interested in a good meal.

Of course most of what we know of the food of the ancients is the food of the wealthy. We know that they enjoyed meats and vegetables fried in olive oil, fish and casseroles baked in woodfired ovens, dainties wrapped in leaves, fish soup and lentils. And all these accompanied by bread. The poor did not have such variety, and are believed to have subsisted on two things. The first was a kind of gruel, the second was another kind of gruel. But the poor would have treats on religious feast days, of which there were many throughout the year. A chicken might be sacrificed, the gods receiving the spirit, the entrails and the fat; the humans the meat. All persons enjoyed sweets, cakes, biscuits and pies.

When Alexander the Great cut his way to India he opened a vein of spices which flowed to the Greek homeland: saffron, nutmeg, cinnamon. These spices had been known, but were too rare to be used in cooking and were only used for medicine. Then came the Romans, who opened up a lively trade of spices and other goods between the eastern Mediterranean and what is now Sri Lanka and the Indian state of Kerala.

Rome fell, yet the Byzantine Empire, of which Greece was a part, continued. The migrations of peoples that were in progress at the time brought new ways and ideas to the kitchen, including Black Sea salt roe and caviar, which is on the table today as taramosalata (fish roe puree). New crops were introduced from the east, such as eggplant and oranges. New cheeses including a salt-cured cheese that would become feta appeared at this time. Distilling, an Arab discovery, was introduced and Greeks used the process to make what would become their national drop, ouzo (aniseed spirit). Christian culinary custom began to shape the Greek diet, giving rise to a reliance on fish that the ancients never even imagined. And perhaps most importantly, as a departure from old ways, cane sugar was introduced, giving rise to the art of confectionery. The sweets eaten then are virtually the same as you may eat today.

The Byzantine Empire did not die a sudden death. It was nibbled away by Arabs, Saracens, Franks, Venetians, Genoese and Turks. And they all had influence on the Greek kitchen. The Arabs brought melons and tarragon, the Franks kippered herring, the Genoese offered Christopher Columbus (Greeks insist that he was born in Genoese held Chios Island). But the chief influences in this era were the Serene Republic of Venice and the Sublime Porte of Istanbul. These two empires struggled over the eastern Mediterranean and both left their marks in the kitchen. The Venetians, with a Columbus connection, brought in New World crops and Italian ways. Hybridising the cardoon they created the artichoke. They introduced pasta. The Turks came with all the abundance of a huge empire. Turkish rule was often egregious, but it was not without benefit. The Turks introduced beans, spinach, rice, and coffee. And it is in this time that we see the introduction of many of the small dishes that will come to be known as mezedhes, those little tasty bits that Greeks take with their ouzo (see Mezedhes later in this chapter).

In 1821 the Greeks began the piecemeal recovery of their independence. It was not until 1947 that the current composition of the Greek national state was realised. And while the struggle was glorious, it was in this epoch that Greek cuisine suffered what might be a worse rout than any army on the field of battle. During this time, and even up to the present day, many Greeks felt that they had to turn away from their past in order to find their future. This attitude manifested itself in many aspects of life, including the kitchen. It reached its peak in the 1920s when a Greek man named Nicholas Tselementes, who had trained as a chef in Paris, decided that it was time to educate his countrymen, bring them into the modern European fold and teach them to eat like the French.

He published a cookbook in which he told his fellows that the spices used in the Byzantine kitchen were naive, even barbaric. He taught them to make sauces on the French model, with chemical precision. He urged the use of butter, and less olive oil. He systematically denuded two thousand years of Greek cookery of its Greekness. He was apparently blissfully unaware that it was the Greeks who taught the Italians, who taught the French, who taught so many others how to cook. His influence is so widely felt that in Greece a tselementes is slang for a cookbook! City Greeks are still recovering. You will see many of them slavishly imitating foreign cooks because they think that's what's sophisticated. A tug of war is in the souls and bellies of many a Greek between the eastern past and the western future. But go to the islands. Go to the mountains. Go to the villages. There Athenaeus still dwells.

SALTADOROI

One of the most searing memories in the Greek national psyche is the German occupation and its attendant hunger during WWII. No one knows the final death toll, but it is believed that over 600,000 Greeks died of starvation or malnutrition, half of them in the winter of 1941-42. Corpses were strewn about the city streets and municipal workers collected them as though it were medieval times of the plague. Country folk often simply died where they lay, to be consumed by other starving creatures.

The ancient Greek practice of gathering horta (wild greens), even in times of abundance, now became a matter of survival. Horta could be the difference between life and death. Sesame seeds, normally used for their taste alone, became sustenance when pounded and mixed with oil, if oil were to be had. Wheat bread virtually disappeared from the Greek diet. Bread made from cornmeal was used when it could be found. To this day older Greeks are loath to eat it because it reminds them of those dark, desperate days.

But there was one small light in this darkness of hunger and despair: the Saltadoroi. From time to time there would appear on a street or an alleyway a sudden offering of big, beautiful loaves of bread. Loaves heavy with nutrition, hope and promise. To some people their appearance was a mystery and a miracle, and they credited the saints. But the saints that brought these loaves were more like divine tricksters. They were young boys, the Saltadoroi.

They worked in bands and, like latter-day Robin Hoods, robbed from the rich German army to provide for the poor of their own nation. As with the Greeks, the staple food of the German army was bread. And everywhere they went they established bakeries to feed the troops. The Saltadoroi quickly learned where the bakeries were, as well as the routes and timetables of the delivery trucks. The strategy called for two or three of the boys to stage a game of football, or a mock fight, in a bend of the road at the time the baker's truck was due. The driver would see the boys and, hopefully, brake to a screeching halt. And while he berated them for blocking his way, the rest of the gang would rush from behind, let down the tailgate, jump aboard and hurl out as many loaves as they could, then jump off and flee with their booty.

If you're invited to a home on a feast day (a real possibility for the Greeks are hugely hospitable), you'll find that festive fare revolves mainly around meat. A spring lamb or suckling pig are the usual favourites, and they'll be surrounded with salad and greens dressed with oil, bread and wine, lots of mezedhes, and an array of sweets. It is at such a feast that you can see the timeline of Greek cookery. The bread, olive, wine and verdure set against the roast represent the feast of antiquity. The elegant and seductive sweets are the legacy of the Byzantine Empire. And the mezedhes, born of the Ottoman time. And there will be plenty of that inescapable symbol of the modern age, Coca-Cola!

FEASTING & FASTING

Many Greek traditions have their roots in ancient times. For example, periods of fasting were necessary for times when certain foods were in short supply. But now, modern methods of food production means people don't have to adhere to fasting periods. But they still do. For if the food were to lose its sanctity, it would lose its flavour.

Bread and water have a sacred place all their own. They are usually referred to with a diminutive form of affection: pso-maki (bread), neraki (water). If you see bread on the street you pick it up so that no one will step on it. Water is always served to visitors. An inhospitable person is described as one who would not even offer a glass of water. Spoon sweets are served with water; coffee is always served with water. Wine is served with water.

Tiny pear spoon sweets at Evie Voutsinas' home, Athens

And wine has all its own traditions. You never fill a glass to the top. Always serve others before yourself. Drink with food. Drinking without food is really frowned upon. Mixing drinks can be terrifying. Serving the last drop of wine to a single person will see them married soon. In fact when drinking wine, if your tablemate gets the last drop from the bottle, say "all the women (or men) for you". If you spill wine at the table it is good luck, a bad stain, but good luck.

Clio Tarazi was born in the Greek community of Alexandria. She now lives in California.

How Greeks Eat

Our mothers and government nutritionists have drilled us in the catechism that breakfast is the most important meal of the day. The Greeks haven't heard of this. Most Greeks think of breakfast as a cigarette and a cup of coffee. If there's time, two cigarettes. Your best recourse is to take to the streets. Not to protest, but to eat. Nobody in Greece would notice yet another protest, it's the national pastime. The pie shops are open early and the range of cheap, delicious pites (pies) are astounding. Street vendors all over the country sell kuluri, a bagel-like ring of baked dough studded with sesame seeds, one of the most common and popular breakfast foods in the country. Many kafenia will be open in the morning and they will also be good places to find a pastry, maybe even a piece of fruit. And speaking of fruit you should betake yourself to the markets twice a week and keep yourself

Kuluri seller, Hania, Crete

supplied. Sally forth in the morning carrying your bananas, stop and buy your tiropita (cheese pie), then go sit down to your coffee. Not exactly what the president or the prime minister would have for breakfast, but it will get you through to lunch. And you'll not have the experience of having struggled up the Acropolis, looked out upon the stunning view, and thought only of eggs and bacon. Learn from us.

The midday meal is the big one. It will not start until about 2pm or later. All in Greece but waiters and cooks set aside their cares and come when called to table. There will be mezedhes including olives, octopus drizzled with oil and vinegar, stuffed vine leaves, dips, spreads and innumerable other culinary bits and bobs. There is no succession of courses. Food is brought to the table as it is ready. Salad will usually come first, but that is because it is ready first. Vegetables will be a part of every meal. Then there may be more substantial fare such as fish or a meat dish like musaka, thickly sliced eggplant and mincemeat arranged in layers, topped with bechamel sauce and baked. For the next two to three hours their world will revolve around food and each other. They will eat and drink and talk and laugh. Life will happen in Greece when all are at the table. In the evening around 10pm, never earlier than 9pm, they will come again and repeat the ritual, though somewhat reduced in calories.

Mezedhes

While mezedhes are a relatively new feature of the Greek table, in their present form at any rate, their concept is as old as Socrates. Bread or other cereal is the basis of the meal, but mezedhes, the little bits of this and that, make it a pleasure rather than mere feeding. Add some ouzo and you double the pleasure. Take it in good company on a bright day on a Greek island and you've got something close to the meaning of life.

What constitutes a meze? Theoretically anything can be served as a meze as long as it is small and goes well with ouzo. Of course 'small' and 'goes well' are open to interpretation, especially in Greece. The Greeks can spend half the day interpreting any given subject under the sun. Indeed they would be positively embarrassed if they came to a consensus on anything. It would mean that nobody is wrong. And if the other guy isn't wrong how can you be right? However, some general agreement can be obtained in time for dinner. Perhaps the most common type of meze would be dips or spreads such as taramosalata or melidzanosalata. Even though these translate as carp roe salad and eggplant salad, they are not salads as we known them. But then, as we have said and will say again, the Greeks do a lot of interpreting. Dolmadhes are always good as a meze, tangy vine leaves stuffed with aromatic rice preparations or with ground meat. Other popular mezedhes include smoked or salted sardines, feta or other cheese, grilled octopus, pickled vegetables and vegetable fritters, fried peppers, cured olives. What most mezedhes have in common is that they are salty, piquant or otherwise assertive on the tongue. This is so they can stand up to the ouzo, the traditional meze tipple. Many mezedhes can be eaten by hand. The salatas, the spreads and dips, are eaten by scooping them up with a crust of bread.

Mezedhes are a bit like Spanish tapas in their size and in the way in which they pair with drink. But tapas are almost always finger food, and you eat them standing up. Except for a pita or kuluri (bagel-like ring of baked dough studded with sesame seeds) no Greek would eat in the vertical. And in a tasca (Spanish tapas bar) you can step in for a quick one and then be on your way. But you won't do anything quick in Greece. That's not what you've come here for.

Melidzanosalata – Eggplant Puree

This is a puree of grilled mashed eggplant, onion, garlic, oil and lemon juice. There are no two cooks who make this stuff alike. It seems to be an immutable law that it must be an individual expression. Some cooks like to char the eggplant skin for a smoky flavour, some like it smooth and some like it chunky. At its simplest, melidzanosalata is nothing more than eggplant, oil and a little lemon juice. But inspired cooks will throw in anything: herbs, spices, garlic or onion. We once heard of a cook on the island of Samos who added hashish. They say he's retired now.

Taramosalata – Fish Roe Puree

This is a thick pink puree of fish roe, bread crumbs, oil and lemon juice. Other common taramosalata additions are parsley and spring onions, maybe some capers. Sometimes mashed potato is substituted for breadcrumbs – a practice frowned upon by experts. Taramosalata is extremely rich and addictive. Greeks enjoy taramosalata during Lent as it can provide for a substantial meatless meal when served with bread, horta, salad and potatoes.

Plate of dips – tzadziki, melidzanosalata, htipiti (cheese dip), patatosalata (potato salad), eleosalata (olive salad), Ouzeri Melathron, Thessaloniki, Macedonia

Tzadziki – Cucumber, Yoghurt & Garlic Puree

This is a dressing or dip made from yoghurt, cucumber and garlic (lots of garlic) and salt. Tzadziki is an excellent thing to have on the table no matter what you're eating. Even though it is rich, it has an uncanny ability to cleanse the palate and stimulate the salivary glands. We salivate as we write!

Saghanaki

The most common form of saghanaki is a sharp, hard cheese that is cut into flat squares and fried until crispy on the outside and soft in the centre. If a menu lists saghanaki this is what you'll get. But you will also see prawn saghanaki and crab or lobster saghanaki, or whatever is fresh today saghanaki. Saghanaki is also the name of a small pan with two handles in which food is cooked and served. The food within may be simple, it may be tarted up with herbs and wine. It may be delicious, it may fall flat. Saghanaki should be translated as 'pot luck'.

Tirokafteri

This is a cheese spread, usually made from feta but can be made from any kind of cheese. It can be spiced up with chilli pepper and garlic, or it can be quite plain.

Keftedhes
These are small rissoles or fritters, often made with minced lamb, pork or veal, onion, egg and herbs (and sometimes ouzo as a moistener). Keftedhes are shaped into flattened balls and fried, but they can be baked. Different regions have their own varieties of keftedhes, and they don't have to be meatbased. Psarokeftedhes are made with fish, and tirokeftedhes with cheese. On Sifnos they can be made with chickpeas and referred to as revithokeftedhes, and on Santorini domatokeftedhes are made with tomatoes. Keftedhes can and are made with anything that can be reduced to a paste and fried. The nonmeat versions are popular among poor folk or during lean times. And they find their way to the tables of the more affluent during Lent. Because they draw on local crops or horta they are a good introduction to regional fare.

Briami
This is a vegetable casserole but also refers to roast vegetables on their own. Roast potatoes, onions, zucchini, eggplant and garlic all make for a fine meze spread.

Deep fried zucchini flowers stuffed with cheese, Apiranthos, Naxos, Cyclades

Bekri Meze
These are meat pieces cooked in tomato and red wine sauce. The name of this dish translates appropriately as 'drunken meze'.

Tsiros
These are small dried mackerel, generally served chargrilled with oil and vinegar. Tsiros were once a traditional snack for shepherds and fishermen who cooked the fish over burning paper torches.

Dolmadhes
These are parcels of aromatic rice wrapped in fruit or vegetable leaves and cooked in water, oil and lemon juice. Classic dolmadhes are vine leaves stuffed with rice, tomato, onion, parsley, mint and fennel, served cold with a sprinkle of lemon juice. Vine leaves are the most common wrapping but fig, cabbage, lettuce and beetroot leaves are also used.

Etiquette

Selecting a place to dine is simple. Just follow your nose. Tavernas are generally open to the street in the warm weather, and the one that smells best to you will likely taste best. It's always wise to count the Greek noses inside, though. If they are few and the foreigners many, the message should be plain: get your bastardised and overpriced fare here. And if you're in heavily touristed areas such as the Plaka in Athens or the mega-resorts you may have to run a gauntlet of waiters standing outside touting their establishments. This is especially true if you are under 30, not bad to look at and wearing a skirt. Greek waiters are notorious for flirting outrageously with foreign women (see the boxed text Ladies Only: The Greek Waiter Syndrome in the Where to Eat & Drink chapter).

Greek table manners and settings are simple. Just take your seat in the taverna, and a waiter will arrive with a basket of bread, paper serviettes and utensils. Sometimes a cruet of olive oil. This will show up on your bill as a small amount. Unless you are in a very smart restaurant you will keep the same knife and fork throughout the meal, and that will be that for your

---

SMOKING

In fine weather Greeks will do most of their dining outdoors, and so should you. It is our firm belief, borne of much coughing, that the Greeks (both men and women) smoke more than any other nation on the face of the earth. They would seem to come out of the womb asking for a light. They smoke all the time, everywhere, through all occasions, and through dinner. They will not only smoke right up to and immediately after a meal. They smoke during the meal. Not only between courses, but during courses! We have actually observed Greek diners take a bite, take a drink, take a drag, repeat. In any establishment at any time at any table, especially the one next to yours, Greeks will be smoking. As if the Athens air were not poison enough.

Most of their consumption is in the form of cigarettes, though great fat Cuban cigars are now a popular status symbol. A few smoke pipes. Thankfully no one seems to 'chaw terbakky'. But you can't just blame the Greek people, you can also blame their government. Taxes on tobacco are the lowest in Europe. This is something in which many Greeks take pride. It allows the poor to shorten their life spans as much as the rich. It also provides gainful employment to otherwise idle smugglers who carry on a lively trade in black market cigarettes with neighboring countries. And in a decade or two the health care industry will begin to reap a rich reward.

METHOD IN THE MADNESS

Greek cookery is often very improvisational. Cooks have long had to respond to changing seasons, times of privation, travel on land and sea. One doesn't always know what one will have to put in the pot. One also doesn't even know if one will have a pot! So how can one always make what's available taste Greek? The obvious thing, of course, is to cook it in olive oil, or add olive oil to it after cooking. No one would complain. Garlic, lemon and parsley also help to keep it Greek. But then there are a host of Greek cooking methods to practice. The cook who masters these, with the help of some oil and garlic, will never have to say in the kitchen "It's all Greek to me".

Kapamas	The method of stewing meat with tomatoes, wine, cinnamon and sometimes red capsicum and cloves.
Kokinistos	'Reddened' Refers to sauteing meat until it browns. Also the method of simmering meat, chicken or rice with tomatoes.
Krasatos	The method of cooking with wine to add flavour and liquid to a dish.
Harti	The method of baking meat and vegetables in parchment or greaseproof paper.
Ladhorighano	The method of cooking with oregano and olive oil.
Lemonatos	The method of cooking with lemon.
Marinatos	The method of marinating meat or fish prior to cooking.
Psitos	The method of roasting meat, chicken and fish. Also an all-purpose term for grilling, baking and barbecuing.
Salmi	The method of preparing stewed game meats such as hare with red wine, vegetables and herbs.
Suvla	'Spit/skewer' The method of chargrilling skewered meat or fish.
Spetsiotico	The method of baking sea fish in a mix of wine, parsley and garlic.
Yahni	The method of stewing food with tomatoes and onions.
Yemistos	The method of stuffing meat, fish or vegetables prior to cooking (pictured).
Yuvetsi	The method of cooking meat or seafood, tomatoes and pasta in a yuvetsi (clay pot).

Yemistos – stuffed tomato and capsicum, Paros, Cyclades

tools of dining. You will have one wine glass and one water glass. You may take as much wine as you like, but you must never appear to be greedy for it. Avoid this unwanted perception by never drinking your glass dry. Always recharge it before it is empty. And never fill the glass more than two thirds. In this way you can drink all you can hold and yet not appear greedy for wine. It is customary for tablemates to pour for each other.

The Greeks have a saying: he eats without leaning on the table, which means he has no zest or enthusiasm for life. So show your zest, tuck in and enjoy. Tipping is not customary. There is a service charge levied. But if you want to show your appreciation just round the bill up to the larger number.

staples
& specialities

The true taste of Greek cuisine depends on fresh, unadulterated staples. Masking or complicating original flavours is not the done thing, especially when you're dealing with oven-fresh bread, wild greens, rosy tomatoes and fresh fish pulled straight from the Mediterranean. And prepare to experience Greece's olive oil, the quantity and quality of which will astound and delight.

STAPLES

Psomi (Bread)

In Greece, life is spoken in the language of bread. It is not merely a commodity or a repetitious and unchanging visitor to the groaning board. In the English-speaking world bread tends to be a lightweight object sliced for the express purpose of encapsulating peanut butter or Marmite. Or in its highest use, to be pulled apart, rolled into little balls and used as ammunition in children's combats. But in Greece bread is not merely the staff of life, it is life, and birth, and death, and all that transpires in between. It marks the seasons and the ages. There is a bread for your name day. There is a bread for Easter. There is a bread for Christmas, for fast days, feast days, birthdays and days of remembrance. There is oven bread, pan bread and pot bread. Wheat, barley and corn bread. Bread in a hundred shapes. Holy bread, profane bread, sweet bread, sour bread. And, by jingo, you can get that lightweight aerated sliced thin stuff we have at home if you really want it. And you can get your peanut butter, Marmite or Vegemite. Sigh.

In the 6th century BC, the wise Athenian leader Solon made it law that wheat bread be eaten only on feast days, and that barley bread be the bread of choice. This was for economic reasons. The soil of what then constituted Greece was unable to support large-scale wheat cultivation, whereas barley thrived in the thin, hilly terrain. Two thousand

Nikos Velonis, a woodfired bakery in the old town of Naxos, Cyclades

CRUSTY VIRGIN

Since the day bread was first made in Greece, it has been imbued with sanctity, mystery, magic and superstition. Eating a special star-shaped bread called **fanouropsomo** will help your wishes to come true or help you to find lost treasures. A pregnant woman traditionally hides a crust under her pillow to ensure a healthy baby.

Many other beliefs surround the mystery of the rising of leavened bread. Make your bread with holy water blessed on Good Friday and it will be sure to rise. Women who are known to have **me heri** (the touch) with bread, those women who can always make it rise, are regarded with a degree of awe approaching that of a witch doctor or a voodoo lady. And many people of tradition believe that a true virgin will always be able to make the bread rise. In other cultures bridal virginity is attested to by the white wedding gown, or a stained bed sheet, or the secret wisdom of a Gypsy shamaness. But in rural Greece the fiancee is put to the test when the boy brings his intended home to meet his mother. If Mother is in doubt about the girl's virtue she will greet her politely, then say "come, let's make some bread together".

Bread baked by the pious for donation to the church, known as **prosforo**, must be imprinted with a special stamp that reads Jesus Christ Triumphs (you can buy these stamps cheaply at any housewares shop, or for substantially more at any souvenir store). These are round loaves weighing as much as ten kilos. They are blessed by the priest and then cut into pieces and distributed to the congregation.

five hundred years later the right-wing dictator Metaxas curried favour with Peloponnesian currant and raisin growers by buying up their whole crop at inflated prices. To recoup the loss, the government required all citizens to purchase a loaf of raisin bread with every loaf of wheat bread. This is why we call a wise lawgiver a Solon, and not a Metaxas.

There was a crisis in the breads of Greece only a very few years ago. And if you read accounts of travellers to the Aegean during the 1980s and early 1990s you may learn of it. The bread sucked! Greek bakers (the big ones, that is) had started producing lightweight aerated breads of little nutritional value and no taste. Just like we get at home! And that was the whole idea! Of course they saved a bit of money in the process, but the fact is they were imitating us. You will see this phenomenon in Greece manifest itself in many different ways (think fast-food, for example). With apologies to our many Greek friends, many Greeks feel painfully their geographical, cultural, economic and societal distance from western Europe. Many Greeks will do a thing, avoid a thing, think a thing or eat a thing because that's what the cool kids in London are doing. And the cool kids in London (and beyond) eat lousy bread. But, irony of irony, at the same time they were 'discovering' the Mediterranean diet. Suddenly the cool kids of London, New York, Vancouver and that place down there with the hoppy animals were eating olive oil and demanding good bread. And when they came to Greece they sought it out, and found it not. The Greeks detected the prevailing wind and quickly returned to their age-old ways of bread. But this begs the question: did they do so because they realised it was the best thing or are they now simply imitating the imitators? The ancient philosophers could have a field day with this one. But, saints be praised, you'll have a good dinner for it.

So what can you expect when you sit down in the taverna? Among the serviettes, salt and pepper will be placed a basket of bread. It will be so full of bread you'll be hard pressed to eat it all. It will be heavy, thickly sliced, aromatic and of a texture so pleasing that merely to feel it is a rich experience. It will have weight in your palm, substance in your mouth and be a presence in your belly. It may be whole wheat or polished white. It may be plain stuff or enriched with eggs, in which case it will taste and feel like a cake made without sugar. Put a little honey on this stuff and you've got a fine dessert. In many places you may specify whether you would like white, whole wheat, or **paksimadya**, what in English is known as rusk.

The single-most common type of bread is **psomi horiatiko**, country bread, peasant bread or even national bread. More of a concept than a recipe, this is bread made by country folk with whatever is available. It is usually wheat bread, but not always. It might incorporate cornmeal, it might be sprinkled with sesame seeds, it might even be enlivened with aniseed or

Holy bread press, Athens

*Freshly baked loaves,
old town of Naxos, Cyclades*

herbs. It will be a sourdough bread, heavy and moist, for this is what has always governed country breads of Greece. Only in modern times have bakers used new yeast for each batch of dough.

Festive breads are simply too numerous to number. Every village and town has its own. But often they are formed into braids before baking, or into rounds and marked with the sign of the cross. You'll recognise them as they're often decorated with strips and gobs of unleavened dough in such a way that they call to mind a tattooed sailor, or pierced punk with green hair. You'll see them in the souvenir shops, pricey and inedible, as though coated with hairspray. But if you see them in the villages, get one and eat it with wine and cheese, and toast your good fortune.

Perhaps the best known Greek bread is **pita**, and we here now must disabuse you of all that you have come to know about pita bread. That stuff you buy at your local supermarket, or have filled with salad or falafel, bears little resemblance to pita in Greece. Yes it's round and flat, but that's where the resemblance ends. Greek pita is thick, often whole grain and absorbent. It does not split at the middle so that you may stuff into it. It is pliable and folds easily so that you may fold it around a tasty filling.

Paksimadya (rusks) are and have been a staple of Greece since ancient days. Our first written reference to rusks is from a writer on food named Paximus, hence the name. This was survival fare, winter food, iron ration and at a pinch could be hurled as a weapon. Today we might call it hardtack, but that would be a calumny as this stuff is actually tasty. It is made from barley flour or whole wheat. After baking it is allowed to cool, but it is then returned to a very slow oven and dried for several hours. This produces a hard, dry loaf that can keep, literally, for years. Archaeologists digging Venetian ruins on the island of Crete have discovered this stuff still edible (they do not report on its taste).

Paksimadya, Greece

STAPLES

Paksimadya nowadays is in vogue and you'll find it in bakeries of every city and town. Most often it is quite plain, but can be prepared with fresh cheese, sugar and spices for Easter or name days. The plain variety is often taken with coffee or water, dipped into the liquid. Sweet paksimadya is enjoyed for dessert or a snack and dipped into Mavrodhafni wine. Our personal favourite is **paksimadya salata** (rusk salad) where rusk is crumbled and tossed with chopped tomato, onion, oil and lemon or vinegar, and topped with crumbled feta cheese. With a jug of wine and a dish of olives it completes a fine lunch.

STAPLES

> **Greek Proverb**
> He has eaten all his bread.
>
> *Describing a man*
> *on his deathbed*

Pites (pies) are among the most common of daily fare in Greece (not to be confused with pita bread; see earlier in this section). Most often pites are made with filo dough, but certainly not always. They can be filled with anything and everything, and they are. They can be homemade monsters cooked by **yaya** (grandma), but the ones you'll see most often are just big enough to fit in your hand. Favourites include **tiropita** (cheese pie) and **spanakopita** (spinach pie). But also look for pites to be stuffed with zucchini, eggplant, tomato, meat or things you won't be able to identify – but they will all be tasty.

Pie shop, Thessaloniki, Macedonia

Filo dough, the basis for most pites, is a paper-thin dough of flour and water, often containing a small amount of olive oil. Every kitchen used to have a couple of long, thin rolling pins that looked like broomsticks for making filo. But it is one of the most labour intensive chores in the kitchen, so nowadays almost everybody buys it ready-made. The word filo means leaf, and it's used in many layers which calls to mind the leaves of a book. It produces a pie crust that's flaky, very flaky. So flaky that you should not eat pites sitting down for at the end you'll be covered with filo flakes. So do as the Greeks: eat them while walking to work or to appointments or just strolling about. But stay on your feet until you've finished.

Tsoureki, Hania, Crete

Elyes & Eleoladho – Olives & Olive Oil

In China it's soy sauce, in England it's Worcestershire, in the US maybe it's ketchup, but the basic sauce for the Greeks is olive oil. Although it is much more than sauce, it is the *sine qua non*, and without it there could be no Greek cuisine as we know it. Olive oil is virtually the only cooking medium. A bit of butter is used in the northern mountains, here and there a spoon of lard where pigs are raised, but most Greeks will sniff at the practice. Olive oil is not only the cooking medium, it is the mustard, relish, ketchup and mayonnaise. It is the sauce, the gravy, the broth and the chief messenger of flavour. Herbs? Who needs 'em? Spices? Down to hell with 'em! We can live lives of fulfilment and satisfaction if we have the olive and its green-gold blood. And maybe some garlic.

Thessaloniki Central Market, Macedonia

Travellers to Greece are often astonished, even disgusted, by the huge amounts of oil they find in their meal. In AD 950 Bishop Liutprand of Cremona, the German prelate and diplomat, wrote that a state dinner he attended was "quite nasty, drunkenly awash in oil". This sentiment still rings true for many visitors. The Greeks know this, and waiters have developed a scale of intolerance for the principal nationalities that come to Greece. The Dutch are said to be the least oil-friendly people of Europe, with the British close behind. But in little tavernas that are ignored by foreigners and loved by Greeks the tables are often set with cruets of oil.

The Greeks simply cannot eat without olive oil. It's as though they must have it to lubricate the oesophagus. In food magazines of the English-speaking world a recipe for a Greek dish typically calls for two tablespoons of oil. That same recipe in an Athenian household calls for half a cup.

Anywhere on Crete it calls for a full cup. An authentic dish will indeed be 'drunkenly awash' in oil. But it will not be 'nasty'! Perhaps you'll say that so much oil makes for too many calories and too much fat. But remember that these recipes are for people who traditionally lead physically demanding lives. They need the fuel. And olive oil is healthy stuff. It keeps down the 'bad' cholesterol, keeps up the 'good' cholesterol and is an antioxidant. All this and it tastes good too.

The olive and its liquid gold are more than food. It is both symbol and substance of Greekness. It permeates Greek culture, history, religion. It has been used in religious rites since pagan days, and as you read this a priest is baptising a child and anointing it with olive oil. It may be scented with rosemary or rose petals for the purpose. When that baby grows up, grows old and then dies, it will be laid to rest in a grave lined with olive branches. For olive is the symbol of life and rebirth. It is also a symbol of victory, of peace, of plenty and the official symbol of the 2004 Olympic games in Athens.

Olive is medicine, olive is soap and olive is hope. Olive is love, backed by the Greek saying: **faei ladi ki ala vradi** (eat olive oil and come to me tonight; if you eat butter, stay home and sleep tight). Hippocrates dressed wounds with olive oil, and Christian Greeks used it as a poultice for sores. Olive oil is mixed into the cement used to make churches. Fishermen pour it on the waves to smooth them so they can see the fish below. It fuels the lamps that illuminate icons in churches. It is even a colour. Something of the colour **ladi** is the colour of olive oil. Ancient Greeks had no soap so they rubbed themselves with oil and then scraped it off with a dull blade. Modern Greeks make soap with olive oil, and in the 19th century nearly the whole French soap industry relied on supplies from Crete. The wood of an old olive tree is excellent fuel for cooking, or as material for cabinets, hope chests or carved mortar & pestle sets.

STAPLES

OIL & THE EVIL EYE

Are you having a run of misfortune? Do you have mysterious aches and pains? Unlucky in love? Tax man looking too closely at your returns? Then perhaps some envious neighbour or malevolent competitor has put a mojo on you, a hex, a curse. They've looked at you with the Evil Eye. Don't try to run. Everyone knows that's futile. It can follow you to the ends of the earth. But you can break the spell. Pour a few drops of olive oil into a beaker of water, then take it to a Wise Woman and have her utter incantations over it. If the oil disperses instead of remaining coagulate, then the bane is lifted. Do not laugh. You may draw the Evil Eye.

Shepherd with his flock in olive grove, Kokohohori, Peloponnese

When you go to the market you'll see olive oil not in small glass bottles measuring one pint. You'll see it in jugs and jerry cans, casks and flasks. Most Greeks live in or near olive producing areas, or they have relatives who do. In November and December families gather what they will need for the year, take it to the village press and wait their turn to convert every five pounds of olives into a pint of oil. City-dwelling members of the Greek civil service can even get paid leave to go home and help with the olive harvest. The country dwellers always set aside some oil for their kinfolk in the city, so that they may have the taste of their ancestral home. For olives, like wine, bear the taste of the soil in which they grow, and no two are quite alike. Nowadays, with so many people residing in the cities and losing touch with their ancient villages, the markets must provide.

The Greeks consume more oil per capita than any other people: 20 litres annually. Greece is the third largest producer of oil, and the largest producer and exporter of extra virgin olive oil. Of all the trees in Greece, 80% are olive trees, and at last count there were more than 127 million. More than 75% of the entire annual production of oil is good enough to be labelled extra virgin. Compare that to 50% for Italy and 30% for Spain. While the olive grows virtually everywhere in Greece there are five major production zones: two areas of the southern Peloponnese, and the islands of Zakynthos, Lesvos and Crete.

There are hundreds of olive varieties, but most Greek olive oil is pressed from the smaller variety of **kalamata**, which is unique to Greece. The larger kalamata olives are used as table olives. To prevent confusion the smaller, oil-bearing variety is known as **koroneiki**. Kalamata may be the best known Greek table olive outside Greece, but **konservolya** is the most common type within Greece. It comes from the central mainland. **Nihaki** is the kalamata table olive from the Peloponnese regions of Messinia and Lakonia. It is usually slit lengthways so that the brine gets well into the flesh. The **gaidhurelya** olive's name translates as donkey olive, which is appropriate due to its large size. It is grown in Halkidiki, near Mt Athos, the monastic land of no women. The **megharitiki** olive is grown in Attica, near Athens. Both green and ripe megharitiki olives are used as table olives. When green they are the standard 'cracked' olive, so called because each one is cracked with a blow from a stone. As with the slit kalamata, this lets in the brine. When ripe they are dry salted. **Stafidholyes** are the easiest olives to recognise. They look like giant raisins as the fully ripe black fruits are harvested then sundried till they are wrinkled. Then they are lightly salted and packed, or immersed in oil.

Contrary to a common misconception, not all olives need to be brine cured in order to be edible. Some varieties lose their bitterness as they ripen and they can actually be eaten fresh off the tree. But many varieties lose their charm when fully ripe so are eaten green and cured.

Olives

Many Greeks prepare their own table olives, and you can do the same. For kalamata olives, simply incise each one from tip to tip, being careful not to touch the stone with the knife, lest you release its bitterness into the flesh. Cover them with pure water, and change the water every day for 12 days. On the 13th day prepare a brine of 1 litre of water and 100 grams of salt for every kilogram of olives and soak the fruits in this for two days. Drain then soak them in mild vinegar for another two days (you can add herbs to the vinegar if you like). Drain and enjoy. You can keep them in vinegar, oil or salted water.

STAPLES

THE GOOD OIL

Olive oil is classified according as its oleic acidity (fatty acid content), the most important element in determining its grade, and to its flavour, colour and aroma. The European Union has defined a specific 30 word vocabulary for the "formal organoleptic assessment and grading of olive oil", which includes such terms as grass (flavour that's reminiscent of freshly mown grass) and positive astringent (the complex drying sensation produced in the mouth by tannins). As with wines, some people will argue persuasively that the oil from no two groves tastes alike.

Hania Central Market, Crete

- **Extra Virgin Olive Oil** is derived from the first cold pressing of olives without refining. It has an oleic acidity level of less than 1%. Greece's ideal climate contributes most favourably to the superiority of its olive oil: richer, fruitier flavour, intense aroma and distinctive green colour. Extra virgin is produced in four styles: regular extra virgin olive oil, organic extra virgin, protected designation of origin (PDO) and protected geographical indication (PGI).

  One reason extra virgin olive oil is so highly regarded is because it offers an almost infinite variety of flavours and aromas. It includes no additives and even in harvest and processing is hardly interfered with. Its fruity taste and complex aroma seem to have almost universal appeal. Its light and delicate consistency make it perfect for dressings. Frying is generally not recommended for extra virgin. It is rich in volatile compounds that high heat will cause to evaporate and you'll lose many of the oil's subtler qualities. Also, the action may perfume your kitchen.

- **Virgin Olive Oil** also comes from the first pressing without refining, but virgin olive oil may have an acidity level of up to 2%. Although its flavour intensity can vary, virgin olive oil is milder than extra virgin.

- **Olive Oil** has an acidity level of no more than 1.5%. At the initial pressing it will be much higher than that, but the level is brought down to its legal limit by blending the refined oil with premium quality extra virgin olive oil. Milder in taste and colour, olive oil is the preferred medium for frying or for flavouring delicate foods that may be overwhelmed by the richness of extra virgin oil.

Meat, Fowl & Fish

In the home meat plays an important, though small, part in the family's diet. Meat is the food for special occasions, for name days, holidays, weddings, Sundays. In earlier, poorer times when Greeks did eat meat, it was most likely to be offal or organ meat, rather than juicy steaks or rib roasts. Popular dishes included **patsas** (offal soup) and **kokoretsi** (offal wrapped in lamb intestines). Earlier travellers from Europe and North America complained they couldn't get enough meat in Greece. You, the modern visitor, will probably never experience a paucity of protein if dining in the public realm. Nevertheless the home kitchen remains largely vegetarian.

Beef is relatively rare as there is very little grazing space for cattle. The most common meats you'll see on the menu are pork and lamb, and their usual method of preparation is in a stew of some kind. This is due partly because the climate is not conducive to the hanging of meat for ageing. Without ageing it's not as tender and so requires lengthy cooking methods of long duration such as stewing. Greek stewing methods often call for large measures of acidity in the forms of wine, lemon or tomato. This helps to hasten the tenderising process and to strike a balance with the abundant olive oil in so many recipes. (Many people, Greeks among them, say that Greek cooks use too much tomato, which smothers other flavours. Somewhat like drowning food in ketchup. You'll have to be the judge.)

Poultry, rabbit and game stall, Thessaloniki Central Market, Macedonia

STAPLES

Samos pork, a speciality of Taverna Kontrabanto, Ermoupolis, Syros, Cyclades

Another method for preparing meat is double cooking. Meat or fowl is first simmered in herb-flavoured water, then fried in oil. Or the reverse: first fried, then simmered. In either case the dish is normally dressed with a garlic or lemon sauce that is made with the simmering water.

Italian-style salami is here and there, especially in the Ionian Islands, but cured meats are not all that common. Again the climate is not suitable. Everybody loves game, so much so that there's very little of it remaining in Greece. Hare and quail are the usual choices. When people can't find hare for a stew they will make do with rabbit. In older days quail were abundant in the wild but hard to catch. Few people had shotguns, so they went hunting with nets, casting them into the sky as the bevy took flight, just as a fisherman casts his net into the water. Quail are farmed these days. They are still extremely tasty, but very small. Make sure you order accordingly.

Stifadho is almost the Greek national dish and, like the Greek character, is difficult to pigeonhole. Every Greek revels in his uniqueness and this is reflected in stifadho. It is traditionally a stew made from hare or rabbit and pearl onions, and it should have a balance of sweet and sour. This everyone will agree upon, except for those who make it with things other than hare or rabbit, such as octopus. Some people put tomatoes in it and some use currants. One cook will add a dry wine and another will swear by sweet Mavrodhafni while another demands mild vinegar. Duels are fought over the choice of cinnamon or cloves or both or neither. It would seem that pearl onions are the only constant in the stifadho pot. We could say that stifadho is a long, slow simmering process, almost an excursus in culinary contemplation, rather than a recipe. You'll never get it the same way twice.

Suvlaki & Yiros

Grilled meats can be had all over the land. Pork, lamb, chicken and even beef are available, grilled on skewers and on huge horizontal or vertical spits. Most often the fuel is charcoal, though nowadays gas and electricity are common. Perhaps the most famous of the grilled meat pantheon is **yiros**, from the Greek verb to spin. In the north of Greece it is some- times known as **doner**. Whatever you call it, like pornography, you'll always know it when you see it. At first glance it appears to be a great haunch of beef turning on a vertical spit. But look closer and see that the haunch is actually about one hun- dred thin slices of meat, tightly

Carving pork yiros in Aristotelous Square, Thessaloniki, Macedonia

stacked in a tower about one metre high and thrust through with the spit. A modern setup is electrically fired and turned, but you'll still see the tradi- tional version mounted next to a metal fire box fitted with shelves kept full of glowing coals. The man (it is always a man at the spit, and there is also something slightly phallic about the whole apparatus) turns it by hand a quarter turn at a time. He lets the fire side of the meat cook for a minute or two, then turns it again. Between turns he deftly slices off paper thin shav- ings of perfectly cooked meat.

It is good enough to eat plain with your fingers right off his knife. And if you ask for a taste he'll give you one. And if you're a pretty woman he'll give you two. Wink and you'll get three. But we digress. Sometimes the meat has been marinated, but more often not. What makes it so delicious is simply the quality of the well-marbled meat. It is so rich in good, hon- est fat that you can literally watch it basting itself as it passes the fire. And so slicing off a handful our man wraps it in a dense, absorbent pita. He adds a bit of tomato and onion, perhaps a pinch of parsley or dill. Always a goodly dollop of tangy **tzadziki** (yoghurt, cucumber and garlic puree), thick and clingy so that it never drips. And lastly a few fried potatoes go into the tasty bundle. Voila! The yiros is meaty, salty, tangy, herby, and goodly greasy. It is the most perfect foil imaginable to a cold beer. It's good even for breakfast and sovereign for a hangover. It's faster than fast-food and infinitely better. It smells great. It's cheap. Get one.

Another grilled meat favourite is **suvlaki**, which is basically cubes of meat on a skewer. Sometimes they get a little fancy and add a bit of onion or sweet pepper. It is cooked over a charcoal or gas grill, then dusted with oregano and served as is. Usually you can get it served with salad and bread. If you want that tasty bundle ask for **suvlaki me pita**.

Pork yiros, Exharia, Athens

Pulerika (Poultry)

Now that prosperity has brought many other animal foods to the table, chicken seems to have taken a back seat, at least in the taverna. It

> ### Socrates' last words
> Crito, I owe a chicken to Asclepius. Will you see the debt paid?

is more common in the north, especially in Epiros. But it was once so common that the limericist Edward Lear, sojourning in Greece, often complained of being fed "everlasting chicken". Turkeys were brought to Greece by the French during their short tenure on the isle of Corfu. Greeks call them **ghalopula** (French chicken) even though they have nothing to do with France, nor Turkey for that matter, being a New World animal. No matter. When off to the market to buy a fat turkey the shopper will often say, "I'm going to get a Frenchman". Turkeys and chickens are traditionally free-range critters, and while flavourful they are on the tough side. So again the cooking technique will most often be stewing. Some rather more novel approaches to tenderising the Frenchman do remain, however. Some Greek cooks are known to slaughter the bird and then immediately soak it, literally 'marinate' (from the Latin *mare*, sea) it in the sea for a few hours. Others rely on brandy. On the bird, that is. A more inspired idea, in our opinion.

Most country folk traditionally keep hens, not so much for the meat as for the **avgha** (eggs). Greeks have been eating omelettes since the bronze age. The most common fillings for omelettes are **horta** (wild greens) and other bounty of forest and field. Potatoes are also good, and it's customary to add crumbled feta or other cheese, maybe a pinch of fresh parsley. If cooks wants to get elaborate they will make a simple sauce, perhaps of garlic and tomato. Few restaurants serve egg dishes. They are considered homely fare. So if you must have an omelette you should get yourself an invitation home to dinner. Eggs also feature prominently at Greek Easter. You know, coloured Easter eggs. Where do you think *we* got the custom?

Psari & Thalasina (Fish & Seafood)

For as long as records have been kept, and for no doubt longer, the people who inhabit the land we now call Greece have been mad for fish. And rightly so in a land of 11,000 islands and innumerable miles of coastline. Greeks are wedded to the sea, its colours, its moods and its creatures. Ancient Greeks spoke of the appetite for fish in the same terms in which they spoke of the appetite for sex. Carp and courtesans came under the same heading when talk at the Lyceum turned to ungovernable desires. And they still lust for their finny fare, as well as lobster, shrimp, mussels, clams and anything else with its house on its back. Although it must be said that with Greece's recent prosperity the people are eating much more meat than they ever have at any time in their history. Indeed Greek travellers of the past used to note with disdain the amounts of meat consumed by western Europeans. But western Europe has arrived in Greece. And many Greeks, in the effort to be good modern western Europeans have increased their consumption of meat by over 150% in the last generation. Consumption of fish has gone down, but not by a corresponding amount. The government says 7%. The biggest decrease in the Greek diet has been in plant foods. It would seem that you could tear them away from their foliage, but not their fish.

Fisherman, Katakolo port near Pyrgos, Peloponnese

In keeping with ancient attitudes, the best way to cook a fish is generally as simply as possible. Catch, kill, expose to fire, eat. A little oil, a squeeze of lemon; if you want to get fancy a pinch of herb, but no, no, no, gloppy sauces, no curry powders, no tartar sauce or ketchup. Bake it, fry it, grill it or boil it. Don't interfere with it. Don't do anything that will mask its fishy flavour. If you don't like the taste of fish, then don't order fish, because we will not accommodate your fussy French ways. Well, actually, they will accommodate your fussy French ways if you happen to be in a resort full of fussy Frenchmen. And you'll get your damned fish & chips with malt vinegar if you are where the English tend to loiter. But if you go for the Greek, for the genuine article and accept no substitutes, you'll get your dish of fish as little adorned as possible and true to its sea-borne taste.

Some of the more common items on the fish menu include **barbunya** (red mullet). This is one of the favourites of the Greek table and quite rightly so. It's about five or six inches long, fat, and red in colour, of course. Red mullet is expensive but possibly the most popular fish in any taverna. It's delicious grilled or fried, as is **melanuri** (sea bream). **Kalamari** (squid) is simply cut into rings and deep fried. You either love it or you hate it. There seems to be no in-between. Grilled **htapodi** (octopus) is so common it's taken for granted. You'll often see it whole, pre-cooked, and hanging from a nail on a wall or a post. When you order it as a meze the tavern keeper will simply hack off a tentacle with a knife, toss it on the fire to warm it then serve it drizzled with oil and lemon. Yummy stuff. Perhaps the most elaborate, maybe the only elaborate, fish dish is **kakavya** (fish soup). You could compare this to the French bouillabaisse, though it tastes more of the sea, while its French cousin tastes more of other French stuff.

Morning's catch, Paros, Cyclades

Greek Proverb

A bride should not eat fish on her wedding day. Otherwise she might flip flop like a fish from man to man for ever more.

Hanging octopus to dry, Naxos, Cyclades

STAPLES

Fruit & Vegetables
Horta (Wild Greens)

Since the days when acorn-eating Neolithic hunter-gatherers roamed what was then known as Achaea (and is now known as Greece) the people of the Aegean basin have loved the wild foods of forest and field. Even today a country family in Epiros will spend a pleasant afternoon on a hunt for mushrooms. In the northern Aegean a kind of sea kelp called **kritamo** grows on coastal rocks. Islanders gather it to eat as a tart, savoury treat like a caper or a pickle. It's good with ouzo or beer, and good cooked with fish. Nuts, berries, roots and tubers are all sought after by individuals and by commercial concerns in order to enrich the Greek table.

But by far the most popular wild foods are greens, and they all come under that same catch-all term of horta. It's useless to try to distinguish this leaf from that blade or another shoot. It just depends on where you are and in what season. Say the word horta and people will assume you are talking about what is being offered in the market and on the table today. It might be poppy shoots if you're dining in spring. It could be thistle or nettle. Amaranth is popular too. It might be some plant you've never heard of nor ever will again. Wild asparagus, long and slender and tender, is often fried in olive oil or baked in a pie. In the mountainous regions where there is greater variety of horta you may be lucky enough to encounter **hortopita** (mixed horta pie), horta rolled in a long tube of filo, twisted into a tight spiral and baked. The gods have smiled on you if you get this dish.

Horta, Athens Central Market

The horta gods do a lot less smiling in the larger cities, though. There the common horta is cultivated and it's nothing to write home about. It all tastes the same: bland. It's just a mess of green stuff boiled into submission, lacking taste and aroma, and we suspect it lacks nutritional virtue as well. But the Greeks must have their horta, and will eat what they are served. So do as they do when in Athens or Thessaloniki or other major towns: drench it in oil, spike it with lemon, and liberally salt it. It will then taste like oil, lemon and salt, which ain't bad, really. Eat it for the fibre, if nothing else. And look forward to better stuff in the villages.

Klimatofilo (Vine Leaves)

Ancient Greeks were fond of cooking with fig leaves. Wrapping fish in fig leaves and grilling them was one common technique. The leaves kept food moist, added flavour and you could just eat the cooking vessel instead of having to clean it. Somewhere between the past and the present the Greeks turned away from fig leaves. We know that by Byzantine times they preferred vine leaves, but we don't know why. Perhaps the newly Christianised Greeks associated fig leaves with the private parts of Adam and Eve and considered it impious to eat things so closely connected to the genitalia of our primordial parents. We can only guess. But we need not guess how delicious vine leaves can be. Even fresh off the vine they have a tangy and cleansing taste. Packed in brine, perhaps with a dash of lemon or vinegar, they are as appetising as oysters, delicious to look at and pleasant to smell. Their most common assignment is to hold packets of aromatic rice in **dolmadhes**. Although dolmadhes need not include rice, as fava beans, chickpeas, fish, almost anything can become a dolma if it is wrapped in a tasty leaf and is small enough to be eaten by hand. It gets extra points if it goes well with ouzo. And don't think that fig leaves are entirely lost to Greek gastronomy. In the Dodecanese they are used to wrap cheeses. We are on the lookout for those in the shape of genitalia.

Fresh vine leaves, Thessaloniki Central Market, Macedonia

Pickled vine leaves, Thessaloniki Central Market, Macedonia

STAPLES

Lahanika (Vegetables)

In the home vegetables make up the bulk of the Greek diet. This is not to say that Greeks are vegetarians, not by any stretch. But poverty and religion have shaped Greek cuisine as much as olives and imagination. Under the traditional Orthodox regime animal foods of any kind are proscribed for as much as half the year (See Feasting, Fasting and the Four Seasons in Culture). And until recently Greece was a downright poor country. Meat was luxury food, festival fare. It was not uncommon for a person to enter the taverna, order **yuvetsi** (roasted meat with pasta) and say, "hold the meat, I'll just have the pasta". Labourers of the Ionian Islands had a breakfast custom that gave them a taste of meat without the full cost. Taking a loaf of bread from home they would stop at a taverna on the way to work and pay a pittance just to dip the bread in a pot of stew.

Artichokes were introduced by the Italians and are a traditional spring dish, often braised with other vegetables, fried in oil, grilled or stuffed. Green beans are summer fare along with stuffed tomatoes and capsicum. Zucchini, as well as zucchini blossoms, are often stuffed or fried. Zucchini is also a common item in savoury pies, as is spinach.

Thessaloniki Central Market, Macedonia

How could you ever go to Greece and not encounter that culinary constant **spanakopita** (spinach pie)? Beets are good winter food. They have been a standard of the table since antiquity when they were taken with such salty counterparts as olives or fish. As was the case then, modern Greeks enjoy both the root and the greens and often combine them in the same dish.

Domates (Tomatoes)

Perhaps the most common vegetable in Greece is the tomato. And yet this is a relative newcomer. The earliest record of tomatoes in Greece is the arrival in 1815 of a packet of tomato seeds delivered to the Capuchin monastery of Plaka in the old district of Athens. We see it next in 1827, in the first ever cookbook to be published in Greek. But this is actually a Greek translation of an Italian book. And at any rate the average Greek

Pickled green tomatoes, Athens Central Market

cook of the time would have been unable to read it whatever language it was in. Those early tomatoes were apparently a yellow variety, and were often grown as ornamental plants, many people believing that they were inedible, even poisonous.

How far the little love apple has come. It is so thoroughly integrated into the Greek cuisine and consciousness that many Greeks are unaware that it is a New World crop. They simply cannot imagine Greek cookery without it. Neither can we, actually. We have never seen a taverna that did not have at least one dish that incorporated tomato. It is prevalent in salads and sauces, it's stewed and fried and made into soup, it can become a spoon sweet, it is dried and kept for winter fare, and it is baked into bread. It seems to be in everything but ice cream. And we are watching for that. **Yemistes domates** is one of the more common tomato preparations, in which the centre is scooped out to be stuffed with rice, cracked wheat or even ground meat.

Patates (Potatoes)

The potato is another thoroughly integrated New World crop. And the Greeks all know it's a New World crop because there was a lot of resistance to it at first.

Ioannis Kapodistrias, first president of Independent Greece, is credited with bringing it to his homeland. He had represented Greece at the Congress of Vienna and travelled widely in Europe where he encountered the tasty tuber. Recognising a useful crop for a poor country he brought it home with him and tried to introduce it to the Greek kitchen. But none would bite. However, knowing his countrymen well, he had several bags of spuds placed in the open and posted a guard over them. He announced that anyone caught stealing them would be whipped. Overnight they disappeared, into the Greek culinary canon. So the story goes.

Nowadays **patates tighanites** (fried potatoes) are the common side dish in any restaurant. And if not that then **patates sto furno** (oven roasted potatoes). At home potatoes are often served mashed alongside a stew, to soak up the gravy. They are cooked with meats and other vegetables. They are braised, oven roasted and baked into casseroles. Predictably they are cooked with a lot of very fine olive oil. The result is that they become so rich and creamy and flavourful that they transcend their humble origin. They become a sybarite's delight. Kapodistrias would be proud.

Bamyes (Okra)

Okra originally comes from west Africa. We're not sure how it found its way to Greece but a seafaring people of long standing (long sailing?) are bound to bring home a few souvenirs. This is another taverna staple. Many people don't care for okra because of the slimy texture of the starch inside the pod. But the variety used in Greece, a small variety, has very little of this, and the Greek cook knows how to get rid of what there is. Okra is most commonly braised with tomatoes, onions and plenty of good oil.

Melidzanes (Eggplant)

This is another common vegetable, one of many that were introduced during Byzantine times. Along with tomatoes, onions and capsicum it is very popular stuffed and baked. It is also an essential of a dish called **briami** (vegetable casserole) sometimes referred to as Greek ratatouille.

Musaka (also known as **moussaka**) is that best known of Greek dishes outside Greece, a casserole of layered ground lamb and sliced eggplant covered with a thick topping of bechamel sauce cooked to a golden crust. Like most Greek recipes it can be made with other ingredients such as ground beef, zucchini, squash or potatoes. Many Greek scholars believe musaka was introduced by the Arabs when they brought the eggplant to Europe. Ironically, many Arab scholars, especially in Lebanon, consider it a Greek dish. To further confuse matters, musaka is also found in Turkey. No one really knows what the origin of musaka is. But we do know the oldest extant written reference to the estimable dish. The 13th century Arabic cookbook known as the *Baghdad Cookery Book* contains the oldest known (at least to us) recipe for musaka.

Imam baildi is a fragrant oil-doused Turkish-inspired dish of eggplant split lengthways stuffed with eggplant pulp, tomato, garlic, onion, parsley and baked. Folklore has it that during the Turkish occupation of Greece an imam (priest) known for his gluttony was invited to dine at the house of a high-ranking official. The official prepared the eggplant in a way that had never been done before. Delighted by the taste, the imam fainted away in sheer ecstasy (**baildi** means swooned). Another version of the story (perhaps the Resistance version) says that the greedy imam ate so much he burst.

Purple eggplant, Athens Central Market

STAPLES

Kremidhia (Onions)

Onions are indispensable in the Greek kitchen. They add taste, aroma, texture and nutrients. They find their way into salads, are taken raw with cheese or bread, and are baked into pies or tarts. Until recently most onions in Greece were those with a purple tint. They are still common, and the traditional preparation for these rather strong onions is to grate them. This exposes more of their flesh to the air, and more of their 'perfume' to your eyes. Read this and weep.

Skordho (Garlic)

Since antiquity, indeed at least since the bronze age, garlic has been food, spice, magic and medicine. Even Homer mentions it. He describes how the god Hermes advises Odysseus to use it as a charm to protect him from the magic powers of Circe. And charm it must have been, rather than repellent, for, the bard tells us, she then found him quite attractive and kept him in council and carouse for a year. Even today folk medicine calls for its use against a host of ailments, including the Evil Eye. Country mothers stick it in the pockets of their children to keep misfortune at bay. Its raw juice is known to have antiseptic qualities, and has been used as such in wartime. But its best and highest use is in the kitchen, and a day without garlic is a day somewhere other than Greece.

Skordhalya (Garlic Sauce)

Ingredients

3	slices dry white bread, soaked in water then pressed dry
½ cup	mashed potatoes
	as much garlic as you like
½ cup	finely chopped walnuts or almonds
1 cup	extra virgin olive oil
1	juice of 1 lemon
	salt

Pound the bread, potatoes, garlic and nuts in the mortar till they are reduced to a paste. Continue pounding as you slowly add the oil, about a teaspoon at a time. Whisk in the lemon juice. Salt to taste.

Serves 6 as a meze

STAPLES

Salata (Salad)

Greeks would be bereft without salad. They have eaten it since ancient days and little has changed in the ways it's prepared. There are a few new ingredients such as tomato, but essentially it's greens, oil and salt, maybe a splash of vinegar or a dash of lemon. As far as we know the Greeks invented salad. They will pour oil on any chlorophyll laden plant and call it salad. The greens can be cooked, the greens can be raw. A salad can be a composition of ingredients or it can be a single horta tossed with oil and lemon. Salad is served.

Horiatiki salata, variously translated as country or village salad, is what we have come to know as Greek salad. Like so much of Greek gastronomy, what goes into Greek salad is widely open to interpretation. The original was nothing more than a slab of feta and some sliced onions dressed with oil, and that alone is an excellent dish. Taken with bread and a little rough red wine it's a Greek ploughman's lunch. On really good days our ploughman might add a few olives to the dish, and in summer maybe a slice of tomato or cucumber. He might even add a few drops of his homemade wine vinegar. He would not

Horiatiki salata, Paros, Cyclades

*Kritamos (pickled green leaves), Chios,
North-Eastern Aegean*

use lettuce. Your restaurant Greek salad is likely to include all of the above and more if they can get away with it. The more stuff they put in, the more they can charge you (and make sure they don't 'forget' the feta). If you want greenery but want to keep it light you can order a **maruli salata** (lettuce salad) or **lahano salata** (cabbage salad).

Salad can serve as a calendar if you're in doubt about the season of the year, for the Greeks prefer to use what's in season. In spring there is an abundance of lettuce including arugula (rocket) and romaine (cos). The leaves are so perfect that they're simply cut into ribbons and dressed with oil. No one would have it otherwise. Summer is the time for tomatoes, tossed with onions or sliced into Greek salad or even plain with oil just like the lettuce. Autumn brings in the bulk of the year's horta, and this is the time of year for variety in salad. Winter salad, you ask? Yes even winter salad, in a manner of speaking. In the northern areas the horta are gathered in summer and hung up to dry. Come winter time they are rehydrated and baked into pies. Not exactly salad perhaps, but made with salad makings. But there is fresh cabbage to be had. It's a sweeter, milder type than is found in the rest of Europe. This stuff is admirable simply shredded and tossed with oil and lemon. To call it coleslaw would be blasphemy.

Fruta (Fruit)

Fruit is such an important and common part of the Greek diet that it is almost taken for granted. It is available everywhere all the time and most often taken fresh and simple. A *yaya* (grandma) will ask children almost reflexively, "have you had your fruit today?" Spoon sweets are mostly made from fruit (see Spoon Sweets later in this chapter). You'll see all the usual fruity suspects at the markets as well as at the neighbourhood grocery. Dried figs have been popular since antiquity. A common snack, one that a

mother will stick into the pockets of her children as they troop off to school, is a dried fig stuffed with almonds. Citrus fruits are especially abundant. Indeed the streets of Athens and other cities are lined with bitter orange trees, their scent mitigating the staggering air pollution. As important as it is, though, fruit is generally not restaurant fare. If you the traveller want any, you'll have to go to the store and buy it. So go.

One of the oldest cash and export crops of Greece is **stafidhes** (currants) of Corinth (the name 'currant' is actually a corruption of Corinth). Indeed currants, along with raisins, were a cornerstone of the pre-industrial economy, with most of the harvest going to Britain. Though originally from Corinth, their production declined after the Ottoman conquest. The Venetians, whom the Ottomans had kicked out of Corinth, took cuttings and replanted them in the Ionian Islands. They are still cultivated here on a large scale. Like their British customers, the Greeks use currants in puddings, bakery goods and sweets, but they also use them in savoury dishes such as tomato sauce and rabbit stew.

Oranges, Nafplio, Peloponnese

STAPLES

Kseri Karpi (Nuts)

Nuts, especially walnuts and almonds are indispensable in baking and desserts, and are also used in many spoon sweets (see Spoon Sweets later in this Chapter). But they are also an ingredient in many savoury dishes. Food historians believe that the Persians taught Mediterranean people to use ground nuts as sauce thickeners. Greeks also incorporate them into stuffing for vegetables. They also just like to eat them plain.

Cart selling a variety of nuts, Plaka, Athens

Ospria (Legumes)

Greek women who bear the name Mary have a special relationship with pulses. Tradition holds that when the Virgin Mary was presented to the Temple of Solomon, Mary's mother distributed pulses to the poor. In remembrance of this act of charity many modern Marys serve lentils on Presentation Day (21 November). Many islanders and country folk rely on various beans or pulses as the foundation of their winter diet. Farmers still come to town to trade some of their cheese or wine or other produce for sacks of beans to see them through the cold months.

The 2nd century writer Athenaeus recommended lentils cooked with hyacinth bulb as "ambrosia in the chilly cold". You'll still find that dish in Athens of a winter's night. In the past there were sellers of bean soups on the streets of the cities and towns. Most of their customers were poor. The poorest of the poor would buy their soup ladled up from the bottom of the pot. If you had an extra drachma you could buy it skimmed from the top where there was plenty of olive oil afloat.

Legumes are even popular as snacks. At the markets you'll see roasted and salted green peas as well as chickpeas sold from bins, scooped into small paper bags to satisfy your hunger as you prowl

Display of pulses and dried beans, Thessaloniki Central Market, Macedonia

STAPLES

the market and haggle over merchandise. Xenophon would recognise the scene and the taste. And he would tell of how his own people of Sparta used beans as a sweet. And beans are not always eaten dry as they are with us. At harvest time they are eaten fresh. Raw fava beans are often removed from the pod, peeled and eaten as a meze with ouzo. Fresh chick peas are eaten in the pod.

There is some confusion about the use of the word 'bean', in Greece. But Greece wouldn't be Greece without a dose of confusion and chaos. In classical Greek, bean specifically means fava bean. It was another legume, the **fasoli**, that came to mean 'bean' in modern Greek, hence **fasoladha** (bean stew). **Fava**, on the other hand, refers not to fava beans, but to a puree of yellow split peas that can be eaten as a porridge with a spoon or as a dip or a spread to be taken with bread. Fava beans are now called **kukya**. To further complicate and confuse things, fasoli nowadays refers to the true beans that are indigenous to the New World. We can take some comfort in the fact that the classical Greek word **chaos** still means exactly that.

Yighandes look like giant white lima beans. You can't avoid them, nor should you try. They are one of the most satisfying, and one of the cheapest, things on the taverna menu. Their most common preparation is in a light tomato sauce seasoned with sweet dill. Yighandes are also served dressed with oil and lemon.

Yighandes (giant beans), Thessaloniki Central Market, Macedonia

Yighandes, Taverna Vlassis, Athens

Zimarika (Pasta)

It will come as a surprise to many that the Greeks are great eaters of pasta. It is believed they acquired the taste for pasta from their former Venetian overlords. Today Greeks are the fourth largest consumers of pasta, per capita, in the world. Although you'll see pasta almost daily on the menus of restaurants, you won't see it in the great variety that you would in Italy or even the US. Most frequently it will be spaghetti with tomato or meat sauce. And there is **pastitsio**, Greek lasagne. Not exactly what you came to Greece for, is it? Don't despair. Another standard taverna item is **yuvetsi**, a hearty dish of roasted meat or poultry, usually lamb, in a sauce of fresh tomato with **kritharaki** (rice-shaped pasta). This is an excellent dish, and is a good taste of Greece.

Here and there you may also come across **varenika** (stuffed pasta), which is rather like ravioli. This is a speciality of the Pontian Greeks, diaspora folk who returned to the homeland from southern Russia and Turkey. The usual stuffing for varenika is cheese, but could be vegetables or meat. Look for such a dish in Macedonia where many of the Pontians have settled. Cretans have a wider variety of pasta. They even have a honey sweetened pasta called **hilofta** that they serve to women who have just given birth.

STAPLES

Pastitsada (beef with tomato paprika sauce), Restaurant Anemomylos, Garitsa, Corfu

Rizi (Rice)

Rice has been known to the Greeks since Alexander made an expedition to India in the 3rd century. But it became a real staple during Ottoman rule. The Turks were potty for pilaf and would have it wherever they went. Greeks joked to each other that heaven in Ottoman eyes was a place where the mountains were made of pilaf. Well the Greeks now love it too, and they're not waiting till they get to Turkish heaven. Pilafs can be made with any kind of meat or fowl, but they are also popular as Lenten fare, made with rice, chickpeas or other legumes. Perhaps the most visible use of rice is as stuffing. Dolmadhes made with vine, cabbage or other leaves are stuffed with rice and braised in tomato sauce. Tomatoes, capsicum and onions are all stuffed with rice and baked. And rice is often cooked with chopped horta, spinach, leeks, cabbage, or a mixture.

Many rice dishes such as **spanakorizo** (rice with spinach) are considered homely fare. It's difficult to find them in the restaurants of cities and resorts. But if you are driving through rural Greece and stop at a village taverna on a Wednesday or Friday, traditional fast days, you should find the wholesome grain on the menu.

Display of rice at store entrance, Monastiraki, Athens

Saltsa (Sauces)

These are not a prominent feature of Greek cookery. Even ancient Greeks tended to pooh pooh such gustatory blandishments. And they looked down at the Romans who were always concocting them. The Greek attitude was and is that a food should taste of what it is. Trying to mask the flavour of a food with rich or spicy sauces might mean that your food is tainted, or that you don't know what to do with it, or that you are a pitiful posturing poseur putting on airs! Down, down to hell with your velouté, says the Greek! Down with your curry, with your hot sauce, and your ketchup!

Well, there are a few very basic sauces that your Greek will tolerate, even embrace. But generally these are quite simple and they tend to enhance rather than mask or compete with the foods they grace. **Saltsa domata** (tomato sauce) is used throughout Greece, especially in the Ionians where the Italian influence is felt more strongly. It is almost always used on spaghetti. It can perk up an omelette. And the Greeks use it often in stewed meats such as stifadho. Unlike Italian versions, Greek tomato sauce often contains sweet ingredients such as currants or raisins, and sweet spices like cinnamon or clove, or even sweet Mavrodhafni wine.

Perhaps the Greek sauce par excellence is **skordhalya** (garlic sauce). It's very much like the Spanish *alioli* wherein raw garlic is pounded in a mortar with olive oil. But the Greek stuff is actually more sophisticated, and more versatile. Skordhalya can be made thin and used like sauce or it can be made thick and used as a dip. It can even be spread on bread for a meze. It can be cooked with vegetables or brushed onto grilled fish or meat. It can even be eaten plain, if you really like your garlic. And the Greeks really like their garlic. A traditional recipe calls for seven cloves of garlic. But we, and many Greeks, are of the opinion that traditional cloves of garlic were bigger than they are today. So feel free to use a whole head of garlic when making this sauce (see the recipe earlier in this chapter).

If skordhalya is the king of Greek sauces, then **avgholemono** (egg and lemon sauce) must be the queen. Its closest relative would have to be the French hollandaise sauce, an egg yolk emulsion flavoured with lemon. But the French sauce contains gobs of butter and that is generally anathema to Greek cooks. Avgholemono is made of egg, lemon and liquid. Traditionally the liquid is the water in which meat or vegetables have been cooked. But tinned or dried stock may be used, even plain water in a pinch. Some cooks will enrich it with milk and thicken it with flour, but that's generally unnecessary. It's easy to recognise a dish in this sauce. It's usually lamb or chicken, and swimming in an yolky yellow bath of lemon scented richness.

Musaka, Hania, Crete

Of course there could be no musaka, at least no Greek musaka, without **saltsa besamel** (bechamel sauce). This is just a basic white sauce made from a roux of butter and flour, milk and a little nutmeg. Cheese can be added to it, but it's not the norm. **Mayoneza** (mayonnaise) made from country eggs and extra virgin olive oil, whisked into a thick emulsion with a pinch of herbs and a dash of lemon, provides an unforgettable taste and a silky texture. **Ladhoksidho**, a Greek version of vinaigrette, is used on both salads and vegetables. The various sweet syrups based on honey or sugar, or both, are a kind of sauce, and the Greeks use them generously. Indeed, a good baklava should be swimming in it.

Ksidhi (Vinegar)

Traditional Greek vinegars are relatively low in acetic acid, and so they are not as strong as those you may be used to. Some of them can even exhibit a slight sweetness, not unlike an Italian *balsamico*. Country folk still make their own vinegar from local wine. They simply leave it open to the air and the process occurs naturally, though your simple Greek farmers often do not understand the process. Since ancient days they believed that spirits caused the souring of wine. This lead to the superstitious practice of never uttering the word **ksidhi** (vinegar) in the vicinity of wine that was meant for drinking. They always refer to it as **ghlikadhi** (the sweet one).

Votana (Herbs)

When cruising the Aegean Sea it is not unusual to smell an island before you see it. So thickly is it cloaked with wild herbs that its scent perfumes the seascape. Even so, Greeks are not want to use excessive amounts of herbs cooking. Perhaps they are satisfied with smelling them all day and night.

Anithos (Dill)

This popular herb is sprinkled onto salads, used in dolmadhes, dropped into soups, baked into pies and as a garnish. Fennel is used if dill is unavailable.

Dhafni (Bay leaves)

Dhafni was the name of a nymph for whom the god Apollo had the hots. Gods being gods they could pretty much have what they wanted, and Apollo tried to get her. She fled. Just before he caught her she cried out to Gaia (Mother Earth), who changed her into a laurel tree, thus foiling the randy deity. To console himself he made a wreath of the aromatic leaves and wore it ever after. Nowadays the leaves are used in soups and bean dishes rather than as headgear. The bay leaves you buy at home are not the same as those in Greece unless the label clearly states that they are of the laurel. The other kind, sometimes known as California bay, are not as sweet.

Dhendrolivano (Rosemary)

Because of its preservative qualities rosemary finds its way into seasoned olives and into flavoured vinegar and a sauce for fish known as **savori**.

Dhyozmos (Mint)

Greek mint (what you may know as spearmint) is prized for its aroma, not surprising as its name means 'sweet smelling'. While not an everyday ingredient in the kitchen, it is used in ground meat preparations, some baked goods and salads.

Faskomilo (Sage)

Sage is one of the most common wild herbs. Its flavour is very strong, even Greek goats seldom eat it. You'll find it used here and there on the island of Crete, but Cretans are more daring than most Greeks. While not popular as a cooking ingredient it is widely used for a herbal tea. It is said to be good for upset nerves.

Maidanos (Parsley)

This is the flat leaf Mediterranean variety, not the curly French stuff. It was thought by many an ancient Greek to be a lucky herb and warriors some-

times wove it into their hair as they went into battle. The worst battle you'll fight in Greece nowadays is with the crazy traffic, and we can report that Athenian traffic has proof against all herbs, as well as charms and spells and curses. But you can still find parsley gracing your table in many forms. It's popular in all kinds of dishes except for sweets. And it makes an admirable salad by itself (see the recipe).

Righani (Oregano)

This might be the most commonly used herb in the kitchen because the ubiquitous Greek salad is usually dusted with it. It's sweeter and milder than the oregano we are used to, and is often confused with marjoram. But for the genuine taste of Greece back at home you should have this. Take some home with you, if your customs officers let you.

Thimari (Thyme)

Thyme makes its appearance at Easter when it is used to season roasted meats. It's as common as sage and the bees love it. And because of the bees' intimate association with thyme it finds its way into Greek honey. You will taste the result.

Oregano hanging to dry, Apiranthos, Naxos, Cyclades

Selinosalata (Parsley Salad)

Ingredients

250g (½lb)	parsley, leaves only	1	small onion, minced
3	cloves garlic, minced	1 Tbs	lemon juice
¼ cup	olive oil	8	kalamata olives
1	hard-boiled egg	1 Tbs	Greek or
	Salt and pepper to taste		balsamic vinegar

Toss together all ingredients except the egg and olives. Chop the egg and olives and sprinkle over the mix. Serve immediately with bread, cheese and wine or ouzo.
   As a meze this will serve four.

Vasilikos (Basil)

This is quite literally the king of herbs. Its name comes from the ancient Greek word **basileus** (king). Champions and victors sometimes crowned themselves with wreaths of it. This is a different variety to what is found in your garden. Greek basil has smaller leaves, a lighter hue of green, and its scent is sweeter and more delicate, yet it carries farther. To this day Orthodox priests take bunches of it, dip it in holy water and use it to bedew the congregation. Villagers hang sprigs of it on their doors for good luck. Householders everywhere grow pots of it as an aromatic ornamental, prizing it as much for its aroma as its appearance. And they seldom use it in their food.

Kapari (Capers)

These delightful little nubbins are the unopened buds of the *Capparis Spinosa*, the caper bush. Its pink and white flowers bloom only one day a year, but all other days the buds can be harvested. Capers can be sun dried, but more commonly they're preserved in brine. After about two weeks the capers are ready to be eaten, and this is how you'll most often encounter them. Some cooks like to drain off the brine and cover them with a mild homemade vinegar, just for a personal touch. Their taste is almost impossible to describe, but it's intense, fresh, flowery and reminiscent of mustard seed. Small capers are used in sauces. The cook will add them just before the dish is done so as to provide bursts of flavour. If they were thoroughly cooked into the dish they would overpower it. Large capers are eaten like pickles and are a popular meze, and are simply magic in your mouth when taken with ouzo.

Baharika (Spices)

Greeks are liable to use spices in baking, sweets and drinks as much as in main dishes. We should also note that the original use of spices was not culinary but mystical and medicinal. Ancient Greeks believed that the various properties of spices were governed by deities. Only later did cooks take them from the priests, doctors and fortune tellers.

Ghlikaniso (Aniseed)

This spice is the main flavouring ingredient of ouzo (see ouzo in the Drinks chapter). It's also commonly used in breads.

Kanela (Cinnamon)

Walk into a bakery selling sweet goods and you're likely to smell cinnamon. It's used in all sorts of cookies, pies and cakes, as well as in the fried pastry sweets the Greeks love. But it's also commonly used in savoury dishes. Every other baklava you encounter will exhude a touch of the sweet spice. Even tomato sauce, sausage and bean dishes are livened up with cinnamon.

Gharifala (Cloves)

Ground cloves are used in pastries, meats, stewed fruits and spoon sweets (see Spoon Sweets later in this chapter).

Piperi (Black Pepper)

Ancient Greeks believed that pepper was governed by Aphrodite, and so they used it in love potions. Pepper's curative powers are reflected in virtually all the ancient pharmacopoeia. Hippocrates prescribed it for feminine disorders and Theophrastus as an antidote to hemlock (Socrates should probably have consulted Theophrastus).

Susami (Sesame)

Possibly the most commonly used spice in Greek gastronomy. You'll see sesame seeds in use virtually every day in Greece, sprinkled on breads, speckled on sweets. Attend a wedding feast and find it in **pasteli** (sweet honey and sesame seed wafers), a symbol of fertility. **Tahini** is a paste made from pounded sesame that can be taken as a meze with bread or used to fortify a soup. Add chocolate and nuts to tahini and you have **halvas**, a popular Lenten sweet.

Safran (Saffron)

The crocus flower yields three bright orange coloured stamens, and this is what saffron is. It takes thousands of them to make an ounce. And that ounce will cost more than an ounce of gold. But a little goes a long way.

STAPLES

Kuluri covered in susami (sesame), Thessaloniki, Macedonia

Greece has a curious relationship with saffron. In ancient times it was widely used as a spice, a medicine and as dye. They even put it in wine. Athenaeus reports that it was used to flavour bread for the symposion (see the Drinks chapter), the classical dinner party. We know that it was used extensively up into Byzantine times. But there its use began to decline. Nowadays it is cultivated in Macedonia and virtually all the harvest is exported to Spain and the Middle East. It is virtually non-existent in modern Greek gastronomy. But as anyone who has travelled in Greece can tell you, this is a land where the past is never quite past. And if you seek, you can find it in little pockets, in tight, dark corners, or even bright spots in the twilight.

Cheese

The French eat their cheese after dinner, the Italians eat it before, the Spanish eat it as a snack, the Americans eat it on their burgers. But the Greeks eat it at any time of day, in any order of sequence, cooked, raw, fresh, aged, plain or dressed for the fair. Cheese to the Greek is not a garnish or a nibble or a food supplement. It is food, to be taken for its nutritional as well as gustatory value. It is a staple, a snack, a comfort food. It travels well and carries the taste of home when the Greek is far away. This has been so since the bronze age. Even Homer talks about cheese and how it is made. He describes the Cyclops making sheep's milk cheese as his chief item of diet. He ate members of Odysseus' crew only as **opson** (they no doubt made for a tasty garnish). A thousand years later Aristotle commented on the making of cheese. He preferred that which uses fig sap to curdle the milk rather than that using the rennet taken from the stomachs of ruminant animals.

When you are in Greece you are going to see cheese every day, even several times per day. Every time you pass by a pie shop you'll be looking at cheese, as the most common kind of pie is **tiropita** (cheese pie). And you'll pass by a lot of pie shops in Greece. Cheese is the original meze. The

Making mizithra cheese in the Peloponnese, the curds hang in cheesecloth balls

ouzeri (bar or taverna which serves ouzo) is never without it. At 23 kilograms per person per year Greeks eat more cheese that any other people in the European Union. Greece is the world's tenth largest importer of cheese. That is a very significant number when you consider that Greece is a small country of only ten million people. That's a lot of cheese landing at the port of Piraeus.

The prominence of cheese in the Greek diet is due to more than the mere love of the stuff. Greece has never been a wealthy country and even today with its new prosperity Greece still has the lowest per capita income of the EU. Flesh foods are dear and always have been. And Greece simply doesn't have the grazing space for large herds of cattle, nor the industrial wherewithal to raise cattle in feedlots. Even fish is costly. The Aegean is overfished so stocks are low, and much of what is taken is exported to Spain and the USA for the higher prices it can fetch there. But Greece can always make cheese. It's a rich source of protein, fat, vitamins and amino acids. It's portable, convenient, tasty, and calorie for calorie it's cheap. Until very recently most Greeks were farmers who worked small plots of land. The milk given by their sheep and goats could not be kept in the heat of the Greek climate. But with a little bronze age technology it could be converted into cheese to help see the family through.

How many different kinds of cheese does Greece produce? The most correct answer would be the same number of villages there are in Greece. Cheese, like wine, is greatly influenced by climate and soil. The innumerable microclimates of Greece produce an infinite variety of organoleptic (taste and smell) qualities in the flora. Those qualities will affect the milk of any mammal that eats them. So just as the Cabernet Sauvignon of the Napa Valley will differ from that of the Barossa Valley, so the **ghravyera** cheeses from Crete and Naxos will differ. Officially, Greece has 20 cheeses under PDO protection, and will apply for more. But we'll just say that Greece has as many different cheeses as you like.

Unfortunately, the culinary chaos that we observe with beans obtains with cheese as well. To wit the hard, aged cheese most Greeks call **kefalotiri** is known in Metsovo as **manuri**. Whereas in Athens and the islands manuri is the name of a soft cream cheese. **Ghravyera** from Naxos is not the same cheese as **ghravyera** from Corfu. The great cheesy touchstone, **feta**, varies in taste and texture throughout the country, and even the recipe for it can vary. However, don't let this confuse you. This is how things are supposed to be. The Greeks like chaos. Just think of it as variety squared. And think of the new taste and smell sensations you will doubtless enjoy as you travel from village to village, island to island, and tuffet to tuffet, eating your curds and whey.

A CHEESE TRIP

Aghrafon This is a fine-textured yellow-white cheese with a mild nutty taste and sensational aroma. Aghrafon is in fact a high-quality **ghravyera** (see below). It is best eaten fresh with fruit, and it is often used as a cheese for melting.

Anthotiros This is a buttery-textured cheese with a piquant taste, and can be made with sheep's, goat's and/or cow's milk. Fresh anthotiros is softer, milder, and is delicious when taken with fruit or honey. Dry anthotiros can be quite hard and is suitable for grating and in cooking. It is also used for pies and pancakes.

Formaela Arahovas Parnasu This cheese is made with sheep's or goat's milk (or a mix). It's a hard cheese aged at least three months and has a deep mellow flavour and an assertive taste.

Ghalotiri A mixed milk cheese that's soft enough to spread on bread like butter. It has a tart flavour and is quite low in fat.

Ghravyera This is one of those cheeses that lends itself to the culinary chaos of Greece. It's generally a hard cheese, with tiny holes and a nutty taste, and is said to be the Greek version of the French Gruyère. On Crete it is made principally from sheep's milk with a touch of goat's. On Naxos it is made from cow's milk with a touch of sheep's or goat's (or both). Then in Metsovo it is made only with sheep's milk. Ghravyera tends to salty but that from Corfu is said to be 'sweeter'. But all of them are suitable for grating and cooking and they melt well, and would make a fine fondue if the Greeks ever wanted to do such a thing.

Kalathaki A sheep's milk cheese that is very similar to feta and is used the same way: fried, baked into pies, taken with ouzo as a meze. It also finds its way into Greek salad. Made in Limnos.

Kaseri A semi-hard, sheep's milk cheese with a mildly tangy flavour. You can recognise it by its faint yellow hue and oily texture. It is good as a table cheese but is also used in cooking.

Kefaloghraviera Not only a mouthful of cheese it's a mouthful to pronounce! As the name would indicate there is some connection to kefalotiri and ghravyera. That connection is that its sharp taste and smell is rather like a mixture of the two. It is a very versatile cheese and can be taken as a table cheese, grated into dishes, fried, or sliced onto pizza.

Kefalotiri This sheep's milk cheese is considered to be the granddaddy of all hard Greek cheeses. It is ripened for at least three months and so acquires a sharp aroma and a rich, salty, tangy taste. It is another of the versatile cheeses. You can do almost anything with kefalotiri but it's the prime choice for frying. The name comes from the Greek word for 'head' and is thought to refer to the size and shape of a typical 'head' of cheese, as opposed to the smaller, cylindrical shaped farm cheeses. It is not, however, to be confused with 'head cheese'. Kefalotiri is known as manuri in Metsovo.

Kopanisti This is a soft, rich, peppery cheese that's matured in clay pots for 12 months. It can be made from sheep's, cow's or goat's milk, and probably any other mammal would qualify as well. Some people say it tastes like a blue cheese, though it is not nearly as fat as a blue. It's usually a table cheese and is baked into pies. Unique to the Cyclades.

Ladhotiri This is a sheep's and goat's milk cheese. It's made in the shape of small spheres and so is sometimes called **kefalaki** (literally, small head). Its proper name refers to olive oil, in which it is aged. It can spend as much as a year in this state and emerge richer and tastier to the point of decadence.

Manuri This is an unsalted soft white sheep's or goat's milk cheese with a rich buttery taste. It can be made either hard or soft, but soft is the norm. Manuri in Metsovo is known as kefalotiri. In Athens and the islands manuri is the name of a soft cream cheese.

Metsovone kapnisto One of the few smoked cheeses of Greece, although it can be had without the smoke. It is made from cow's milk, but sometimes with the addition of a little sheep's or goat's milk. Smoking is traditionally done with a slow fire of vine cuttings. The more creative of the Epirot cheesemakers also add mountain herbs to the fire.

Mizithra This cheese is made all over Greece from sheep's or goat's milk, and comes in two forms. The fresh, ricotta-like unsalted (or lightly salted) version is eaten within hours, or at the most, days, after it is made. The dried version is well salted and aged until hard, making it good for grating and cooking. The Cretans use it in baking and sweets. Mizithra can be distinguished by its woven markings created by the little wicker baskets in which the cheese drains and sets.

Mizithra

Tirovolya A soft, sweet ricotta-style cheese. Made in Mykonos.

Tulumotiri This moist, snow-white cheese prepared in bags made from goat's or sheep's skin.

STAPLES

Feta

Feta is the national cheese of Greece. Foreigners and Greeks alike think of feta when they think of Greek cheese. We don't know how long Greeks have made feta, but the oldest known record dates back to Venetian times in the city of Chandia (Hania). No surprise at the name, then, for the word feta is the Italian word for slice. All feta is made from sheep's milk, though it may contain up to 30% goat's milk. Most feta comes from mountainous areas, where pesticides and other agricultural chemicals are rare. However, in this high environment grazing is limited so the flocks have to cover great distances in order to feed adequately. This is a double advantage for the cheese. Because of the wide grazing pattern the sheep feed on a wider variety of plants, and they transmit their characteristics to the milk. Secondly, because the sheep are constantly in motion they don't get fat, hence their milk is less fat, thus the cheese is less fat and has its characteristic dazzling white colour. Feta made outside Greece must be chemically treated to achieve the same whiteness.

Once the milk is curdled it is moulded in baskets or sieves and allowed to drain, without the use of pressure. It is then lightly salted and left to rest. During this resting stage various microflora grow on the surfaces of the

Milk drums are steam-cleaned and returned to the farmers for tomorrow's milk delivery

curds, giving them more regional characteristics. Now the cheese is immersed in a 7% brine solution which kills the microflora and gives the cheese its well known tang. It is then sent to market in its barrels of brine and sold to be eaten quickly.

People eat feta in innumerable ways. It's baked into pies, it's part of well-known **horiatiki salata** (Greek salad), it's crumbled on omelettes and stuffed into fish. It's even dredged in flour and fried to make **saghanaki**. But perhaps the best way, the true feta lover's way, is to lay a thick slab on a plate and drizzle it liberally with olive oil. Maybe a pinch of fresh oregano. Take this with a piece of stout Greek bread and a glass of ouzo, and you'll have a uniquely Greek moment to savour for a long time.

FETA MAKING IN THE PELOPONNESE

It takes 4kg of milk to make 1kg of feta cheese. First the pasteurised sheep's and goat's milk is heated in a large vat to 65°C and then cooled to 35°C. While cooling the cheesemaker stirs the milk with an implement much like a wooden stick. A culture is added to the milk and it is allowed to stand for one hour to form the curd. The curd is cut into small cubes with a 'koftis' – a large wire cutter that resembles a guitar. After the cut curd has sat for a further 15 minutes, the curd is cut again, this time into smaller pieces, and stirred for five minutes to bring the bottom of the mixture to the top. A 'vacuum' or large hose is placed into the vat to siphon off most of the whey (liquid) and the curd is then transferred into perforated metal moulds.

Coarse salt is sprinkled over the surface of the curd in each mould and the moulds are tilted on an angle to assist the draining of excess whey. They are rotated and drained again overnight. After more salting the cheese is cut into three pieces vertically for easy handling. The cheese is layered with salt in wooden barrels and left for three days. On the fourth day, it is washed, salted again, and then the barrels are closed and the cheese is then matured for about 15 days. At this stage the cheese is ready.

Note: It can only legally be called Greek feta if it is stored in wooden barrels during this salting process.

Yaurti (Yoghurt)

Yoghurt in Greece is something about which to swoon. This stuff is like no other yoghurt anywhere, and we urge you to eat lots of it while you're in Greece because you won't get it at home. Normally made from sheep's milk, Greek yoghurt is thick, rich, fat and flavourful. The Greeks often eat it plain at any time of day, as a snack, side dish or dip. They bake it into pies. On Crete they serve it with fried potatoes, a strange yet addictive combination. The Cretans also use it in cooking rabbit and hare. Greek yoghurt is what makes tzadziki something more than a mere vehicle for garlic. It is a common breakfast food, featured on the menus of virtually any taverna open of a morning. Have it with thyme honey and your mouth will remember it forever.

Besides its being made from sheep's milk, Greek yoghurt is also strained. You can approximate the texture and richness by straining

Honey poured over yoghurt with nuts

your own commercially available yoghurt. Empty a pint of it into a sieve lined with cheesecloth or a coffee filter, and stir in a teaspoon of salt. Place the sieve in a bowl and refrigerate overnight. Most of the water and all of the salt will drain out, leaving you with the richest, creamiest yoghurt in your neighbourhood.

Before the plastic age reached Greece in the 1970s, yoghurt was sold by men who traipsed through the neighbourhood or village bearing clay pots full of the stuff. Like the milkman of yore he delivered it to the household and received the cleaned empty pot he had dropped off the day before. Shepherds and labourers carried it in goatskin bags, very much like wineskins but with larger mouths. Or they might dilute it with water or milk to make a substantial and nutritious drink. Nowadays it is almost always delivered in plastic containers with foil seals. It looks like an industrial product out of Chicago or Birmingham. But it's not. Honest.

Sweets
Meli (Honey)

The original and quintessential Greek sweet and sweetener is honey. Cane sugar did not come into Greece until Byzantine times when it was introduced by the Arabs. Greek honey is unique, and you'll realise this as soon as you see it. It is darker than most commercially available honey, yet possesses a clarity such that you can almost see through it, like stained glass. You will know when you smell it for its aroma is suggestive of flowers and fields. Most importantly you will know it when you taste it. It's flavour is more intense yet less sweet. It is full in the mouth yet doesn't cloy. You are persuaded that you are eating not a sweet, but a perfect natural food that happens to be sweet.

The reasons for this uniqueness are many and include Greece's intense sunlight, rich diversity of native flora, and the extended flowering period available to Greece's plants and trees. The abundance of thyme and other herbs growing wild provides for many single flower honeys, the most common being thyme. You will see this stuff for sale all over Greece. Perhaps the most common way to enjoy it is at breakfast where it is drizzled onto the equally unique Greek yoghurt.

Honey-flavoured sweets are also very common. There is a huge variety of sweets made with honey, with some of them being little more than sesame seeds or chopped nuts bound up in honey and cooked to semi-hardness. Or they might be nougat flavoured with honey and studded with bits of orange peel. There are biscuits made with honey, and an infinite universe of **ghlyka tapsyu**, cakes and pies and pan sweets made with filo. And then there is **koliva**, boiled cracked wheat sweetened with honey and served as funerary fare (see the boxed text Sweets for the Deceased in the Celebrating chapter).

One of the oldest sweets in Greek culture is **melomakarona**, made from flour, fruit, oil, eggs and honey and baked in the oven. The name is often translated as honey-cookie, honey-biscuit or even as honey-buns. In Byzantine times they were known as **finikia** or **phoenikia**, the former referring to the colour of dates which the dark brown cookies call to mind; the latter meaning Phoenician, suggesting that they originated in what is now Lebanon. In ancient times melomakarona fell into the category of **plakous**, a variety of honey cakes served with wine during the symposion. To this day in western Crete they prepare honey-cakes called **plakoundia**. Nowadays melomakarona is a standard Christmas treat, made at home by mothers and **yayas** (grandmas). But you can buy it year round from the bins in sweet shops and even in packages at the supermarket. Try them with a little sweet Cretan wine.

Native Greek honey and yoghurt

STAPLES

Ghlika Kutalyu (Spoon Sweets)

As with much of Greek confectionery spoon sweets date to the Byzantine era when refined cane sugar was introduced to the empire through contact with the Arabs. This is home cookery and the domain of women and you generally will not find it in restaurants. Although you will find it commercially prepared, packaged and offered for sale wherever tourists are dragged, such as the airport duty-free, bus stops along major routes, hotel and ferry gift shops, and by the souvenir hawkers who line the waterfronts all over Greece. In fairness, none of these commercial products are bad, some are quite good. But none are those sugary acts of love performed by women in their own domains.

The spoon sweet custom is thought to have been started by highborn ladies of Constantinople. This makes sense as sugar would have been the prerogative of the rich at the time. But many scholars believe it was simply a sweet addition to an already ancient tradition. Spoon sweets, you see, are not just candy, nor something to spread on a piece of bread and eat as a snack or with an afternoon cup of tea. They began as an essential to Greek **philoxenia** (hospitality), itself an essential to Greek culture. Ancient Greeks held that strangers were sent into their midst by Zeus, and so they were loathe to mistreat them lest the stranger give a bad report of them on Mount Olympus. Strangers who called on the homestead were always given cool water to drink and something to eat, often a dried fig. With the advent of Christianity the custom was no less compelling and the explanation virtually the same. The stranger might be a saint in disguise, sent by God to test your heart. So whether the spoon sweet began in the parlour or the farmhouse seems moot. Even if there were no sugar in the whole world and all the bees flew away the Greeks both high and low, rich and poor would have something up their culinary sleeve with which to purchase a good report in heaven.

THE LANGUAGE OF FOOD

A popular and very traditional spoon sweet is **visino ghliko**, sour cherry preserves in syrup. Confectioners know how difficult it can be to achieve a perfect fruit syrup, to get it to thicken properly without the use of a candy thermometer. Such devices are very new to the Greek kitchen, and so it was a not infrequent occurrence for a woman's **visino** (syrup) to fail. Hence the question asked of a woman in a bad mood: **den sou edese to visino?** Wattsa matter with ya? Your syrup didn't thicken?

Presentation is as important as taste in spoon sweets. You can see this immediately. The colours are vivid, the fruit without blemish, the syrup shimmering. If the fruit is cut, it's cut into pleasing and interesting shapes. Bergamot peel is cut into ribbons and rolled into little bundles. Bitter orange segments are geometrically perfect, varieties of fruit are chosen for their complementary colours and shapes. Even vegetables are used if they are pleasing to the eye and take sugar well: little green tomatoes, baby egg-plant, chunks of pumpkin. Even walnuts are used.

The elaborate services of crystal or silver further attest to the aesthetic importance of the spoon sweet. In Constantinople there was an entire industry dedicated to their production. You can still see them in many homes. Usually they come in small bowls with demitasse spoons hanging from the edge. It is accompanied by a set of tiny saucers and delicate glass tumblers for water. The custom is for your hostess to pour you a glass of water, and let you take a spoonful of the sweet and place it on your saucer. First you drink the water. Then, little by little, barely more than licking the spoon, you eat the sweet. When you're finished you put the spoon in the glass. If your visit is to continue you'll then be served coffee. Spoon sweet services are often heirlooms. Even poor families treasure them and will keep them locked up in hope chests or steamer trunks, awaiting the day a saint or other stranger arrives.

Spoon sweets, Thessaloniki, Macedonia

There are a few regional variations on spoon sweets, perhaps the best known being that on Chios. There it is known as **ipovrihion** (submarine). Rather than fruit it is a sugar fondant flavoured with native **masticha** (gum mastic) or sometimes with vanilla. It is always white in colour and you can buy it at the ferry landing in Chios Town. The custom here is to take a spoonful of the thick fondant and drop it, spoon and all, into your glass of water. Then you can take the spoon leisurely from the water, have a lick of the fondant, then return it to the water where it will keep together rather than flow off the spoon. Your submarine dives and surfaces until you have eaten it all.

Lukumi (Greek/Turkish Delight)

Quinces are a common fruit in Greece and form the basis of many a spoon sweet. But even more commonly they are used to make that inescapable staple of the Greek sweet shop that we of the west call Turkish Delight. Nobody really knows if the Turks invented this stuff or if they were simply delighted by it. A lot of this delightful sweet comes from Syros, and some Greeks say that's where the Turks pinched their idea. But for as much as the Greeks eat of it, it might as well be called Greek Delight. Young boys seem to delight in it especially. Roly-poly boys are often referred to as **lukumia**.

Lukumi (Greek/Turkish Delight)

Ingredients

500g (1lb)	quinces
750g (1½lb)	sugar
1 Tbs	rose water
	icing/confectioner's sugar

In a saucepan, cover the quinces with water and simmer until soft. Remove, drain and cool, then peel and core before pureeing them in a food processor. Return the quinces to the pan and add the sugar. Bring to the simmer, stirring, and cook to a thick smooth consistency. Stir in the rose water. Pour the mixture into a square pan and cool overnight so it sets like gelatine. Cut it into manageable squares and roll it in confectioner's sugar. Leave overnight and roll it again. Delightful.

Makes as many as you cut.

Baklava

It's hard to mention Greek sweets without this. Although we don't really know where it originated. It is a staple of the dessert table throughout the middle east. And there are few variations on it. Baklava is baklava whether in Athens or Beirut or Cairo. Layers of filo dough, well buttered or oiled, are alternated with layers of chopped nuts, and perhaps raisins or currants. They might or might not be dusted with cinnamon or cloves or allspice. The whole thing is baked and then soaked with sugar syrup or honey. As simple as it is, it can be hauntingly delicious. It can, however, be quite forgettable. The quality of the butter or oil used is crucial to its success. And it is at its best two or three days after baking.

drinks
of greece

Retsina and ouzo may be Greece's most famous (or infamous) tipples, but there are plenty of other quaffable options to be found. Wine has been produced here since ancient times, and innumerable springs provide locals with natural refreshment. Then there's the

Alcoholic Drinks
Krasi (Wine)

Wine in Greece predates written record. According to legend, the wine god Dionysus, son of the great god Zeus, was tramping the vintage even before the bronze age. Neolithic peoples in what is now called

Greece worshipped him and indulged in his works during winter festivals. When writing finally emerges we find that the cult and culture of wine is already widespread. Historians believe that wine displaced an even older beer culture. And if the tales of Dionysus are any guide it was a violent process. Dionysus made war constantly during his travels on earth. He spread joy and terror wherever he went and all who opposed him were either killed or driven mad. His cult was especially popular among women. Their rites included wine drinking (of course) and a ceremony that bears a remarkable resemblance to Christian communion. Further foreshadowing Christianity Dionysus, died and was resurrected. In childhood he was torn to pieces then boiled in a pot. But you can't keep a good god down. He was put back together, and then to hide him from his enemies he was raised to adulthood in the guise of a girl. Ancient depictions show someone with a marked ability to accessorise. No wonder the ladies liked him.

Wine in ancient times was a quite different tipple than it is today. While a modern connoisseur might call a certain vintage divine, the ancients actually believed that by drinking wine they were imbibing the essence of a deity. They didn't say you must have white wine with fish and red with meat, for wine to them was not a part of the meal proper. It was more like dessert, it came after the repast with a few sweets and lots of good talk.

The epitome (a fine Greek word) of Greek wine culture is in the Athenian **symposion**. Loosely translated as 'drinking party', the symposion might better be thought of as a wine ceremony, as its purpose went well beyond the mere enjoyment of the grape, and it was invested with numerous rules and protocols. The symposion elevated and educated

*Chardonnay vines at Semeli Winery,
Northern Attica near Kifissia, Athens*

DRINKS

its attendees, established social bonds and promoted community. Which is not to say that it never degenerated into a piss-up. At one symposion the drinkers got so drunk they became convinced they were on a ship at sea in a storm. To keep the ship afloat they began hurling furniture and other 'cargo' overboard, and several passers by were conked on the noggin. The shore patrol were summoned and the seasick sailors clapped in irons and thrown in the brig on charges of disturbing the peace. The neighbours thereafter referred to the house in which the party took place as 'the ship'. One wonders what might have been in the wine.

We don't know precisely what the wines of old tasted like, and we don't know much about what grape varieties were grown where. However, we do have the ancient wine lexicon still in use today. The Greeks were very early to develop a vocabulary with which they could discuss wine in a meaningful way. That vocabulary has seen changes and additions over the centuries, but Pericles and Plato would probably get the gist of what you were saying if you used terms like **anthosmia** (bouquet), **eftonos** (well-toned, firm, vigorous) and **inodis** (vinous) to describe a drop. Oenologists suppose that most of the fine wines, those drunk in symposia, were sweet and often of a rosé style. They were also high in alcohol, around 16%. For this reason the symposion drinkers mixed it with water. There was a running debate in Athenian society about the mix, and even over whether the **symposiarch** (the toastmaster) should pour water into wine or the other way round. This was serious business, for only barbarians drank unmixed wine. Even Plato weighs in on this in an essay called, appropriately enough, *Symposion*.

Despite the widespread devotion of women to Dionysus, and one assumes a taste for wine, the symposion was generally an all-male affair. Sometimes there would be 'flute girls' to entertain, both musically and otherwise. And there might be female attendants to serve the sweets. But in the main it was boys night out at the symposion. They would meet at 'the hour of lamplighting'. They reclined in pairs on couches arranged in a circle and were served a meal which they took in business-like fashion. They might talk casually, but none would let fly his best witticisms before the main event. Once detritus was cleared, incense lit, garlands donned and sweets served, the wine was presented. The symposiarch poured a bit of wine on the floor as a libation, the guests sang a **paean** (hymn), the wine was mixed in a special bowl called a **krater** and ladled into painted cups, and the party began. The symposiarch presided over the talk, encouraging one, cutting short another, asking this one to recite a poem and that one to comment on a speech in the assembly. After the third krater of wine was consumed the party was over, for the symposiarch would heed the advice of Dionysus, as penned by the playwright Eubulus: one krater for health, the second for love and pleasure, the third for sleep. After which, the wise go home.

The symposion, as well as other pagan practices, disappeared in Byzantine times. But wine never lost its religious character. It was always a part of the Christian religious service, and remains part of many religious rituals. But in Byzantine times wine did go through many changes. The use of amphorae to transport wine fell away in favour of barrels. Flavouring wine with spices or gum mastic fell out of favour, though in Ottoman times these would be applied to ouzo and **masticha** (see Tsipuro later in this chapter). People eventually stopped mixing wine with water, for the most part. Sweet wines still fetched higher prices; dry wine was a poor man's dram. But new styles of wine emerged that are still on the market today such as Monemvasya.

UNREQUITED LOVE IN A GLASS

We know the Mavrodhafni grape is indigenous to Greece, but how it got its name remains a point of contention. The best theory harks back to the early 19th century, when a number of Bavarians came to Greece on the coat-tails of Greece's new King Othon (himself a Bavarian). One of these carpetbaggers set himself up as a vineyardist, and had a penchant for a black and sweet local grape that produced an equally black and sweet wine. He had an even greater penchant for a woman who worked in his vineyard named Dhafni. She was quite dark in complexion. And we are told that she was quite sweet in disposition. And as Apollo pursued a Dhafni of old, our German wine grower pursued the new Dhafni. And as the old one spurned the advances of the god, the new one spurned the advances of the human. One day Dhafni died. Our grower was disconsolate, so he named this sweet black grape and the wine it yielded, after his unattainable Mavrodhafni, his Black Dhafni. Think about that when you sip this wine.

The Byzantine era was very chaotic, with numerous invasions, incursions, outrages and disasters. Wine growing suffered for it, and at a time when some of the great vineyards of France and Germany were being established, many in Greece were disappearing. Then came the Ottomans in 1453 and wine production shrank dramatically. The Turks did not ban wine, but they taxed it, putting it out of reach of many people. For a time one of the biggest growing regions was Mt Athos, where the monks had permission from the Sultan to grow and consume their wine untaxed. Ironically, the dearth of wine made it even more important in Greek culture. For to drink wine was to imbibe 'Greekness'. Drinking wine was a way of saying, "I am not Turk, I am Greek".

L 1001214

Λτήμα Τσέλεπου

GEWÜRZTRAMINER

2000

Τοπικός Οίνος Αρκαδίας
λευκός ξηρός

ΟΙΝΟΠΟΙΗΘΗΚΕ ΚΑΙ ΕΜΦΙΑΛΩΘΗΚΕ ΣΕ 11.800 ΦΙΑΛΕΣ
ΣΤΟ ΚΤΗΜΑ ΤΗΣ ΟΙΚΟΓΕΝΕΙΑΣ ΤΣΕΛΕΠΟΥ
ΑΔ.ΕΜΦ. 1/95 ΔΧΥ ΑΡΚΑΔΙΑΣ • ΕΛΛΗΝΙΚΟ ΠΡΟΪΟΝ

500 ML / 12 % VOL

AP 009844 00

By the time of Greek independence in 1829 there was little of what could be called a wine industry. Farmers grew small vineyards alongside their chief crops and made wine for their own consumption and a little for trade. It was such a casual business that those who supplied the tavernas didn't even have bottles or cellars. They crushed the grapes, drained the must into barrels, sealed them and hauled them off to the buyer still fermenting. When the taverna keeper could no longer hear the bubbly fermentation process within, he drove a tap into the barrel and sold the wine by the glass or jug. If a customer wanted to take some home he'd fill his wineskin, bottle, cooking pot or old boot if that was what he had. Needless to say, new wine was the norm, as ageing in an old boot would deny the owner of its use.

And that is about how things remained until very recently. The Greek Wine Institute was established in 1938, though little happened as a result. Its members were a few wealthy people whose efforts had little impact on the lives of the general population. Then came WWII and the civil war. And the farmers continued to haul their still-fermenting wine by horse and dray even into the neighbourhoods of Athens. It wasn't until about 1970 that new thinking began to emerge in the Greek wine mind. The reasons are many, not the least of which are the migrations to the cities (especially Athens), the growing prosperity and the increased literacy rates. About this time we see a number of people with the time, money and interest in making superior wine in Greece for the first time in 1000 years.

But this is all very new in Greece. The great bulk of production is still **krasi vareli** (barrel wine), what we would call jug wine or plonk. That might be a bit unkind, though, for krasi vareli is almost always well made and enjoyably drinkable. And it has the admirable virtue of being cheap. If a taverna has only one barrel wine it will be white, and it may be retsina. If retsina doesn't float your boat it's wise to ask before taking a seat. The barrel wines are all made with indigenous grapes. These local grapes can stand up to the heat of the Greek climate without losing their acidity. They are light in body and tart on the tongue, perfect for the rich Greek food. And did we mention that they're cheap?

Many barrel wines exhibit a hint of acetic acid, the stuff of vinegar. A modern wine snob would thunder against this. Yet a 19th century wine snob might complain if acetic acid wasn't detectable in certain wines. In those days a common thirst quencher was a pint of water mixed with a dash of vinegar. It stimulates the salivary glands and aids digestion. Tastes change and change again. But give the barrel wines a chance. They're very appetising. And did we say that they're cheap? So cheap that if you don't like it the taverna keeper is likely to take it back and not charge you for it. And furthermore, as of old, the taverna will sell it to you to take home in any vessel you bring along. Even an old boot.

A Gewurztraminer produced in the Peloponnese

Retsina

Retsina is the best known, nay, perhaps the only known Greek wine outside of Greece. It is the native wine of Attica. Just as the name implies, retsina is wine that has been flavoured with the resin of pine trees. People who don't care for it say it tastes like turpentine, and they're not joking. It does taste like turpentine. But we like to think that it tastes pleasantly like turpentine. If that makes any sense. Not that we think turpentine tastes pleasant. Work with us here.

Retsina is arguably the oldest continuously produced wine in the world. Some folk have postulated that when the Persians were marching on Athens and the populace had to flee they adulterated their wine with pine resin. This was so that those pesky Persians would get a rude shock should they drink it. This seems a bit wasteful of time in the midst of a mass evacuation. Others say it was the use of pine-wood barrels to store the wine; that the resin leached into the wine and over time the Athenians came to like it that way. But the amount of resin that would be leached from seasoned wood into the wine would not equal the amount the Greek guzzlers came to prefer. Perhaps the most plausible theory is that the unglazed ceramic amphorae used to transport wine were often lined with pine resin.

If you should happen to go walking through a pine forest in Attica you will see the resin being collected. The harvesters use an axe to cut away a small oval of bark to expose the wood. They then hang a container and the resin slowly oozes into it. The winemaker next adds the resin to the wine as it ferments. The amount varies, it can be anywhere from a tablespoon to a cup of resin per barrel. Some independent producers, who are making it just for home use, use chips of pine wood, or sometimes even pine cones instead of resin.

Travellers have been denouncing retsina for centuries. Merchants and ambassadors to Constantinople have written, very feelingly, that the resin was so strong that it took the skin off their lips. And we know that in the past it was quite strong indeed. But in the last few decades vintners have been scaling down their use of resin so that many retsinas have just enough for a teasing perfume. The usual grape for retsina is the white Savatiano, but any wine can be retsina, even red, or even champagne. And be aware that Savatiano is not always made into retsina. If a wine contains resin, it will be so labelled. Retsina goes very well with Greek food (especially seafood) and it also makes a fine aperitif. It is cleansing on the palate, stimulating to the salivary glands, and good for digestion. It is said to take some getting used to. And from our experience we agree. It takes about one full glass.

RETSINA ROAD

When reminiscing about hitchhiking through Greece, I realise it's the food I miss the most. Town markets would supply me with bags of olives, crumbly goat-cheese, perhaps a flaky **spanakopita** (spinach pie). So many memorable flavours. However, for better or worse, my main memory harks from the island of Aegina, where I was baptised into the ritual of retsina. Certain comestibles stand out in the memory for their very ghastliness upon first consumption. Thailand's durian, Chinese sea cucumber and Japanese natto. And the retsina of Aegina. I speak of the resin peeled off of pine trees, smashed into alcohol, left to vegetate for a few weeks like an errant child standing in a corner, and finally served in great greyish glasses to men of the sea and the islands. I speak of the retsina served on Aegina, poured from bottles with no labels, not poured smoothly but with chunky amber-brown globules, one of which was served to me.

No liquor this, but a torture of fermented tar, the alcohol biting the tongue, the resin sticking to the upper mouth, the odorous brew, rather than being swallowed, clinging to the throat like a leech before dropping down into the screaming gullet.

"Well?" said Nicholas, my host in the taverna, anxiously waiting for my reaction.

"Delicious", I said. "Absolutely scrumptious." And then I gagged, not for telling a lie, but because the retsina had made a sudden jump back into the throat as if to escape, an alcoholic incubus ready for a night out.

I swallowed again, and again expressed my appreciation. But no more words were needed. Already, another unlabelled carafe was pulled from the shelf, a large dusty rag was slapped against the glass. Then the cork was pulled away.

"Another", said Nicholas. It was a command. The brownish liquor glared at me. Nicholas glared at me.

"To your health", he said.

"Thanks for the blessing," I said. And down went the retsina. With the second gulp, my inhibitions gave out, and I asked the inevitable.

"Who in hell ...?"

Nicholas gazed at me and poured out another glass. He waited for the sentence to be finished, but I had forgotten the question. Then it came.

"Who on earth invented this?"

Nicholas translated for the others now gathering around and filling up from the carafe. Nicholas had no answer, but one fishermen rattled away in some ancient Attic language, and it came out that retsina was – in Nicholas's words – a mistake, an accident.

And with the fourth carafe of retsina, I found my legs pushing off the floor and my body falling to the floor. Others in the taverna laughed (I was laughing too, of course), and my legs and body were put back

Men playing backgammon, Pyrgi, Chios, North-Eastern Aegean

together. I faced the retsina again. Nuts and honey and a paper-thin pastry were also pushed into my mouth.

Next I was hoisted upon shoulders, thrown into the back of a truck and taken to an old barn where music was playing. The barn had no lights. Just a few candles burning. And the music? It was called **rebetika** and was like retsina: sour, loud, unpalatable, jumpy in rhythm. I began to whirl with the music. I fell and was helped up by my arms. A dosing of retsina kept me awake. The brew resembled jellied vodka spiked with razor blades. No carafe this time. The retsina was wheeled over in an old oak barrel and ladled into my glass.

Some of the older men simply went to sleep, but others insisted on dancing, and so I danced with them. I suppose I must have danced with them. It all became a clamorous dream in the darkness as my arms were held up and one slow foot went in front of the other. I must have fallen a dozen times, but soon a group of us were dancing out to the port, where boats bobbed under the half-moon. Dancing on the port, walking nowhere, with shouts and music. I was a young zombie meandering along the quayside, with a concertina-player following, his notes as wayward as my legs.

And that was all I remembered. The next morning I woke on a bed in a little bare room. I had been well looked after. Apparently my own clownish excesses an entertainment to people who love to be entertained.

Harry Rolnick, New York

GRAPE VARIETIES

The effort to identify and classify the grapes indigenous to Greece is a fairly recent effort, but as of writing there are now about 300 listed cultivars. This is nowhere near the number for Greece's near neighbours in the wine world. But Italy was never invaded by Venetians, nor France occupied by Ottomans. There are also ongoing efforts to revive some of the nearly extinct varieties known to have been grown in Byzantine times.

White Grape Varieties

Aidhani Aspro is a grape with an aromatic quality reminiscent of jasmine flowers. It does especially well in volcanic soil, and so is well suited to Santorini island where it's often blended with Asirtiko and Athiri. This grape is thought to have originated in Syria.

Asirtiko is considered by many to be Greece's queen of white grapes. Its high tannin content helps it to age well, and it develops a flowery, honeysuckle bouquet. It's believed to have been brought to the Cyclades after the eruption of Santorini in 1640 BC. Asirtiko wine is often made by sun drying the grapes to produce its rich, sherry-like aroma. It can be made in a lighter, drier style.

Athiri is the most widely planted grape on the island of Rhodes, though it is also plentiful in other regions. Its wine is usually high in alcohol and low in acid, yet it develops a 'creamy' body and gives a fruity, melon-like aroma. When blended with Asirtiko it achieves a fine balance.

Debina is the best known white grape of Epiros. It yields a wine that has a green apple aroma and a colour often described as silver. The wine is generally low in alcohol and high in acidity, and can be made in a range of styles including dry, semi dry and lightly sparkling. It is light, undemanding, and makes for a good picnic wine.

Monemvasya (also known as Malvasia) is arguably the most famous grape to emerge during the Byzantine era. It took its name from the Peloponnesian port town. The modern wine from this grape is sweet, low in acidity and high in alcohol, not unlike a tawny port. Excellent for sipping at sunset or after dinner.

Moshato (also known as **Muscat**) was well appreciated in ancient times, but is now more popular in France. Production of this grape seems to be falling off in spite of demand, as it is a difficult grape to care for. Also the bees love it and get in the way of the vineyardists.

Moshato Aleksandhrias is a highly versatile grape grown mainly on the island of Limnos. It is often used to make a *vin de liqueur* highly prized for its intense, perfumey bouquet recalling raisins and dates. It also yields a dry wine with a fruity nose that's excellent with seafood. In its dessert wine avatar it is often spicy and honey like, though with a surprisingly short finish. It is also blended to perk up otherwise good but unremarkable wines.

Robola, the most famous grape of the island of Kefallonia, yields a wine with a lemony taste. It was thought that it was a variant of Italian *Ribolla,* brought to Greece by the Venetians. Research has proved there's no relationship between the two, but that doesn't stop slick merchants from labelling the wine as 'Italian' and flogging it as a fancy import. Read the label carefully. Robola is Greek and *Ribolla* is Italian.

Rodhitis is a very temperamental grape. If its growing conditions are not just so, it yields a flat and thin wine. Rodhitis is grown mainly in mountainous regions where the air is cooler and where vineyards are usually on north-facing slopes, to keep their exposure to sun limited. It is a white grape with a green skin, yielding a wine that is, at its best, rich like a Chardonnay, with a green apple nose and a long, intense finish.

Savatiano is the quintessential white grape used to make most retsina. Its low acidity makes it especially receptive to pine resin. On its own, Savatiano is a very appetising wine and good with all kinds of Greek food. The grape can produce dry, sweet and sparkling wines.

Rosé wine from Semeli Winery, Northern Attica near Kifissia, Athens

Red Grape Varieties

Ayoryitiko (Saint George; also known as **Mavroudi**) is the king of indigenous red grapes. It produces a range of wines from dry to sweet, all rich in colour and very fruity. Ayoryitiko benefits greatly from cask ageing but is also good when new, and is even made in *vin nouveaux* style. Its most common expression is in a style very similar to a Merlot. Excellent sipping wine.

Kotsifali produces a wine low in tannins and acidity and high in alcohol. It's most often blended with a tart, light wine so its natural spicy character is brought out.

Krasato is commonly grown in the foothills of Mount Olympus. It yields a dry wine that is low in alcohol and acidity, and is most often blended with Ksinomavro and Stavroto.

Lyatiko (literally July wine, when it ripens) yields wines low in acidity. When treated skilfully the wine will mature into something very like Spanish *Rioja*. Lyatiko wine can be sweet or dry, but is most often dry.

Mandhilarya is dispersed throughout the southern Aegean. It is very dark, so dark that it has been used as a dye. Don't spill this on your white shirt. Mandhilarya can be dry or sweet. It is used extensively for blending to give body and character to lesser wines.

Mavrodhafni (also known as Black Laurel) is well distributed, and gets a lot of attention from vintners, with full cask ageing and extended bottle ageing. A good Mavrodhafni is a lot like a ruby port. This is one of the more common bottled wines you will see in Greece (see the boxed text Unrequited Love in a Glass earlier in this chapter).

Wines from Crete

Rosé wine from Crete

Wines from Paros, Cyclades

Negoska (also known as Popolka) is originally from Macedonia. It has a strong aroma of berries and is widely used in blending in order to bring down acidity and increase alcohol. Its common companion in the bottle is Ksinomavro, where it brightens the colour and softens the tannins.

Ksinomavro is the premier grape of northern Greece. It is very versatile, providing for a wide range of styles. This is one of the best wines of Greece for ageing as it improves in the bottle for at least five, and as much as 12 years. Ksinomavro wine has a dark colour and high acidity.

Winemaker analysing the wine, Mercouri Estate,
Korakochori Ilia near Pyrgos, Peloponnese

WINE CLASSIFICATION

The Greek Ministry of Agriculture promulgated the nation's wine laws in 1971, and in 1981 they were further modified into the Appellation Control laws, when Greece joined the European Union. Greek wines are labelled in a variety of languages, but appellation designations are often likely to be in French. Look for *Appellation d'Origine Controlee* (AOC). Wines sold under this classification must meet criteria regarding such elements as varietal content, local growing practices, vinification techniques, degree of alcohol and yield per hectare. The Greek law also recognises a sub-set appellation called Appellation of High Quality Origin (AO). There are 28 Appellations in Greece at the time of writing, 20 of which are AO wines. Among the lesser wines (a relative term) Greek law recognises Table Wines in two categories: Commercial Wines are any wine sold under a brand name rather than a varietal or AOC. Wines sold under the Appellation by Tradition include retsina wines and certain old blends like Verdea of Zakynthos. And finally there are Country Wines (or *Vin de Pays)*, sold with the designation of their local commune or co-operative. Their content and production are only loosely controlled, but they are wines that have come to be associated with their producers.

(AOC) label on a Semeli wine bottle, Northern Attica near Kifissia, Athens

Wine regions

When it comes to barrel wine, region doesn't make much difference. There are so many small holdings, so many microclimates, and so many wine-makers doing so many things differently that region simply doesn't play much of a role. Even the new generation of vintners like to say that the grower transcends region. To a great extent this is true. But the coastal low-land of Lesvos island will yield a different product than the mountains of Epiros. The sea breeze and the north wind, Zephyrus and Boreas, will treat the same grape differently.

Wine making is oldest in central Greece. It was in Attica that Dionysus is said to have taught winemaking for the first time. Attica is most famous for its retsina, so praised by Greeks and damned by all the rest of the world (or so it would seem). The Savatiano grape dominates here, as well as in neighbouring Viotia and Evia, and is the variety most often used in making retsina. Despite this millennia old tradition, a few inconoclasts are experimenting with Syrah, Grenache and Carignan and are getting good results. From the foothills of Mount Olympus comes Rapsani wine, made from a combination of Ksinomavro, Krasato and Stavroto. The area of nearby Krania is a good place to look for regional wines made of Cabernet Sauvignon and Merlot.

The Ksinomavro dominates in northern Greece. It can be deep and bold, but here and there it provides a light red wine with a fruity bouquet. In the higher elevations of Macedonia the climate is friendly to international varieties like Chardonnay and Sauvignon blanc. Thrace was said to be the birthplace of Aries, God of War, and of fierce men who painted themselves blue before going into battle. Now it's better known for AOC

Vine leaves

THE VINTNER

A few miles north of Athens, near the battlefield of Marathon, lies the village of Stamata. The word stamata means stop, and legend has it that the herald who ran from the battlefield with the news of victory ran through here. The inhabitants urged him to stop and take some rest and water. He refused and went on to deliver his message, collapse and die. The villagers named their abode for his mistake.

And here lives Anne Kokotos. She doesn't stop either. She was born and raised British but has made her life in Greece with husband George. Together they operate a few enterprises, but George concentrates mainly on the hotel while Anne breathes new life into Greek wine. She is the manager of Stamata's Kokotos winery and Semeli vineyards, and is growing wine where wine began in Greece. Using the most modern techniques and technologies, yet completely organic; planting the oldest varieties, yet also some of the newest to be brought to Greece.

She takes us on a walk through the vineyards, planted with Savatiano and Ayoryitiko, as well as Cabernet Sauvignon and Chardonnay.

"Look down there", she says, pointing to the Savatiano vineyard nestled between two hills. "That's where the Greek army camped on the eve of the battle of Marathon. The battlefield itself is just over that hill".

Further down the path she points to the village. "This is where King Icarius saw a vision of Dionysus, and he taught the king to make wine. And here on these hills is where he made it. The first wine in Greece."

Wine has been grown here continuously since that time. And while the winery has been called Kokotos, the vineyard is called Semeli, named after the mother of Dionysus.

As we walk about we see both ancient and modern approaches to viniculture. Ribbons attached to vines do the work of scarecrows. Rose bushes planted among the vines give early indication of mildew. Only natural fertilisers are used, if any. Then there's the stainless steel wine press and temperature-controlled fermenting vats. She splits the difference in the fermenting process, inoculating the white wines and letting the reds ferment naturally. In the packing room we ask about the peculiar design of the wine boxes. Anne explains that unless you stand the box precariously on end the bottles always lie on their sides.

"Barrel wine is still the norm in Greece. Most people don't even equate wine with bottles. To be fair, corked bottles are a relatively recent invention, taken in the long view. Many Greeks don't know that upright storage will dry the cork and spoil the wine. So we make it difficult to store it upright."

We taste some of the wines, including the Savatiano grown on the army camp. Though Savatiano is the principal grape for retsina, we note that this stuff is in its natural state.

"Yes" says Anne. "Some 'modern' innovations we don't employ."

Wine bottles, Semeli Winery, Northern Attica near Kifissia, Athens

wines made with the Ksinomavro as well as blends of indigenous varieties like Asirtiko, Athiri and Rodhitis. Due to Balkan politics and emigration to the cities, Epiros has shrunk in population yet has grown in the amount and quality of its wines. It is especially known for its 'quiet' sparkling white wines from Zitsa, made with Debina grapes. Zitsa white wine was well known in the region during Turkish rule, loved by the reprobate Ottoman governor Ali Pasha as well as the reprobate poet Lord Byron.

In the Peloponnese thrives what many consider to be the 'noblest' of the indigenous grapes, the red Ayoryitiko. But there are so many microclimates around the Nemea zone that almost any wine could be grown. For this it could be compared to California's Napa Valley. Achaïa also has numerous microclimates, due to its wide range of altitudes. Many of the AOC wines from here are made from the Rodhitis grape. Other parts of the Peloponnese are given over to the sweet Mavrodhafni. This wine's aroma, the result of years of ageing in oak barrels, is not unlike a rich porto.

In the Agean, the world's oldest wine press was discovered on the island of Crete. They pressed the grape here before they wrote in Linear B. Except for Samos, Cretan wines are probably the most written of and talked about of any of the finer Greek wines. Dry Dafnes is made from the early harvest of the red Lyatiko grape. The sweet Dafnes comes from the late harvest of the same variety. These wines go back to Venetian times. Samian wine was written about and praised by virtually every generation of ancient wine snobs. The most popular grape there is the white Moshato, producing wines with a wide range of sweetness and body. The volcanic soil of Santorini is perfect for the white Asirtiko grape. Often blended with white Athiri and Aidhani it gives the distinctive dry white AOC Santorini. The chalky soil of Limnos gives a dry Moshato, as well as some sweet variations. Paros is known for its white Monemvasya, and Rhodes for the red Mandhilarya.

Tsipuro

When wine grapes are harvested and pressed there are usually two ways in which the remaining grape skins and stems can be put to use. They can be spread on the vineyard as fertiliser, or fermented and distilled. It is then blended with water for a highly potent though unremarkable drink known as **tsipuro**. The same drink is known as *raki* in Turkey and as *tsikouda* on the island of Crete.

Tsipuro, Syros, Cyclades

Tsipuro is almost anything that the distiller says it is, and people have certainly experimented with ways to flavour the stuff, using herbs, spices, even the bark of aromatic trees. On the island of Chios it is flavoured with gum mastic and called **masticha**. Tsipuro can even be flavoured with a bit of aniseed, and turn white with water, but not as white as ouzo. Tsipuro is often stronger than ouzo, the result of a second distillation. When drinking tsipuro, drink slowly, with lots of water.

Tsipuro, served with kukia beans, cucumber and olives, Agios Nikolaos, Crete

Ouzo

Like tsipuro, ouzo is made from distilled grapes, but while any given ouzo may have many flavourings (including mint, fennel, even hazelnut) the chief among them is always aniseed. And no matter what the distiller may add, there is always a touchstone to let you know that it's the real thing: when you add water to ouzo (which is the proper way to drink it) it turns a milky white. This is because the aniseed oil forms microscopic crystals when mixed with water. Many people like to have it on ice, but only one or two cubes at most. When the ouzo gets too cold those tiny crystals begin to coagulate and form little lumps, giving the drink the appearance of curds and whey.

Glass of ouzo in an ouzeri, Chania, Crete

Although they are always flavoured with anise, no two ouzos are alike, and it can be difficult to keep track of them. Ouzeri and taverna keepers, especially in the villages, often buy in bulk and serve it from whatever bottle they may have. And it's not uncommon to mix two or more brands in order to fill the bottle. The only way to know that you are getting a certain brand is to buy it from sealed bottles. Some people make their own ouzo at home, and if that's what you find yourself drinking you may be getting it from a ladle or an old boot. But in our experience there is no such thing as a bad ouzo, just some that are better than others. Many people say that the island of Lesvos produces the best ouzo. Common brand names are Mini, Aphrodite and Metaxa.

Ouzo is a superb appetiser. It stimulates the gastric juices and induces a calm, good mood. Of course at an ouzeri it is the beverage of choice with your meal. This is the only distilled spirit in the world, as far as we know, and we look into these things, that is an admirable companion to dinner. Many Greeks in taverna have ouzo to start things off, then have wine with the main repast. Afterwards they may enjoy brandy or more wine, but not more ouzo. The Greeks always say "no ouzo after wine". Many a time we have scandalised the Greeks by flouting this custom. We find ouzo to be an admirable digestive. And we're going to keep doing it.

Maratho me Uzo Supa (Ouzo & Fennel Soup)
You'll find ouzo everywhere in Greece. On Rhodes, in Athens and in soup!

Ingredients

500g (20oz)	fennel
1 cup	dry white wine
¾ cup	water
1 tsp	salt
100g (4oz)	smoked chicken breasts
1	chicken stock cube
½ cup	sour cream
2 Tbs	ouzo

Trim the fennel stalks down to the bulb. Cut the leaves into small pieces. Cut the bulb in small pieces and boil them together with the dry white wine, water and salt. When the fennel is tender transfer it and the liquid into a food processor, blend and let it cool. Cut the chicken breasts into thin slices, add to the soup and reheat. Add the sour cream and two tablespoons of ouzo. Stir well. Garnish with fennel leaves.

DRINKS

Brandy

Greece produces a number of brandies. The dominant brand on the market is Metaxa (absolutely no relationship to the dictator). Greek brandies tend to be flowery in the nose, and sweet. Some are deliberately sweetened by the addition of Monemvasya or other sweet grapes.

Metaxa brandy

Tipota (Nothing)

Greeks are exceedingly social people. Lives of solitude are not for them, and hermits are few and far between. They may have nothing but water to drink when they gather together, but gather they will and drink water, or less. The story goes of a keeper of a poor man's taverna in Thessaloniki. His food was simple, his drinks rough, and all on the cheap. But times were so bad that only one of every four customers could afford anything. But loving company, the penniless would come with he who had a penny, take seats and talk. The taverna keeper would come to the table for their orders, and he who had money might order a glass of wine or ouzo and nurse it through the night.

"And what will you have?" the host would ask of the others.

"Oh, nothing", said they. Night after night this scenario would play itself out.

"Oh, nothing to drink. Nothing for me", each poor man would say. "Tipota". Nothing.

Our host grew tired of this. Irony being a Greek word, and hospitality and generosity being Greek virtues, he smiled to himself and said, "I'll give them *nothing*". He took some tsipuro, mixed it with water and poured it into carafes. When next his impecunious guests asked for nothing he served them this brew.

"Here now. What's this?" they asked.

"Why that's tipota", he replied. "Nothing. I call it nothing." And that is what he charged them. Nothing.

Tipota is still produced in Greece. If you are in the Peloponnese you can even visit a distillery that makes it. The Biris Distillery is at 12 Ermou Street, Tripolis.

Cumquat liqueur made from cumquats soaked in brandy, Corfu

Beer

There is good and bad news for lovers of suds. The good news is that Greece, while still strongly a culture of the grape, is also awash in barley and hops. And the Greeks serve it cold. But then, when it's scorching in the shade even an Englishman would not take it at room temperature. So much for the good news.

The bad news is of the pitiful, damnable lack of variety. Greece just doesn't brew beer to speak of and imports are few. Of course in the bars where idle Greek youth hang out, and at the resorts where Euroyouth go to dance, rut and drink till they puke there's a bit more choice. Corona

beer from Mexico is a regular, and the American brewer's equivalent of fast-food, Bud Light, is making inroads. But for the most part your choice will be between Amstel and Heineken. Both are brewed locally under license, and you will find them both plentiful and predictable.

There are a few very small independent breweries in Greece. The most common one is Mythos, producing a pilsner type brew in a distinctive green bottle. We once saw an empty bottle labelled Aegean Lager, but we never saw a full one. And another seldom seen brew is Alpha. Cyprus exports a beer called Keo, and you might see it if you look hard. But we should not be surprised at this situation. Remember that Greece was originally a beer culture. But then came Dionysus with his wine and he made war on the brewers. And all his enemies were either killed or driven mad.

Mythos beer

Non-Alcoholic Drinks
Coffee

Greek coffee used to be known by the universal term, Turkish coffee. But in 1974 Turkey invaded Cyprus and that upset the Greeks a lot. So much so that they stopped calling it Turkish coffee and thereafter called it Greek coffee. In our opinion they should have simply stopped drinking it. To us Greek coffee tastes, smells and has the texture of mud. Yes, a slurry of soil and hot water. Drink a cup of this stuff and you may have to pick your teeth. You don't exactly sip Greek coffee, it's more like you break off a piece and chew it. It's so gritty it provides you with dietary fibre. But that's us. The Greeks gulp it with gusto. They find it very comforting, with an assertive taste and a rich aroma. Greek coffee is said to have 30 variations but most people refer to only four: **sketos** (without sugar, strong and bitter); **metrios** (medium, usually with one teaspoon of sugar); **ghlikos** or **varighlikos** (almost honey sweet); **ghlikivrastos** (sweet but boiled again so it loses most of its froth).

Greek coffee and the bill, Chios, North-Eastern Aegean Islands

DRINKS

Kafes Elinikos (Greek Coffee)

In the spirit of fairness, we're going to show you how Greek coffee is made. It does look exotic and delicious, but don't be fooled. It's really just a cup o' mud. A finer grind of coffee and a better grade of bean would yield a completely different beverage. But the Greeks would have it no other way.

It all begins in a **briki**, a tall, cone-shaped container with a long handle and a lip, traditionally made of brass or copper. Along with the briki you need some demitasse cups, intrinsic to the enjoyment of this biting brew. Using one of the cups as a measure, pour 4 cups of water into the briki and add a teaspoon of coffee per cup.

For a metrios coffee add 4 teaspoons of sugar. Put the briki on a low flame and stir. Holding the briki handle, swirl the brew gently as it begins to simmer. You'll see the coffee begin to bubble and foam. Be careful not to let it boil over. Once the coffee starts rising, remove it from the heat and leave for a minute to allow the grounds to settle (they will never settle completely). Pour a little liquid into each cup so as to distribute the froth, then fill them completely. Don't stir the coffee once it has been poured. Sip (or chew) until you reach the thick sludge. As with any Greek beverage, serve it with a glass of cold water.

Greek coffee, Café Loxadra, Thessaloniki

Frappe

This is where it really gets ridiculous. The single-most common beverage throughout the land of Homer and Maria Callas is a mix of instant coffee, sugar and condensed milk whipped into a frothy mess and garnished with two (always two) plastic straws. At a distance it looks like a chocolate milk-shake. But it's nothing but instant coffee and canned cow.

Ice is added to a glass of frappe

Stroll by any outdoor cafe anywhere in Greece and you'll see frappe occupying almost all the tables. This could lead you to think that the Greeks, the people who taught Europe to read, write, war and wassail have become degenerate in taste. But no. Look closely. They hardly ever leave an empty glass when they depart the table. And we have never seen anybody drink two. They haven't come for coffee crystals or milk from a can. They have come to visit. The cafe is the communal parlour, living room, conversation pit. Instead of calling on a friend at home they ring up and arrange to meet for a frappe. Apartments are small, and meant for family, not entertaining. But you can't use the cafe's tables for free, so frappe is the price of admission. And as long as you buy one you may nurse it till the cows come home.

DRINKS

FRAPPOUZO

I can't convince any of my Greek friends that this is one of the greatest drinks on the planet. I called it Frappouzo. You order **frappe me ghala metrios** (iced coffee with milk and sugar). You also order an ouzo. As soon as the waiter turns his back, pour the ouzo into the frappe. You won't believe how good it tastes, and the feeling isn't bad either. If you are feeling low and don't want to waste precious vacation time being depressed, one or two of these will do the trick. Any more and you're on your own.

Matt Barrett lives on the island of Lesvos and is the author of
I Married a Lesbian

Espresso

Espresso is now available in almost every cafe, bar and pie shop. All the better taverna offer it. Curiously, many kafenia do not. Many do, but many do not. The traditional drink here is Greek coffee. Cappuccino has been discovered and you can find it almost anywhere that idle Greek youth are idling. In Athens there are a number of shops selling superior coffee beans from around the world. If you're going to be in town a while you might like to pick some up (see the Athens map).

Tsai (Tea)

Tea is a sorry story in Greece. Greeks just don't drink it. Ask for cuppa in a taverna or cafe and you'll get some indifferently heated water and a teabag full of suspect leaves. If you want a proper cup of tea we recommend that you bring your own. Herbal teas, however, have been in wide use since antiquity. But they are taken as a remedy more than as 'the cup that cheers but does not inebriate'.

Nero (Water)

After wine, and perhaps even before wine, water is the Hellenic favourite. Always has been. If you arrive at someone's house for a visit you will be offered a sweet or a coffee or something, and a nice glass of cool water. No matter what you order in a bar or restaurant or taverna you will always be given a glass of cool water. Greece's diverse topography ensures a huge variety of springs. Every region has its own unique, refreshing bottled spring water on the market. The Greeks so love water that they even speak of it in the diminutive. The word for water is **nero**, but ask a waiter for **neraki**, roughly translated as 'my dear little glass of water'. No Greek can help but smile when hearing this request. Really. Try it.

Now as to tap water, that's a drink of a different order. We can assure you that tap water in Greece will not kill you. It meets European sanitation standards. In the major cities it is quite drinkable, if unremarkable. But in small coastal towns, and especially on many of the islands, it tastes like harbour water. And that is basically what it is. The water tables here are close to the surface and the sea leaches in. You can survive a shower in this stuff. But you don't want to drink it. A cup of Greek coffee made with Chios tap water is like ... like ... nothing you have ever tasted! Think of seaweed boiled in mud. It's a shocker. If you are ever served this, as well you might be, do not be offended. Run to the street and spit it out. Then tell your waiter that you would like your coffee remade with bottled water. You will get no argument, no resentment, and no extra charge. Just a cup of mud made with good water. We are mystified as to why they do not do this in the first place.

home cooking
& traditions

t's impossible to say with marksman's accuracy where the home kitchen ends and the public domain begins. Cooking can be as ocial as dining. It often takes place in the open, where friends and amily can learn or have a hand in culinary creations.

In the cities, Greek dwellings are mostly rather small, they are not air-conditioned, and the weather can be beastly hot. People have a need to betake themselves out of doors regularly just for some elbow room and breathing space and some cool breezes and shade. And they need to be together. So the taverna, the ouzeri, the kafenion become extensions of the home, the living room and the kitchen. They are necessities of successful communal living, not luxuries or idle entertainments. Greeks visit them regularly. Restaurants are as integral to life as food itself. People feel at home there.

Inside an Athenian apartment within the vast urban sprawl, the kitchen is no remarkable construction. It might consist of no more than a two burner gas or electric cooker, a cutting board and a few pots. Even a more elaborate affair may not have a convection oven, though it might have a microwave or a toaster. All in all it looks like a kitchen in many European apartments. Until just recently, a Greek kitchen would have two or three rolling pins, long and narrow like broomsticks, used for making filo

Sacred bread presses, Athens

dough. But these days most people buy readymade filo at the supermarket, and it is as good as most. The modern home cook will still make **prosforo** - sacred bread to be blessed by the priest. A few of the wooden stamps for the purpose will be found in her kitchen drawers. A well equipped kitchen will have a few **saghanaki**, the metal or ceramic dish used to prepare individual size casseroles. There will be a tin beaker for olive oil, and a mortar and pestle. And there will always be the **briki** with its bits and bobs for making the damnable Greek coffee.

*Rigani (oregano) growing in an olive tin,
Mesta, Chios, North-Eastern Aegean*

Now a traditional country kitchen is another kettle of fish. Part of it, even most of it, will be outside. It might be built into an outer wall, or could be a separate little building next to a well, reached by a path of stepping stones. It will have a raised hearth on which a fire burns, a pile of wood or charcoal beside. The walls will be black with age and soot. A tripod over the fire holds a blackened cooking pot, and the heat is adjusted by raising and lowering the pot by means of a chain and pulley. For kneading bread dough the cook places it in a special wooden trough, often built into the wall. The flour for the bread is stored in a trunk, along with oil, spices, pasta and beans. The cook may have a wood-fire **furnos** (oven), but if not the dough will be taken to the bakery or communal oven to be transformed into bread. Pots and pans, and braids of onions and garlic hang on the wall. Perishables are stored under the eaves where the air circulates most freely. An altar honouring the Virgin Mary always has a few sprigs of herbs lying on it. Athenaeus would recognise this kitchen. He would simply assume that the figure of the altar was Hestia, goddess of the hearth.

As in most cultures, homely fare will differ somewhat from restaurant offerings. There will be a greater variety of horta, for example, as the family is more likely to go out into the woods and gather it themselves. The home kitchen will also tend to offer a greater variety of cheese, whereas a restaurant is likely to offer only feta. The oil used in most home kitchens comes from small family owned groves. They will harvest and press the olives themselves if it is nearby. If it's far away it will be sent to them by relatives. And the home kitchen may be similarly supplied with cheese, honey, wine and fruit. A home kitchen offers the taste of native soil. And, just as importantly, it can also offer the taste of the native sea, when it's situated nearby.

Barbunya Psita Stonanitho
(Red Mullet on a Bed of Dill)

The most common Greek practice with fish is to interfere with it as little as possible. Herbs and spices are not often used. This recipe shows the Byzantine mind at work. The fish is not cooked with the herb, merely next to it.

Take a few red mullet, cleaned but heads intact. Sprinkle them with salt and squeeze some lemon juice over them. Build a fire and let it burn down to coals. On a portable grill lay down a bed of fresh dill sprigs. Brush the fish with oil and lay them atop the dill and set it over the fire at a height of about 8cm (3 inches). Cook for five minutes per side.

THE EPIPHANY

My first encounter with Greek food changed my life. I was 25 years old, travelling through Europe on my way to India and was glad to finally be in Greece, meeting up with 'K', a friend from my graduate program. K and Pop, her father, collected me from the Hania airport on Crete. She was five feet tall, as was he. His enormous belly swung before him.

We set out for the beach house. Like many Greeks, Pop drove in darkness with the headlights off. This supposedly helped save on the car battery, but basically just provided some cheap thrills. Some ouzo kept me detached, and my cultural exposure to reincarnation came in handy as we hurtled along the winding road. Finally we passed the last village before descending to the beach house. My friend shouted greetings of reassurance up and down the road, receiving slightly hostile rumbles of recognition in exchange.

I awoke the next morning to the smell of coffee. The thick brew was served unfiltered in small cups, accompanied by fruit, bread, butter, honey and **mizithra**, a wonderfully tangy cheese. My experience of cheese until then had been limited to cheddar, cream cheese and Swiss. Following instructions, I layered honey and mizithra on thick chunks of bread, a previously incomprehensible combination for me. It was delicious. The family procured a variety of other cheeses: sharp, nutty **ghravyera** and **kefalotiri**, the standard feta and also sheep's milk yoghurt, as thick and pungent as cheese.

The charm of any beach house is, of course, eating fresh seafood. Every afternoon Pop met with returning fishermen. He brought back thick purple octopus, monkfish, and lobster that resembled armoured tanks. The seafood was grilled, sauteed, steamed and poached. No breading or deep frying. This first immersion into the essence of fish reminded me ecstatically of certain amorous encounters with humans.

An appetite for internal organs was strongly evident in this family, and everyone cleaned out their fish heads except me. Determining that I had indeed rejected my portion, K grabbed the head and sucked it clean. Similarly, every spindly leg of the lobster was lovingly cracked and consumed.

I surrendered my unwanted rejects, content to sip my red wine. This household cultivated grapes and pressed their own wine, adding to a vat that included distillations 10 years old. Until now, American jug wines had defined the extent of my experience. This wine was exquisite: ruby red, dense, fruity, full-bodied. Pop warned me that it was rationed so I had to make do with one glass a day. Unrationed spirits included retsina and ouzo. I had no complaints.

Unbeknownst to me, K had a reputation as a woman with balls, and so, long before the main meal, we were each presented with a single s sphere of dark meat. She popped this item nonchalantly into her mouth. "What is it?" I asked, probing with my fork.

"Eat!" barked Pop, who watched me chew, then held up his ouzo in salute. Kidney? Liver? My friend revealed the mystery meat as a cock's testicle. I looked up with a start, which caused the men to laugh appreciatively and regard me with renewed interest.

Locals stopped by the house after lunch, inviting us to join them in diving for sea urchin roe. My friend jumped at the chance, and I accompanied her. Sea urchin roe are considered on par with caviar, and I had tasted neither. We travelled to a beautiful bay with crystal clear water. The divers needed unmuddied shallows to escape being punctured by the sea urchin spines. The operation of locating pregnant specimens was entirely hit-and-miss. But once the egg-loaded spheres were split open, they revealed their bounty in orange-red veins. By sunset, the treasure amounted to three tablespoons' worth of roe. Around us were littered the remains of dozens of spiny creatures. The precious booty was transported home, rinsed and liberally garnished with lemon juice and olive oil. Finally, we were ready for the tasting.

The first impact on the tongue was salty. But then, rolling and mashing the roe in my mouth, an iridescent rainbow of tastes shot out and blended into one another in breathtaking profusion: sweet crab, sour citrus, bitter liquor, meaty wild mushrooms, searing horseradish ... it felt as though I had chewed through a kitchenful of food. The sticky essence lingered for an eternity, transforming, coalescing, then mutating again all the way down the resonant tunnel of my throat. I was in shock. I felt drained, my body post-orgasmic in its stupor. I felt full to bursting. I could not bear the thought of any other food. I wanted to be alone. As I struggled to focus on the others, I realised there was silence at the table, a rare event for my boisterous host family. I wasn't the only one who had been transported by this magical food.

We admired the effortless local beauty and pledged to hunt down more sea urchins the next day. But clearly our luck had run out and I left Greece without tasting that wondrous food again. Once in a while that rainbow of tastes re-ignites on my tongue, bringing my vivid initiation into Greek pleasures rushing back, and I thank the Greek Gods for fate, chance, destiny and the sacred talent of sensual enjoyment.

Ginu Kamani is a professor of English
at Mills College in Oakland, California

celebrating

with food

n Greece, history, religion and identity are intrinsically entwined, and this is no more evident than in the nation's celebratory foods. Every morsel is laced with symbolism, from Christmas biscuits to the spit-roast lamb of Easter. Even the fasting days of Lent have

Carnival

In Greek, carnival is called **apokries** (abstinence from meat) and refers to the three weeks before Lent. This is a time for indulgence, as going without meat (and the other delights that individuals may forswear for Lent) would otherwise be too hard to bear. And it isn't just the selfish desire to consume that obtains in this near month of partying. This celebration has its roots in Dionysian or Bacchanalian celebrations that were meant to help stimulate the fecundity of the earth after the long death of winter. All of nature bursts forth at this time, and humans, no less a part of it, must do their bit to ensure the continuance of the process. Lest there be any doubt, November is a busy month for the midwife. The church was never able to contain this spring fever, so the learned fathers incorporated many of its aspects into the paschal observances that we know today. So partaaay!

Militinia (Aegean cheesecakes), Paros, Cyclades

In the first week of carnival, the family will slaughter a pig if they have one. Or something else if they don't. And they'll even buy something if they must. In the second week all are free to eat as much meat as they like. Even on Wednesday and Friday for Heaven's sake! And the whole land is befogged with the smell of roasting meat. Week three is **tirofaghos** (cheese week) during which many a cheese pie, cheesecake and slab of feta are gobbled with delight.

Even the dearly departed are invited to the party during carnival. On **Psihosavato** (Saturday of the Souls) ladies carry **koliva** to the graves of those who have departed in the last year, and encourage them to do their part in rejuvenating the earth (see the boxed text).

Family lunch, Chios, North-Eastern Aegean

SWEETS FOR THE DECEASED

In Greek culture, death is marked by special foods, with koliva being the most important. After the church service koliva is what mourners are served as it symbolises the cycle of life. Women have always been responsible for death rituals, and in accordance with this, koliva is prepared by old women, grandmas or aunts. If a family is bereft of a koliva maker, one is contacted through the church. Once the order is placed, the koliva will appear on the day of the funeral.

To make koliva, soft-boiled wheat kernels are mixed with dried fruit, pomegranate seeds, sugar and nuts. The fruit symbolises joy and sweetness; the pomegranate seeds, fertility. The main ingredient, wheat, is a symbol of the Resurrection: *unless the grain of wheat falls into the earth and dies, it remains alone, but if it dies it bears much fruit* (John 12:24). The mixture is placed on a silver platter in the shape of a mound, covered with icing sugar and studded with almonds to form the shape of a cross.

All during the funeral the anticipation is unbearable. The tears, the prayers and the grief are all worth the koliva that the priest gives everyone as they leave. The koliva takes away the awkwardness, sweetens the pain, makes it part of life. As you take the koliva you say "life to the living, may God forgive the deceased soul and may their memory be eternal".

Clio Tarazi was born in the Greek community of Alexandria.
She now lives in California.

Clean Monday

The first day of Lent is when cooks scrub their pots and pans clean of any trace of animal fat, because they are embarking on 40 days of strict observance. This day marks the start of a spiritual and physical inner cleansing and the restoring of 'balance' into the lives of Orthodox congregants. After the gut-busting, meat-eating days of carnival, many find Lent something of a relief. It's a day to ease oneself into Lent. And what could be more delicious or indulgent, while still eschewing meat and dairy, than a meal of fish-roe salad, horta, seasonal vegetables, all kinds of seafood, stuffed vine leaves, pickles and **laghana**, a long flat loaf sprinkled with sesame seeds baked just for this day. And though it be Lent, the wine flows.

Lent

The 40 days of Lent are days of prayer and reflection. One does not marry, start a business, go on a journey, laugh too much nor eat meat during this time. This is not a time for indulgence. Ah, but this is Greece, and Greeks have subtle and creative minds, and demanding palates. This is the best time of the year to eat vegetarian fare, as this is when the native Greek genius is most taxed, challenged and vindicated. Rich, almost sinful, dishes such as **yemitsa** (stuffed vegetables), **dolmadhes** (stuffed vine leaves), wild greens and sweets are available to the pious Greek sinner who is vitiating any malfeasance by avoiding bangers and bacon. Hah! And of course there are exceptions allowed in the regimen such as on the Feast of the Annunciation (25 March; which is also simultaneously Greek Independence Day) when folk may gorge themselves on platters of fish and tankards of wine, and stagger home with a belly full. Lent, you say? Bring it on!

Dolmadhes with yoghurt, Hania, Crete

Greek Proverb

An oven has fallen
(a death or disaster has occurred)

Easter

This is the big one. This is the most important time of the Greek calendar. People plan for this through the entire year. And after 40 days of abstinence they are ready for it. Despite the feasting and gaiety, Holy Week (the week leading up to Easter) is a time of reflection, even of mourning, for the loss of Christ and virtue on earth. Many people take no food at all for the first three days. Entertainment is limited to passion plays, moralities and religious dramas. And everyone knows they'll be over in a week.

On Good Wednesday housekeepers call on their priests to have the eggs and flour blessed. These ingredients will become the sacred breads of Easter. On Good Thursday preparations start in earnest: the sacred breads are baked, scented with mastic, sweet spices, honey, rosemary, bay, or whatever the bountiful earth provides can find its way into Easter bread, cookies and cakes and biscuits.

Good Thursday is often called Red Thursday, and every household will prepare red-dyed Easter eggs. Eggs have always been symbols of renewal and continuity, and the red dye symbolises Christ's blood. These eggs are given as gifts, baked into breads and also wielded vigorously in knock-out tournaments following Easter mass. Contenders select an egg and take turns to smash an opponent's egg using the pointy (less vulnerable) end as a weapon-head. Last egg standing is the winner.

And then comes Good Friday, a national holiday on which absolutely no work may be done. Even taxi drivers take this seriously, so beware if you are a visitor. On this day no meat or dairy will appear on the table. And no olive oil or fruit juice, nothing that has to be crushed or deformed, in memory of the tortures Christ's body went through. On this day no one will hammer a nail or hang laundry in respect for his sufferings. But there will be vinegar dressing on the vegetables to commemorate that which was given to Jesus on the cross.

Good Saturday is the day to slaughter the Easter lamb. In most parts of Greece it will be dressed and prepared for the spit. In the Dodecanese it will be stuffed with rice or bulgur, nuts and raisins, then trussed and placed in the communal oven to roast ever so slowly until the next afternoon. With the innards of the lamb people make **mayiritsa** (lamb's offal soup). But this is still a fast day, so the soup will be set aside until after midnight mass. Even the non-religious and irreligious attend this mass. Soldiers will shine their boots, girls will don their finery and the priest will be in his richest vestments. At midnight the bells ring, the people shout and the boys light fireworks. Be careful if you're at this festival, for some of the naughty ones will hurl sticks of dynamite and casualties are not unknown. High explosives are illegal in Greece, but it's hard to stem the exuberance.

A church at Elounda, Crete

Easter Sunday is the main event. The menfolk will dig a pit, kindle a fire within and have the lamb turning on the spit by mid-morning. Women will keep them supplied with coffee, water and little things to nibble, and tell them that at noon they will bring them wine or ouzo. By about 11 o'clock the men will decide that it's noon somewhere in the world and that's good enough for them. The spirit of Dionysus is soon felt across the land. By mid-afternoon the lamb is cooked and so are a few of the men. The table is set with other traditional Easter dishes such as cheese pies and salads, but it is the lamb, after so many meatless days, that is the centrepiece.

Kuluria Astipalitika (Saffron Biscuits of Astypalea)

Most Easter breads and biscuits are sweet, but these are savoury, containing no sugar. And sugar being a relatively recent addition to the Greek kitchen we are sure that this is indeed a very old recipe.

Ingredients

1 tsp	saffron threads
1 cup	milk
1 cup	full fat cottage cheese
30g (1oz)	butter
¼ cup	olive oil
1	egg yolk
½ tsp	allspice
4 cups	all purpose flour
½ tsp	white pepper
½ tsp	salt
1	packet dry active yeast
¼ tsp	baking powder

Add the saffron to the milk and simmer in a saucepan until the milk takes on the saffron's colour. Set aside. Beat together the cheese, butter, oil and egg. Whisk the milk into this mixture, then mix in one cup of the flour.

In a mixing bowl add allspice, pepper, salt, yeast and baking powder to the remaining flour and mix well. Make a well in the centre and pour in the milk mixture. Mix until a good dough is obtained then let it rest, covered, for one hour. Preheat the oven to 200°C (400°F).

Take the dough by handfuls and roll them into cylinders about eight inches long and half an inch thick (20cm by 1cm). Connect their ends to form a bagel shape. Place them onto oiled baking sheets, leaving room for them to swell, and bake for 25 minutes. Remove and let them cool completely. Return them to the oven at 80°C (175°F) for four hours, or until they're completely dry. They will keep for months in tins or Tupperware.

Makes 2 dozen.

Weddings & Name Days

There aren't many holidays in the summer months, but many weddings are celebrated, as well as the days of the saints for whom people are named. Name Day celebrations can be anything from a festive dinner to dinner and a show. Weddings, however, have many a custom and comestible surrounding them. In some traditional villages the nuptial bed is prepared by relatives, in some others by unmarried girls. They stuff the mattress with lamb's wool and sew it up with special needles and thread. They lay out the sheets and blankets. Atop that they place trays of sweets, the kinds that symbolise fertility, such as sesame candy, sugared almonds, or breads moulded in highly suggestive shapes. Then they smash a pomegranate against the front door. This has been a symbol of fertility, prosperity and renewal since the cult of Dionysus.

The chief food of the wedding feast, indeed of most Greek feasts, is a spit-roast lamb. It's Easter all over. The lamb is trussed and put over the fire even as the ceremony is taking place. If you are in the church at this time, watch the feet of the bride and groom. Just before the priest pronounces them to be husband and wife one of them will gently but unmistakably step on the other's foot. That first 'step' on the road that is marriage indicates who the dominant partner shall be. And it could go either way. After the ceremony and feast, the bride is taken to the groom's family home. It is there that her new mother-in-law will feed her a spoonful of sugar to ensure her of a sweet disposition.

Saint Efstratios church, Thymiana, Chios, North-Eastern Aegean

GREEKS DO IT BETTER

They are excessively fond of amusement and display ... the number of holidays seriously interferes with the industry and prosperity of the people. Scarcely two thirds of the year are occupied by working days. Then the people give themselves wholly up to pleasure; which consists in an unusual modicum of bell-ringing, martial music, discharges of cannon, permabulation in the streets in holiday attire and fireworks.

Charles Tuckerman, 1873

Christmas & New Year

The end of the year brings on another 40 days of fasting prior to Christmas. An element of Halloween is evident during December. At this time you may meet **kalikandzari**, dreadful little creatures (like ugly leprechauns) who reside in the bowels of the earth. In dark, cold December they swarm out and do all manner of mischief, plaguing the good and delighting the evil. But they are shallow creatures, with a sweet tooth. It's easy to buy them off. Just leave some candies or sweets out for them and they'll leave you alone. And if they don't take the sweets, you may eat them.

Near Christmas the carollers make the rounds, singing **kalanda** (folk songs) so as to wish all prosperity and happiness. People give them **melo-makarona** (honey-biscuits), festive breads and honey sweets. On Christmas day those who have one slaughter and roast a piglet. Others buy one or go to the taverna and order succulent roast pork dishes. The custom of eating roast pork at this time of year predates Christianity – it was also a part of the Dionysian celebrations. There's a lot of history in a suckling pig.

New Year celebrations are much like Christmas, even an extension of it. But the sweets change. Those symbolising fertility are favoured: pomegranates, almonds and other nuts, honey and sesame candies. A golden-glazed bread called **vasilopita** is baked with a coin inside. At midnight the family tears into it, and whoever finds the coin can expect good fortune throughout the ensuing year.

regional
variations

Greece defies accurate division into distinct regions of gastronomy. Any such division we might make will be met with objections by those whom we have divided. "No", they will say. "It's not like that. It's like this." Even Greeks don't agree very much beyond a few topographical certitudes, undeniable when consulting the map.

Consider this: there are about 15 million Greeks in the world, one third live outside Greece, one third live in Athens and Thessaloniki, and the remaining third are spread throughout the land. This situation is the result of only the most recent of many migrations of Greeks during their long, long history. They have always been a people who travel. In ancient times they sent colonies out across the whole of the Mediterranean, and from that grew the greater socio-linguistic community they called **Magna Grecia** (Greater Greece). Even then they were criss-crossing back and forth, exchanging goods, ideas, hostilities, alliances, arts and kitchen craft. The unique wines of Crete became necessities of Syracuse. The Athenian way with fish became the standard. All ate hard, dry **paksimadya** (rusks).

REGIONS

BULGARIA

FORMER YUGOSLAV
REPUBLIC OF
MACEDONIA

Black Sea

Adriatic
Sea

ALBANIA

Thessaloniki

Thracian
Sea

Sea of
Marmara

Corfu   Ioannina

Ionian
Sea

G R E E C E

Mytilini

ATHENS

Aegean
Sea

TURKEY

Nafplio

Ermoupolis

Mirtoön
Sea

Mediterranean
Sea

Sea of Crete

Hania   Iraklio

| | Aegean Islands | | Ionian Islands | | Southern Greece |
| | Crete | | Northern Greece | | |

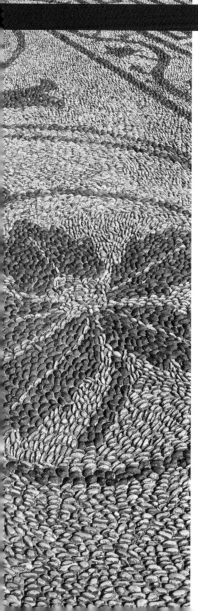

About the only thing that didn't travel was the infamous black broth of the Spartans, a soup of pig's blood, vinegar and salt.

Greeks ventured east in the wake of Alexander the Great, always sending home new things. Roman conquests carried them north and south, and they brought home yet more of the world and suffused it throughout their homelands. And then came the Ottoman conquest, and like a huge wind blew them all across the face the globe in what is known as the Greek Diaspora. Greeks scattered to the Black Sea, Romania, the Austro-Hungarian empire, Russia, to the great cities of Europe and to the New World. They even spread throughout the Ottoman empire.

As the Ottoman empire collapsed many of the diaspora Greeks began to return, though not always to ancestral lands, but wherever they could make a living. In 1922 independent Greece and the Republic of Turkey exchanged populations of one and a half million people, and Greeks of Asia Minor brought their distinct kitchen customs to the mainland. After the fall of the Soviet Union, Greeks from Pontus returned, settling mainly in Macedonia where they have been transforming the local cuisine. And since the 1960s people all over the country have been abandoning the farms, villages and islands to seek a better life in the cities.

Pebble mosaic, Saint Efstratios church, Thymiana, Chios, North-Eastern Aegean

Aegean Islands

The Aegean Sea is the geographic, historic, and cultural heart of Greece. Tourism has brought some new wealth to the region (and we include port calls by NATO navies), but before the 1960s these islands were poor, some wretchedly poor. Many have thin soil and little water. Tourism has been a blessing and a curse. It has lifted the people up out of a life of want, and slowed the exodus of Aegean youth. But it has brought a plague of fast-food, binge drinking, drinks with paper umbrellas, spam, corned beef and tinned spaghetti. And did we mention fast-food?

When you do find the genuine article in the Aegean you'll discover a cuisine based on eggs, pulses, potatoes and bread. These staples are supplemented by locally grown fruit, vegetables, as well as **horta** (wild greens). Being such a stripped down, basic kind of cookery you will find that cooks here can extract the most pleasure and benefit from humble ingredients.

REGIONAL VARIATIONS

SALTY SARDINES

Sardines are seasonal. In July and August the sardines are the perfect size. Visitors who come to Lesvos in September and October may have a hard time finding them at all. If you're lucky enough to find a place selling salted sardines, be sure to watch them being prepared. The general method is to put down a layer of sea salt, then a layer of sardines, then another layer of salt, and so on. It sounds simple, but many makers claim that their personal touch makes all the difference. One cook told me his sardines tasted better because he placed the fish with their bellies up.

Eating salted sardines is easily mastered. Firstly, hold the fish body between forefinger and thumb of your left hand (if you are right-handed). Take hold of the tiny head with your other hand and bend it down towards the belly. As the spinal column breaks and the head is severed, pull it towards the tail so that the guts come with it when it is fully detached. Throw this to the cats that surround your table. Peel the skin from the fish using a rubbing motion of your thumb. Line the fish up and season with olive oil (some people add lemon or vinegar), or ask the proprietor to season it his own special way. In most cases preparation will have been done for you by the cafe worker in the kitchen and your salted sardines will already look like giant skinless anchovies.

As for eating the sardines this is a matter of experimentation. It's a fact that they go well with ouzo but they can also be eaten as a meal. But ouzo and salted sardines certainly complement each other and in my opinion there is no better meze.

Matt Barlett lives on the island of Lesvos and is the author of I Married a Lesbian

Sieving and sorting dried oregano leaves, Pyrgi, Chios, North-Eastern Aegean

For example, climate and soil are ideal for growing tomatoes, and so much attention is paid to them. They are taken raw in salads, strung on braids and sun dried for winter and made into soups and sauces. And they are often baked with nothing but a pinch of herbs, not even a drop of oil. And they are the taste of sunshine itself.

Fish has always been an important supplement to the Aegean diet, though in recent years this has been changing. Overfishing has reduced available stocks and fisherfolk can fetch a better price in Athens or beyond. This leaves locals with imported frozen fish from Israel, North Africa, even Brazil. The one tasty and traditional import is **bakalyaros**, salt cod from Iceland or Norway. Aegean cooks can do amazing things with this stuff, but the most common way is to fry it in oil with lots of garlic.

Salt cod, Thessaloniki Central Market, Macedonia

Skumbri se Klimatofila (Mackerel in Vine Leaves)

This is a popular dish on the island of Lesvos. It's delicious either hot for dinner, or cold for a picnic or meze.

Ingredients

12	small mackerel, cleaned, heads removed
2	onions, chopped
1 tsp	oregano
30	fresh vine leaves
1	juice of 1 lemon
¹/₂ cup	olive oil
	Salt and pepper to taste

Sprinkle salt in the cavities of the fish and let sit for 15 minutes. Mix the onion, oregano and some salt and pepper and fill the fish with it. Wrap each fish in two vine leaves and set them in an oiled ovenproof dish. Drizzle with oil and lemon. Bake at 180°C (375°F) for 30 minutes.

Serves 6 as a meze, 3 as a meal.

You will rarely see this on the tourist trail, it being thought too humble. But seek and ye shall find.

Sardines, tuna and octopus are all enjoyed as both meze and main course. People dig for **pines**, a kind of razor clam, and they go diving for **ahyini** (sea urchins). Their roe is delicious. To make a small catch of fish go a long way, locals make **kakavya**, fish soup that is the forerunner of French bouillabaisse.

A crop unique to the island of Chios is gum mastic. It grows nowhere else in the world. It can be chewed as gum right off the tree, but more often it's used as a flavouring in spirits, spoon sweets and festive breads. In ancient and Byzantine times it was highly favoured. But since Ottoman times it has played a larger role in the economy than in the cuisine. As part of the price for privileges Chiots were given by the Sultan, they had to turn over the entire mastic crop. Taking a chunk for personal use would result

REGIONAL VARIATIONS

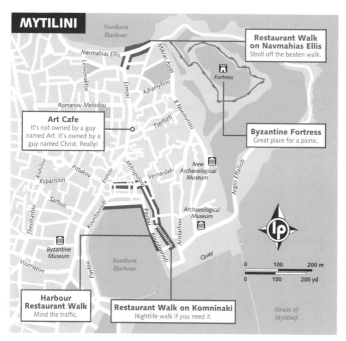

MYTILINI

Northern Harbour

Navmahias Ellis

Lesvonaktos

Ermou

Mikras Asias

Adramytiou

Fortress

Restaurant Walk on Navmahias Ellis
Stroll off the beaten walk.

Romanou Melodou

Tsertseti

8 Noemvriou

Art Cafe
It's not owned by a guy named Art. It's owned by a guy named Christ. Really!

Byzantine Fortress
Great place for a picnic.

Aishiou

Pittakou

Ermou

Mitropoleos

Vernardaki

New Archaeological Museum

Agiri Eftaliou

Kyparision

Sarfous

Kountouriou

Pavlou Kountouriou

Aristarhou

Archaeological Museum

Theofrastou

Vournazon

Byzantine Museum

Pavlou

Southern Harbour

Quay

100   200 m
100   200 yd

Harbour Restaurant Walk
Mind the traffic.

Restaurant Walk on Komninaki
Nightlife walk if you need it.

Straits of Mytilinif

in a severe flogging. Stealing a commercial amount would result in your head on a pole. Even today the majority of the crop goes to where it went in Ottoman days: the Middle East, where it is used as perfume, incense and chewing gum. But you can buy all you like at shops by the ferry landing of Chios Town.

On a few of the Aegean islands saffron grows wild, and when they're in bloom, women go wandering through the hills, plucking the pretty little flowers. Once they've returned home with a full basket the real work begins, for the stamens can only be removed by deft fingers. There's no way to shake them out or otherwise cull them from the flower. And there is no machine that can do it. Even the large saffron farms of the north employ nimble fingered workers to collect the spice. The islands yield relatively few crocus flowers, but the resulting spice is more intense than the cultivated variety. The stamens of one flower are sufficient to flavour an island pilaf.

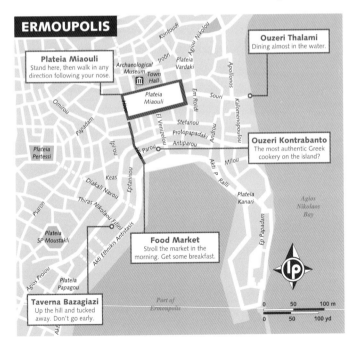

ERMOUPOLIS

Ouzeri Thalami
Dining almost in the water.

Plateia Miaouli
Stand here, then walk in any direction following your nose.

Kontoudi

Agiou Nikolou

Iroön

Plateia Vardaki

Archaeological Museum Town Hall

Apollonos

Plateia Miaouli

Em Roïdi

Souri

Kalomenopoulou

Omirou

Papadam

El Venizelou

Stefanou

Protopapadaki

Antiparou

Ipirou

Parou

Aïptorou

Ouzeri Kontrabanto
The most authentic Greek cookery on the island?

Plateia Pertessi

Keas

Akti P. Ralli

Milou

Plateia Kanari

Psaron

Diakali Naxou

Thiras Nikolaou Filini

Eptanisou

Ep Papadam

Agios Nikolaos Bay

Plateia SP Moustakli

Akti Ethnikis Antistasis

Food Market
Stroll the market in the morning. Get some breakfast.

Agios Proïou

Plateia Papagou

Taverna Bazagiazi
Up the hill and tucked away. Don't go early.

Port of Ermoupolis

0   50   100 m
0   50   100 yd

THE CONSERVATOR – Faces of Gastromony

Jasmine Zahariou drags on her cigarette, blows a smoke ring and smiles.

"Women are new to this sport", she says. "Only since my generation do women smoke. Before, if a woman smoked she was thought to be loose. I like to smoke. Yes, it's a new thing. But I do little else that is new".

Jasmine and her partner, Maria Papantzima, own and operate the Ouzeri Kontrabanto in Ermoupolis on the island of Syros. They are on their own little crusade to keep alive Greece's culinary traditions that they see diminishing with every passing year. They've been at it since 1993.

Jasmine is the chef and Maria serves at table. Maria is quick to smile, but not so quick to speak. Jasmine tells you anything you want to know. If business is slow she'll even sit down and have a glass of tsipuro with you. She takes the fiery drink neat.

"Water is a crime", says she.

"Then criminalise my ouzo", says I.

She adds a dollop of water and the ouzo billows white. Educated as a historian it is fitting that Jasmine is trying to preserve her country's gastronomic history.

"Here we use only Greek methods and products. I'm always searching for old recipes. So I don't read cookery books, they're full of novelties and foreign influence. Instead, I talk to old ladies. That's the way to do it in Greece. We've always had mothers and grandmothers who passed down their skills. These days so many women work and have no time to cook. There are few opportunities to pass on the recipes of generations. And now it's all in danger of being lost. It's my job to see it doesn't happen."

The little Ouzeri Kontrabanto seems a small place for such a mighty task. It holds only eight small tables tucked away into a little side street. And the kitchen is tiny.

"My kitchen may be small, but it's a shelter to me. There is history in there, as in any good Greek kitchen. Because it is so small I couldn't try anything French or Chinese even if I wanted to", she says with a wink.

She goes on to explain some of her culinary principles: she will only grill fish because other methods dilute or diminish its natural flavour. Meat cooked for holidays must be done in the oven. She bans popular foreign products such as cream, milk, bacon, even soy sauce.

"I don't dislike foreigners, nor their food. Sometimes I eat it. But I don't cook it. But I *do* love it when foreign tourists come here to get real Greek food. And we stay open all year. Many places close when the tourists go home. But we're cooking for a Greek palate, and need the feedback."

As I pour more water into my ouzo and she sips her neat tsipuro she says, "and I don't cook with water either. Only wine. Wine gives itself to the food. Water only takes away."

So I take a swallow of ouzo neat. Maybe she has a point.

Richard Sterling

DON'T MISS – Aegean Islands

- The many forms of mastic on Chios
- Tomatoes, tomatoes tomatoes!
- Watching European tourists get drunk and dance topless on the beach
- Kuluria Astipalitika – Saffron Biscuits of Astypalea

A pilaf is an ancient dish, but not as ancient as **kuluria astypalitika**, the Easter biscuits made on the island of Astypalea. Most Easter breads and biscuits are sweet, but this one is savoury, containing no sugar. And sugar being a relatively recent addition to the Greek kitchen (middle Byzantine times) we are persuaded that theirs is indeed a very old recipe. It is also a rusk and so will keep for months. So the women bake huge quantities, taking their dough to the local bakery where the ovens are large enough to accommodate what will be a year's worth of saffron bread. Some of it they'll send to relatives on the mainland. But most of it will stay on the island, to be eaten with cheese or coffee, or on its own. (See the recipe in the Celebrating chapter.)

Crete

Every dietician in the western world praises the Mediterranean diet in general, and the Cretan diet in particular. We can describe the Cretan diet and culture in a word: more. There are many commonalities of the general Mediterranean diet: grains, legumes, fruit, fish and goodly amounts of wine. But to these Crete adds more olives, more olive oil, more honey, more fruit and horta. Greeks consume more cheese that any other Europeans, but Cretans consume more than other Greeks. With this diet, and a low-stress lifestyle, the Cretans outlive almost all the other peoples of the world. But be warned, a Cretan dish literally floats in olive oil. A Cretan farmer will get one third of his daily calories from oil.

Lying between Europe, Africa and Asia Minor, Crete has always benefited culinarily from being in the middle of trans-continental trade. Dates

HANIA

Sea of Crete

Zambeliou
Stand here, then walk in any direction following your nose.

Venetian Port

Naval Museum

Mosque of the Janissaries

Ancient Kydonia

Plateia Katehaki

Akti Enosis

Kalergon

Epimenidou

0   50   100 m
0   50   100 yd

Theotokopoulou

Akti Koundourioti

Apostolidou

Lithinou

Ag Markou

Kanevaro

Sifaka

Arholeon

Kalistou

Sifaka

Patriarhou Ioanikiou

Pireos

Douka

Plateia Venizelou

Karaoli Dimitriou

Kondylaki

Archaeological Museum

Hrys Episkopou

Potie

Cavaladon

Kafenion Kolompos
Relaxation amidst the intensity of holiday making.

Patriarhou Gerasimou

M Melaxaki

Piga

Folklore Museum

Siavo Bastion

Haliadon

Orthodox Cathedral

Skrydlof

Plateia Hortatson

Mihali Dalani

Tsouderon

Plateia Markopoulou

Nikiforou Episkopou

Nikiforou Foka

El Venizelou

Kyrilou

Giannari

Plateia 1866

Kriari

Koraka

Plastira

Tzanakaki

Food Market
The cutest little market in the country. Great for breakfast.

Ancient Kafenion
An ancient nameless kafenion, sitting next to a modern cyber cafe.

Kydonias

Ionias

Smyrnis

P Kalaïdi

Zymvrakidon

Sfakonmanli

Apokoronou

Dining Area
An area completely devoid of tourists.

Sfakion

Kornarou

Public Garden & Zoo

Konstandinoupoleos

MAKING FILO PASTRY – Hania, Crete

In a small shop behind the central market in Hania, filo pastry is made by hand six days a week. You can tell the shop is open by the curtain in the front window – if the curtain is knotted the shop is open, but if it is hanging straight the shop is closed.

The ingredients used to make filo are flour, water and salt. These are kneaded into a dough using a simple machine that resembles a mangle. This ensures the dough is incredibly elastic. The dough is then weighed into 500g pieces and formed into balls. After resting for approximately 20 to 30 minutes, these balls are rolled into flat disks using a heavy rolling pin.

The village of Plaka near Elounda, Crete

Now it really gets impressive. Each disk is rotated furiously by hand, and in very short space of time the disk increases in size to become a very thin, large, round sheet. Suddenly, as though it was a fishing net, the sheet is flung on to the centre of a table covered with a coarse linen cloth. As it lands it catches the air and forms a dome. It is then stretched by being gently tugged, pulled and coaxed towards the edge of the table until, within a few minutes, it covers the entire surface of the table.

Hania, Crete

The edges are then trimmed to form a perfect square (the trimmings are gathered together and re-used). The trimmed filo is covered with another sheet of linen and left to dry slightly for about 15 to 45 minutes, depending on the weather. After drying, the filo is cut into 16 identically sized rectangular pieces. Each piece is then lightly covered in flour and stacked one on top of the other. It is then ready for sale to the steady stream of customers that come into the shop.

and plums came from Egypt and Syria. The sea voyages that the early Cretans made saw the invention of jams and preserves to sustain the sailors on long voyages. Such preserves still feature as a filler for Cretan pies and sweets. Both Byzantine and Venetian influence is still evident today, such as in the popularity of such pasta dishes as cannelloni.

Most Greeks are fond of snails, but the Cretans more so. Elsewhere in Greece they are a tasty snack or a meze, but on Crete they are a staple. After rain, snails are easily plucked from the ground by eager children who bring them home to be readied for the table. They will already be delicious because they have been feeding on the herbs that grow wild all over the island, but they will be given a diet of meal and more herbs for a few days before being condemned to the pot.

There's a surfeit of greens on Crete, including purslane, artichokes and chicory, which is eaten as part of a salad or boiled and dressed with lemon.

DON'T MISS – Crete

- A dish of snails
- Cretan quantities of olive oil
- Sweet Cretan wines
- Living longer on a Cretan diet

Kukya me Aghriangginares
(Broad Beans with Artichokes)

Pulses are one of the pillars of the Cretan diet. So are artichokes, both domestic and wild.

Ingredients

500g (1lb)	dried broad beans, soaked, then simmered for 30 minutes and drained.
1kg (2lb)	wild artichokes, trimmed and cleaned
¼ cup	fennel, chopped
1	onion, chopped
4	tomatoes, peeled, seeded and chopped
1 cup	olive oil
	Salt and pepper to taste

Heat the oil in a pot and brown the onions. Add all the other ingredients and heat through. Reduce the heat and simmer for one hour or until the beans are tender.

Serves 4

Artichoke

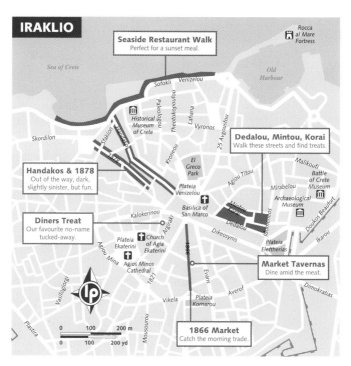

IRAKLIO

Rocca al Mare Fortress

Sea of Crete

Old Harbour

Seaside Restaurant Walk
Perfect for a sunset meal.

Sofokli Venizelou

Paleologou Theotokopoulou Lahana

Vyronos

Historical Museum of Crete

25 Avgoustou

Skordilon

Stadiou Handakos 1878

Dedalou, Mintou, Korai
Walk these streets and find treats.

Malikouti

Battle of Crete Museum

Agiou Titou

Mirabelou

El Greco Park

Handakos & 1878
Out of the way, dark, slightly sinister, but fun.

Plateia Venizelou

Archaeological Museum

Doukos Beaufort

Ikarou

Basilica of San Marco

Mintou Korai

Idomeneos

Kalokerinou

Dedalou

Diners Treat
Our favourite no-name tucked-away.

Angiraki

Dikeosynis

Plateia Eleftherias

Agiou Mina

Plateia Ekaterini

Church of Agia Ekaterini

1866

Market Tavernas
Dine amid the meat.

Agios Minos Cathedral

Dimokratias

Vasilogiorgi

1821

Evans

Averof

Vikela

Plateia Kornarou

Plastira

Mousourou

0   100   200 m
0   100   200 yd

1866 Market
Catch the morning trade.

Legumes are a cornerstone of the Cretan diet, and cooks get very creative, even with leftovers. If beans go uneaten at dinner they will appear again, though hardly recognisable, for they will have been 'married' with other foods. They might be wed to rice, betrothed to meat, conjoined with tomatoes, and the dish will bear its married name: **pandremeni**. On the 5 January an ancient ritual is played out using pulses. In ancient days celebrants honoured the gods with dishes of peas and pulses. Today a dish of mixed pulses called **polispora** is served, not only to the family but to the farm animals. At the meal's end the women scatter leftovers for the birds.

Cheeses such as **mizithra** make many a dish. And **tiropita** (cheese pies) are often made quite differently on Crete. They may be baked, but they may also be fried. And pies that we think of as sweets, such as pumpkin, will be made savoury.

Ionian Islands

This is the most European part of Greece. With the exception of a brief (in historical terms) Turkish occupation of a couple of the islands they have always been western looking. Italy, France, Russia and Britain have all lorded over the islands at some stage. But do not think that these islands are any less Greek. Throughout history the eastern Mediterranean has seen vast changes in religion, language and arts, as peoples and empires have come and gone. But the single-most constant constant has been the Greeks. Their language has evolved, but is still the same. Their religion

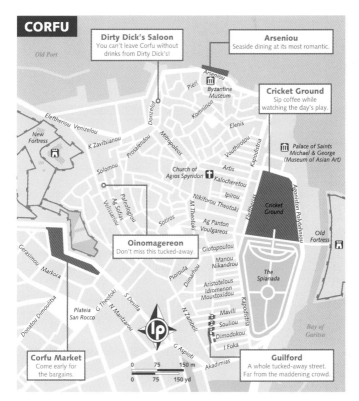

CORFU

Dirty Dick's Saloon
You can't leave Corfu without drinks from Dirty Dick's!

Arseniou
Seaside dining at its most romantic.

Old Port

Arseniou

Pieri

Byzantine Museum

Cricket Ground
Sip coffee while watching the day's play.

Komninon

Elenis

Eleftheriou Venizelou

New Fortress

K Zavitsianou

Prosalendou

Donzelot

Mitropoleos

Vouthirotou

Kapodistria

Palace of Saints Michael & George (Museum of Asian Art)

Solomou

Artis

Church of Agios Spyridon

Kalocheretou

Ipirou

Agoniston Polytechniou

Paleologou

Ag Sofias

Velissariou

Nikiforou Theotoki

M Theotoki

Sotiros

Ag Panton Voulgareos

Cricket Ground

Old Fortress

Oinomagereon
Don't miss this tucked-away.

Giotopoulou

Gerasimou Markora

Manou Nikandrou

The Spianada

Psoroula

Dinarhou

Aristotelous Idromenon Moustoxidou

Kapodistria

Donatou Dimoulitsa

Plateia San Rocco

G Theotoki

S Desilla

N Mantzarou

N Zambeli

Mavili

Souliou

Dimodokou

i Foka

Bay of Garitsa

Corfu Market
Come early for the bargains.

0   75   150 m
0   75   150 yd

G Aspioti

Akadimias

Guilford
A whole tucked-away street. Far from the maddening crowd.

Sofrito (veal with garlic sauce), Doukades, Corfu, Ionian Islands

DON'T MISS – Ionian Islands

- The view of Liapades Bay from Lakones, Corfu, Ionian Islands
- The spiciest food of Greece
- Kefallonia for Greece's oldest operating winery
- An afternoon of beer and cricket on Corfu

still resembles its antecedent. And both the cooks of antiquity and those of today could talk to each other with much understanding.

For the visitor the most important non-Greek gastronomic influence is the Italian. This is the only part of Greece that uses large amounts of red pepper. Other Italian crossovers include salami, **sofrito** (veal sliced thin and cooked in tangy sauce), pasta dishes and a red-hot fish stew called **burdheto** (see the recipe). But don't be misled into thinking that any of these dishes will bear the taste of Italy. For they are only informed by the boot-shaped neighbour. They still taste of Greece, and you could tell the difference blindfolded. The olive oil of this region is very often different. In most of Greece the fruit is beaten off the branch by means of a long stick, for it is harvested before it is fully ripe. But in the Ionian Islands the olives are often left to fully ripen and fall off the tree. This gives a quite different taste to the finished product, and it leads the men to say that they beat neither their wives nor their trees.

The British held the island for 50 years in the 19th century and their mark is lasting. Fortunately not in the home kitchen. But they did leave the people with the game of cricket, and if not exactly a taste for beer then a willingness to provide it.

Bakalyaros Burdheto (Salt Cod Stew)

The word burdheto is actually a corruption of *brodetto,* the Venetian word for soup. But then this recipe is not exactly a soup. And it isn't always made with salt cod, or any other fish. Sometimes the fish is omitted altogether and a delicious vegetarian dish is obtained.

Ingredients

1½kg (3lb) salt cod, soaked and ready to cook,
            cut into manageable pieces
2 tsp   cayenne pepper
1 cup   oil
½ tsp   black pepper
1   onion, chopped
1   full head garlic, chopped
1   large tomato, peeled, seeded and chopped
1kg (2lb)   potatoes, peeled and quartered
1 cup   water or white wine
            chopped parsley and black olives for garnish

Heat the oil in a pan and saute the onion, garlic and cayenne until soft. Add the tomato, potatoes and black pepper. Add water or wine almost to cover, leave a bit exposed. Cover the pan and simmer for 10 minutes. Lay the fish on top of the mix then cover and simmer for a further 30 minutes.
   Serves 8

Salt cod

Northern Greece

Seekers of sun, sand and sex rarely even think of Northern Greece. A lot of Greeks don't think of northern Greece. This fact alone makes it attractive to us. There is little or none of that contrived Greece designed to attract flocks of migratory European moneybirds. Here the terrain is as different from the sunny isles as can be. This is a land of mountain mists, narrow twisting roads and lonely vistas. Lakes, fields and streams provide foods that other Greeks have never tasted. Being a border region, cultures inevitably mix, clash, advance and retreat. Pine forests and bulrushes, spicy grills of meat, smoked fish and fiery tsipuro inform the gastronomy of northern Greece, as well as Albanians, Bulgarians and Turks. Animal protein features more in the diet, because this is where more animals live.

As you travel northward from Athens watch for the restaurants serving **peinirli**. This dish is somewhat like a pizza, but rather than flat it is shaped into a trough resembling a boat and is filled with goodness such as cheese and ground meats and herbs. And the farther north you go the more game and freshwater fish you'll encounter. Greeks have only recently taken to

REGIONAL VARIATIONS

Yaurtopita Tizdhramas (Yoghurt Pie with Vine Leaves)

This dish is unique to Macedonia, specifically the region of Drama. It may be of Turkish origin, but maybe the Turks just liked and made it often.

Ingredients

500g (1lb)	strained yoghurt, preferably sheep's milk.
½ cup	finely ground cornmeal
½ cup	spring onion, minced
½ cup	fresh dill, minced
½ cup	fresh mint, minced
¼ tsp	white pepper
25	vine leaves (drained and rinsed if packed in brine)
¼ cup	olive oil
salt	

Mix together the yoghurt, cornmeal, spring onion, dill, mint, salt and pepper. Oil a pie tin and line the bottom and sides with half the vine leaves. Brush those with oil and pour in the yoghurt mixture. Cover the mixture with the remaining leaves, tucking them down into the sides to form a good 'crust'. Brush the top with oil and cover loosely with aluminium foil. Bake at 180°C (375°F) for 45 minutes. This recipe can also be made in individual ramekins.

Serves 4–6

Sausage display, Thessaloniki Central Market, Macedonia

eating trout and carp and other lake fish. They have always thought of it as unclean, food for famine. Perhaps in other days the waters in which the fish lived were unclean. But these days European standards of purity are in force. At any rate smoked trout is now considered a delicacy. There are now mountain tavernas dedicated to the cooking of freshwater fish, they are called **paradhosiaki psarotaverna**. And along with the trout, frog legs are enjoying increasing popularity. Formerly almost the entire catch of frogs went to France. Somehow the Greeks have awakened to this tasty treat.

Vegetable foods are still important despite the abundance of meat in this region. Mushrooms are more plentiful and more popular here than in most of Greece. Many Greeks regard mushrooms with suspicion, believing

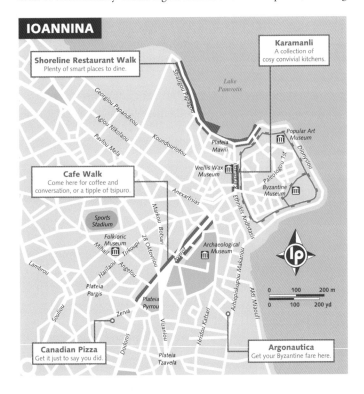

IOANNINA

Karamanli
A collection of cosy convivial kitchens.

Shoreline Restaurant Walk
Plenty of smart places to dine.

Lake Pamvotis

Georgiou Papandreou

Agiou Nikolaou

Pavlou Mela

Stratigou Papagou

Koundouriotou

Plateia Mavili

Popular Art Museum

Dionysiou

Vrellis Wax Museum

Paleologou 1st

Byzantine Museum

Cafe Walk
Come here for coffee and conversation, or a tipple of tsipuro.

Anexartisias

Ethnikis Andistasis

Markou Botsari

Sports Stadium

Folkloric Museum

Mihail Trikoupi

Harilaou Angelou

28 Oktovriou

Avgou

Archaeological Museum

Antiepiskopou Makariou

Akti Miaouli

0   100   200 m
0   100   200 yd

Lambrou

Plateia Pargis

Plateia Pyrrou

Souliou

Zerva

Dokonis

Vizaniou

Hristou Katsari

Canadian Pizza
Get it just to say you did.

Plateia Tzavela

Argonautica
Get your Byzantine fare here.

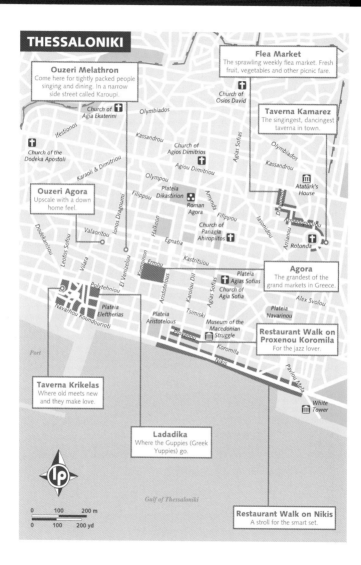

THESSALONIKI

Ouzeri Melathron
Come here for tightly packed people singing and dining. In a narrow side street called Karoupi.

Flea Market
The sprawling weekly flea market. Fresh fruit, vegetables and other picnic fare.

Church of Osios David

Taverna Kamarez
The singingest, dancingest taverna in town.

Church of Agia Ekaterini

Olymbiados

Olymbiados

Ifestionos

Kassandrou

Agias Sofias

Kassandrou

Church of the Dodeka Apostoli

Church of Agios Dimitrios

Atatürk's House

Agiou Dimitriou

Karaoli & Dimitriou

Olympou

Ouzeri Agora
Upscale with a down home feel.

Filippou

Plateia Dikastirion

Amynda

Ionos Dragoumi

Roman Agora

Filippou

Iasonidou

Dragoumi

Antigonidon

Valaoritou

Haltaou

Church of Panagia Ahiropiitos

Rotonda

Dodekanisou

Arianou

Egnatia

Leofos Sofou

Vilara

Kastritsiou

El Venizelou

Kommninon

Ermou

Plateia Agias Sofias

Agora
The grandest of the grand markets in Greece.

Polytehniou

Aristotelous

Katolou Dil

Church of Agia Sofia

Alex Svolou

Agias Sofias

Navarhou Koundourioti

Plateia Eleftherias

Tsimiski

Plateia Navarinou

Plateia Aristotelous

Museum of the Macedonian Struggle

Restaurant Walk on Proxenou Koromila
For the jazz lover.

Port

Proxenou

Koromila

Pavlou Mela

Nikis

Taverna Krikelas
Where old meets new and they make love.

White Tower

Ladadika
Where the Guppies (Greek Yuppies) go.

Restaurant Walk on Nikis
A stroll for the smart set.

Gulf of Thessaloniki

0   100   200 m
0   100   200 yd

LP

them to all be poisonous or even magically empowered. But mountain families go out on mushroom hunts. There are more kinds of horta here than elsewhere in Greece as well. A famous dish is the local variety of **hortopita** (mixed horta pie) made with seven, eight or even nine different wild plants. In keeping with the custom of mixing vegetable foods, **briami** (vegetable casserole) is especially tasty here, often made with a mix of both wild and domestic greenery. And the general Greek love of pulses is evident in dishes of beans, lentils and chickpeas. All especially good of a winter's night in a cosy fire-warmed taverna.

A distinctive kind of meat cookery in this region is known as **ghastra**, sometimes translated as charcoal baking. If you have ever been a boy scout

Arni Kleftiko (Lamb in a Clay Pot)

This recipe was famously, if not traditionally, prepared in an earthenware water jug during the Turkish occupation. While the men were fighting in the mountains, the women kept them fed by cutting the meat and other ingredients into small pieces and stuffing them into the narrow mouth of a water jug. This they sealed with dough and put the whole affair into the oven to bake. Then they would leave the innocuous looking jug near a fountain and the warriors would come out from hiding to collect their rations.

Ingredients

500g (1lb)	boneless lamb cut into bite-size pieces
1	large eggplant cut into bite size pieces
1	large potato cut into bite size pieces
1	capsicum, chopped
2	tomatoes, peeled, seeded and finely chopped
1/4 cup	olive oil
1/2 tsp	cayenne pepper
2	onions, chopped
1	bay leaf
1 tsp	oregano
1 tsp	thyme
3	cloves garlic, chopped

Combine lamb, oil, pepper, bay, oregano, thyme and onion. Cover and refrigerate overnight. Salt the eggplant and drain in a colander then wipe dry. Combine all ingredients together in a water jug (any ovenproof dish will do), cover and bake at 220°C (425°F) for 30 minutes. Uncover and toss the stew, reduce heat to 180°C (375°F) and bake for 1 1/2 hours.

Serves 4

REGIONAL VARIATIONS

DON'T MISS – Northern Greece

- Finish off dinner in the Thessaloniki market with some sweet loukamades
- Fresh and smoked trout
- Frogs' legs
- Winter evenings by the fire in tavernas

or accomplished camp cook you'll recognise the principal behind the technique. Meat, potatoes, perhaps other vegetables and oil go into a metal pot called the ghastra. This is closed and set on top of glowing coals. The lid is then covered with coals. In this method the food is slowly cooked by a means of 'moist roasting' until it is so tender it nearly falls apart.

Southern Greece

Southern Greece is dominated by Athens. All of Greece is dominated by Athens, for all of Greece comes to Athens. At the grand market on Athenas Street signs proudly proclaim "All our fish are from the Aegean". The olives of Kalamata in the Peloponnese are here. Trout from the mountain lakes of the north, wines and fruit from Crete, turkeys from Corfu, horta from all over. As well as imports from all around the Mediterranean. So Athens, while a tasty town, can be a bit confusing to the hungry traveller.

The food in this region is largely what most non-Greeks think of when they think of Greek food. This is the home of retsina. Though it is made elsewhere, it was made here first. This is also where most of the best olive oil comes from, pressed from the smaller kalamata. No one knows for sure but **avgholemono** (egg and lemon sauce) is said to have originated in this area. **Paksimadya** (rusks) are thought to have first been made here too. Notwithstanding the Spartans and their much maligned black broth, this is where we find the cradle of Greek cuisine. This is where we find that mother kitchen to the western world. What will you have in this region? Well, the real question is, what would you like? There is nothing more to say.

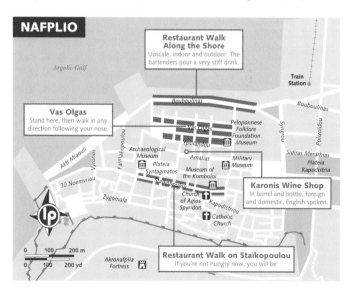

*Cooking lunch on the grill, Taverna Kokkalis,
Stamata, near Kifissia, Athens*

REGIONAL VARIATIONS

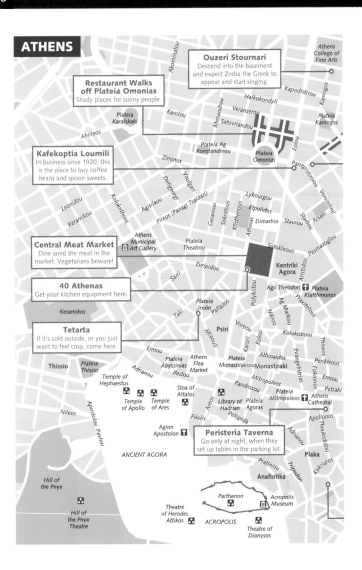

ATHENS

Athens College of Fine Arts

Ouzeri Stournari
Descend into the basement and expect Zorba the Greek to appear and start singing.

Restaurant Walks off Plateia Omonias
Shady places for sunny people.

Kafekoptia Loumili
In business since 1920, this is the place to buy coffee beans and spoon sweets.

Central Meat Market
Dine amid the meat in the market. Vegetarians beware!

40 Athenas
Get your kitchen equipment here.

Tetarta
If it's cold outside, or you just want to feel cosy, come here.

Peristeria Taverna
Go only at night, when they set up tables in the parking lot.

Akominatou
Kapodistriou
Kaningos
Plateia Kaningos
Halkokondyli
Menandrou
Veranzerou
Satovriandou
Plateia Karaiskaki
Karolou
Ahilleos
Plateia Ag Konstandinou
Plateia Omonias
Eolou
Panepistimiou Venizelou
Zinonos
Deligeorgi
Voulgari
Agisilaou
Pireos (Panagi Tsaldari)
Geraniou
Sokratous
Kristhenous
Athinas
Lykourgou
Efpolidos
Dimarhio
Stavrou
Stadiou
Arsaki
Leonidou
Kolokinthous
Keramikou
Athens Municipal Art Gallery
Plateia Theatrou
Sofokleous
Pesmazoglou
Evripidou
Sarri
Kentriki Agora
Aristidou
Agii Theodori
Plateia Klafthmonos
Keramikos
Taki
Plateia Iroön
Pallados
Polyklitou
Ag Markou
Praxitelous
Nikiou
Kolokotroni
Psiri
Misouli
Voreou
Karori
Eolou
Thiseos
Perikleous
Foktonos
Tetarta
Ermou
Plateia Abyssinias
Athens Flea Market
Ifestou
Adrianou
Plateia Monastirakiou
Athinaidos
Monastiraki
Evangelistrias
Petraki
Thissio
Plateia Thissio
Temple of Hephaestus
Stoa of Attalos
Mitropoleos
Pandrosou
Library of Hadrian
Plateia Agoras
Plateia Mitropoleos
Athens Cathedral
Apollonos
Nileos
Temple of Apollo
Temple of Ares
Areos
Pikilis
Pelopida
Pikilis
Apostolou Pavlou
Agion Apostolon
ANCIENT AGORA
Pratiniou
Plaka
Anafiotika
Theoukididou
Adrianou
Tripodon
Kekropos
Hill of the Pnyx
Hill of the Pnyx Theatre
Theatre of Herodes Attikos
Parthenon
ACROPOLIS
Acropolis Museum
Theatre of Dionysos

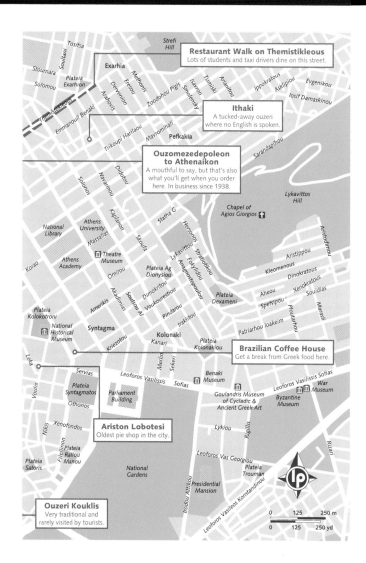

Tositsa

Strefi Hill

Soultani

Restaurant Walk on Themistikleous
Lots of students and taxi drivers dine on this street.

Stournara

Exarhia

Methonis

Solomou

Plateia Exarhion

Eresou

Devernion

Zoodohou Pigis

Tsamaki

Arantinou

Ippokratous

Asklipiou

Evgenikou

Iosif Damaskinou

Aralovis

Smolensky

Kavron

Emmanouil Benaki

Themistokleous

Trikoupi Harilaou

Mavromihali

Pefkakia

Ithaki
A tucked-away ouzeri where no English is spoken.

Sarandapihou

Ouzomezedepoleon to Athenaikon
A mouthful to say, but that's also what you'll get when you order here. In business since 1938.

Didotou

Solonos

Navarinou

Kaplanon

Statha G

Heronon

Stratiotou

Chapel of Agios Giorgios ✝

Lykavittos Hill

National Library

Athens University

Massalias

🏛 Theatre Museum

Skoufa

Lykavittou

Fokylidou

Anagnostopoulou

Aristodimou

Korao

Athens Academy

Omirou

Plateia Ag Dionysiou

Dimokritou

Voukourestiou

Plateia Dexameni

Aristippou

Kleomenous

Dinokratous

Aheou

Xenokratous

Souidias

Marasli

Plateia Kolokotroni

Amerikis

Akadimias

Soukton Al

Pindarou

Irakitou

Patriarhou Ioakeim

Ploutarhou

Spetsipou

🏛 National Historical Museum

Syntagma

Knezotou

Kolonaki

Kanari

Plateia Kolonakiou

Brazilian Coffee House
Get a break from Greek food here.

Leka

Servias

Merlin

Sekeri

Benaki 🏛 Museum

Leoforos Vasilissis Sofias

War 🏛 Museum

Voulis

Plateia Syntagmatos

Othonos

Leoforos Vasilissis

Sofias

Goulandris Museum of Cycladic & Ancient Greek Art

Byzantine 🏛 Museum

Nikis

Xenofondos

Fillelinon

Parliament Building

Ariston Lobotesi
Oldest pie shop in the city.

Lykiou

Rigillis

Plateia Satoris

Plateia Rallou Manou

National Gardens

Presidential Mansion

Leoforos Vas Georgiou

Plateia Trouman

Rizari

Ouzeri Kouklis
Very traditional and rarely visited by tourists.

Triodou Attikou

Leoforos Vasileos Konstandinou

0   125   250 m

0   125   250 yd

LP

REGIONAL VARIATIONS

DON'T MISS – Southern Greece

ΚΑΛΑΜΑΡΙΑ
ΝΤΟΠΙΑ- ΦΡΕΣΚ.
1998

- Dinner in the Athens market
- Retsina
- Tipota (a drink of nothing)
- A tasty tour of Kalamata

JIMMY THE GREEK

Walk into his taverna and he greets you like a long lost relative. He is genuinely glad to see you. Every day he feels as though he's just returned from one of the long sea voyages of his maritime days. Like every other man in Greece Jimmy spent several years as a sailor in the merchant marines. Greeks just can't get the sea out of their blood.

Here in the village of Katacolo Ilias (in the northern Peloponnese), and very near Mercouri Estate, Jimmy has come home to retire from the sea and serve you lunch or dinner in his appropriately named taverna, Jimmy's. As in any traditional taverna the first thing to do is go inside and look at the menu board. Make your selection, then betake yourself to an outdoor table under the awning, amid the refreshing green pots of basil.

"I always kept a pot of this growing on the ships I sailed in", Jimmy says. He fluffs one of the plants, looks at us and smiles. Suddenly we can smell it from several feet away.

"You see. It's the smell of home. Wherever I was on my voyages I could caress the basil plant and smell home. Lots of sailors do this."

Having been a sailor and resort worker, Jimmy has had a lot of contact with foreigners over the years. He speaks pretty good English, he knows foreign customs and tastes, and he wants you to have the best possible experience of his country. And he knows that you probably don't want your food to be as oily as a Greek would, but if you tell him that you want it in true Greek fashion he will be overjoyed, he will give you his best and he will try to adopt you.

"Bring us your native best", we say. "We want none of the oil reduced rations that the Dutch would call for. And bring us a wine that you can respect." Jimmy is a **meraklis**: a man who does things with passion and gusto. If, as the poet said, living well is the best revenge, then the meraklis is a man of good vengeance. He has a passion for food and drinks his wine slowly. A meraklis like Jimmy makes his own wine.

"Wine is a living thing, and you must get to know it intimately. I know a priest in a mountain village that makes the best wine and I learn from him. We talk for hours about the wine."

Jimmy sets the table with a clutter and clatter of little dishes of fried sardines, kalamari, tomato fritters, horta, clams in wine, crusty bread and his own homemade retsina.

"I make this wine every year. Two barrels, sometimes three. I don't use the pure pine resin. I put two large pine cones in each barrel as they ferment. And I only use old whisky barrels from Scotland."

We ask "do you know that the whisky barrels of Scotland come from Spain and were used first for sherry? And they came originally from Tennessee in the US?"

Jimmy takes all this in with the mind of a meraklis.

"Then we must drink to Scotland, Spain and the US", he replies.

We toast, then eat and drink. And when we are ready to depart, Jimmy gives us a two litre bottle of his special retsina. "So that you can continue to drink to Scotland, Spain and the US", he explains. "But please, have a drink for Greece, too."

Fetes Psaryu me Domata ke Stafidhes
(Fish with Tomato and Currants)

This recipe makes use of one of the oldest and most important crops in the Peloponnese, the currant. It has Venetian influence in its relative complexity, use of red pepper and the fact that it was made originally with cod, which was introduced from Spain by way of Venice.

Ingredients

6	fish steaks, each weighing about 200g (7oz)
	oil for frying
	flour for dredging
¼ cup	olive oil
2	onions, sliced
3	cloves garlic, minced
½ tsp	cayenne pepper
½ cup	dry red wine
3	tomatoes, peeled, seeded and finely chopped
1 cup	currants
½ cup	parsley, minced
	salt to taste

Dredge the fish in flour and fry in hot oil until brown. Set aside in a baking dish. Heat the olive oil and saute the onions, garlic and pepper. Add the wine and cook for one minute, then add the tomato and cook over low heat until the sauce thickens, then stir in the currants and remove from the heat. Pour the sauce over the fish and bake at 180°C (375°F) for 20 minutes.

Serves 6

shopping
& markets

Modern shopping may have arrived in Greece, but the smells and sounds of traditional, colourful commerce can still be found. Fish are still sold on the pier, oranges are still sold from the back of a truck. And today's grand markets can be just as manic as they were in the age of Pericles.

"The isles of Greece, the isles of Greece!" sang Lord Byron when he arrived in the Aegean for the first time. Later he was more subdued when he discovered the Levantine bazaar instead of the Athenian assembly. And you should no longer expect even the Levantine bazaar. You should expect the supermarket, the convenience store, all the perks of modern European living. And why not? The Greeks like modernity. As they say, "ours is not that culture buried in the ground". Yet there are institutions that just never die. Just as there are gods who never die, they just assume a new name and a different shape. The spirit of the **agora** (market) has never gone away. You'll hear its echoes on the islands where small farmers set up shop with a pair of primitive scales under a palm tree. Gypsies in old trucks pull over to the side of the road and sell their goods to passers-by. Peddlers come to the ferry docks to sell bread,

Canned food, Ladadika, Thessaloniki, Macedonia

sweets and local produce to passengers. Fisherfolk still land their catch on the ancient pier and sell to all who come. And once a week in many city neighbourhoods a farmers' market convenes. It may be upscale and elegant as in Kolonaki in Athens, it may be sprawling and vast, teeming with gypsies and Albanian refugees as in the centre of Thessaloniki; it may be small, humble and convivial as in Nafplio.

The grand market still stands in some cities, such as in Athens, Thessaloniki, Hania, Iraklio and a few others. Here the houses of commerce still pulsate with the energy of exchange. Every fresh product the kitchen could require is here. Meat, fish, fruit, vegetables, preserves, olives, tinned foods, fresh foods, salted foods, dried foods ... but no frozen foods. No fast-foods. Nothing that you would ever see advertised on television.

Mobile pussy, Hania Central Market, Crete

Onions and garlic are market essentials

The market of Athens at 50 Athenas Street is about 100 years old in its current incarnation. It would be within sight of the ancient agora at the foot of the Acropolis were it not for the buildings that interfere. You can visit the ruins of the ancient agora and ponder how things have changed, and also how they have not. The 'new' market is laid out in concentric squares, like boxes within boxes. As you approach you can see that the market has burst its seams. Commerce has spilled out onto the sidewalk and into the alleyways along the outer wall. Here you'll find stacks of ready-to-eat foods: olives, roasted and salted pulses and nuts, prepared tuna and sardines, fruits and sweets.

Once inside the market you'll find vegetables and a few housewares. Go another level deeper and you're in the land of meat: carcasses hanging, splayed, laid out, being reduced to manageable pieces by knife-wielding men, as expert as surgeons. Look closely at their instruments. The most common knife used is a **tsatira**, which has a long, triangular blade fitted to a wooden handle. You can see this exact same instrument depicted on ancient Grecian pottery, and being turned to the same purpose, in the very same setting.

Now venture deeper into the centre of the market. Given the Greek addiction to fish it is fitting that the market's heart is the fishmongers' stalls. In here the atmosphere is intense. Merchants are chopping and hacking, customers are crushed into narrow aisles but are undaunted as they seek those culinary treasures of the Aegean. Fishwives are singing out the quality of their goods and proudly announcing their low price "for today only!". The concrete floors are wet with the continuously melting ice that keeps the fish fresh. And the deeper you go into this whirling centre of commerce the louder the shouts become as they echo off the stone walls. Ultimately you must escape. So face the north wall, and in its middle you can see your way to relative calm and succour. For there you'll find the three market tavernas.

Butcher at work, Thessaloniki Central Market, Macedonia

All the grand markets of Greece have a taverna situated right next to the butchers. This is a very old custom, and wise. Unless you are a vegetarian the smell of fresh meat will eventually induce hunger. The sight of it all may shock you, especially when the entrails are well displayed, but sooner or later the smell will have you thinking about eating. In Athens the market tavernas are open 24 hours a day, in Thessaloniki 22 hours a day and others that close in the evening are open early, so these are good places to come for a hearty breakfast. This is where the butchers come for breakfast. You might not get eggs and bacon, but you will get **patsas** (offal soup) and other hearty fare.

SOMETHING FISHY?

Morning's catch, Paros, Cyclades

The Greeks do have, and have had since antiquity, a curious relationship with the sellers of fish. Fishmongers are generally regarded as liars, cheats, mountebanks, charlatans, frauds and all-round bad apples. Even ancient comedies portray this popular attitude toward the fishmonger. When you go to the market they are assumed to be offering you yesterday's catch, artfully presented to look and smell like freshly caught fare. Perhaps the funerary arts are applied. The wise shopper is urged to take nothing for granted, to probe and pinch each potential purchase, to look it in the mouth and in the eye (the seller as well as the fish) and to accept nothing but the freshest, plumpest, prettiest fish or go elsewhere. In all fairness, the Greek climate is one that will tax the ability of any food to keep. Before the introduction of ice, the only way to be sure of quality was to see the fish flapping. In keeping with the ancient equation of sexual desire and the desire for the taste of fish, it is not surprising that the fish seller should be held in the same esteem as the pimp.

While the Athens market tavernas are popular places for people ending a long evening's revels, the Glentadiko taverna in Thessaloniki market is itself the place for revels. This is one of the best nightspots in town. Although that is not its purpose; it just works out that way. All day and night the Glentadiko taverna has been feeding people. Some of the Glentadiko's tables are so close to the butchers that you can talk to them as you dine and they cut meat. It's actually rather swanky for a taverna: the tables are covered with cloth! But this is Thessaloniki, the most cosmopolitan city of Greece, so we have tablecloths.

By about 6pm the butchers and most of the merchants have closed up shop, but the taverna still hums with business. People come for a coffee after work, a drink on their way to visit grandma. Around 9pm the early diners arrive, and so begins the dinner service that will last for as long as anyone is hungry. Diners dine amid photographs of local celebrities – politicians, TV stars, radio personalities and Art Agnos, the Greek-American former mayor of San Francisco. The kitchen is the size of a sailboat's galley. The food is on display at the front. No menu needed to select mussel pilaf, cheese-stuffed squid, **yemista** (stuffed vegetables), grilled octopus, fish and suvlaki.

Grilling octopus outside, Syros, Cyclades

It's a family operation. Mother, aunt and daughter work the grill, the men serve, constantly passing on orders to the kitchenhand, receiving the ready viands. The pace gets manic yet they hold it together. The party begins around 2am when revellers begin filtering in. Music begins to pulsate. A few selections are contemporary, but most of it is Greko-pop, a modernistic rendition of Middle Eastern music. Soon the women are dancing with each other. It's a sort of belly dance, replete with flailing scarves. The men are sitting, drinking, talking, eating.

A waiter picks up a tambourine and begins to play. Soon the men are dancing, too. It's hard to tell if anybody is dancing with anybody. Or perhaps they are all dancing with each other. Now they are dancing on the tables. The revellers know the lyrics to many of the songs, and they sing along. A waiter takes a moment for a quick smoke. The three women at the

grill all share a match, tuck their cigarettes into the corners of their mouths and carry on. One slices a leg from an octopus hanging on the wall, then splits a large sardine and throws both on the grill. They hit with a sizzle. Another prepares **saghanaki** (fried cheese) by throwing a slab of feta on the fire. Smoke rises and the scent of onion fills the air. The third woman lines up orders on a tray and ladles salad onto each dish. The music plays, the revellers dance. One falls off a table. No problem. Get back up and dance some more. They will eat, drink, sing and dance here in the marketplace till they can do no more.

Feta on sale at Athens Central Market, Athens

Walk through the markets or commercial district of any Greek city and you'll pass **zaharoplastio** (patisserie or sweet shops), for the Greeks have a keen sweet tooth and will see it satisfied. Such establishments offer an astounding variety of Byzantine pastries, biscuits, cookies and candies, as well as spoon sweets. With such a bounty of sugar, honey and the sweet baking spices you may well smell these places before you see them. So follow your nose. As you prowl the streets of any city, town or village you'll pass **furnos** (bakeries). As you drive the highways and the back roads you'll pass bakeries. You will smell bread everywhere you go in Greece. Wherever you are in Greece you are not far from a place where you may purchase bread, pies, cakes or other tasty things baked in the oven. If you should hire a car, you'll always be able to find lunch at a roadside bakery. If you have a large party, purchase one of the monster 10-kilo loaves, just for the thrill of it.

Fresh bread at Nikos Velonis, a woodfired bakery in the old town of Naxos, Cyclades

A Greek Picnic

The food, climate and terrain of Greece is perfect for outdoor eating. Bakeries are on every street corner, and they usually also sell yoghurt, cheese and soft drinks. You'll see all the usual fruity suspects at the grand markets as well as at the neighbourhood grocery. As important as it is, though, fruit is generally not restaurant fare. If you want any, you'll have to go to the store and buy it. So go. And go to the grand market for tinned fish, dried foods, cheese and nuts. Of course if you're going to have a cook-out the grand market is the best place to buy your fresh fish, fowl and meat. And naturally the ubiquitous sweet shops are good for sweets.

Wine is both easy and difficult to find. Bottle shops are not common. Most wine in Greece is barrel wine. Bottled wines, as well as ouzo and brandy, are usually available in supermarkets and tourist traps, as well as at many of the ferry landings. Shortly after harvest you'll see people on the side of the road selling new wine from barrels. Just bring your own container. Some of it will be rough stuff, but it will always be a bargain. And you can always take wine away from a taverna in your jug, thermos or old army helmet.

Kalamata olives, cheese and wine, Semeli Winery, North Attica near Kifissia, Athens

Things to Take Home

If you enjoy a proper Greek coffee, or even if you don't, the coffee set is a fine souvenir. It is beautiful to look at, portable, and easy to appreciate as an artefact. You'll want a **briki**, the long-handled metal pot used for making Greek coffee, as well as some cups, a tray, a whisk and a measure. And the little hand-turned coffee grinder is a must. They are usually made of brass and look rather like a pepper mill. You can even use it as such, and as a general spice grinder. You'll find these things in tourist shops. In such places you can also find the little olive oil lamps that are used to illuminate icons in churches.

Greek coffee pots, Athens

Wooden spoons and forks, Athens

All sizes of scoops, Athens

Greek wine glasses, Athens

Greek kitchen equipment is good to have and to give. A mortar and pestle set carved from vine wood is both stunning and practical. Just for the taste of memory you might like to have one of the little tin wine pots that are the usual serving vessel in tavernas. Throw in a brace of those Greek wine glasses that look more like shot glasses. A couple of saghanaki pans will cook up a Greek meal for two. They are cheap and fit easily in your bag. And if you've got plenty of room, kitchen ceramic wares are very attractive. One thing is certain: you will be using more olive oil when you return, so buy a tin oil pitcher. You can find all these things in any houseware shop. And the grand markets of the major cities all have houseware dealers clinging to the edges.

To take home a bit of the Greek spirit, both ancient and modern, visit a church. You'll have no problem finding one. They are everywhere and usually open for business. Even between services people stop in to pray or just have a quiet moment. Beautiful, slender, golden candles made of beeswax are always burning and filling the air with their honey scent. Next to the urn in which they burn you'll see a box of them. They cost but a pittance, usually just a donation. Put a few pittances in the coin box, collect a few candles, light one and take the others home. Then on some night when you long for the isles Greece, extinguish all your lamps, touch a flame to your candle, and marvel that the light it sheds came all the way from Greece. And its honey smell began as Greek flowers. And remember that it was the Nymph Melissa, who was loved by the bees, that gave her name to the honey of Greece: **meli**.

Assorted wine jugs and pots, Athens

Spoon sweet, Evie Voutsinas' home, Athens

As for edible souvenirs, you can't go wrong with some of that gift of Melissa. Both honey and spoon sweets are for sale at the duty free. But if you should make a friend while in Greece (and that is easily done) ask for some from the friend's kitchen. They will be flattered. And it will taste so much better when you are home.

So many ouzos to choose from, Athens Central Market, Athens

Your favourite ouzo is probably not exported, so we recommend extensive tasting to find the one you want to take home. If you really want the taste of the soil, get some oil. Greece produces some of the finest olive oil in the world. Buy a few varieties so you can appreciate their subtleties and nuances (see Olives & Olive Oil in the Staples & Specialities chapter).

where to
eat & drink

Where to eat and drink in Greece? Perhaps the question should be
'where not to?' Greeks live to eat and drink. They dream about i
nd talk about it in bed when others are addressing other appetites
Wherever you go in Greece you might not find lodging, accurate
clocks, punctual flights or a good cup of tea, but by Zeus you wil

Where to Eat
Suvlatzidhiko (Suvlaki Seller)

Greece's original fast-food can be found at any of the nation's suvlatzidhiko. These are easily spotted by the joint of meat being grilled on a spit at the front of the shop. **Yiros** (carved spit-roast meat served in pita with salad and tzadziki) is traditionally eaten standing, or walking, or at any rate outdoors. But because tourists are so taken with yiros, many restaurants carry it on the menu. Be careful when ordering yiros or **suvlaki** (skewered and chargrilled cubes of meat) in a proper sit-down restaurant. If you want that tasty bread and meat bundle, be sure to ask for **me pita** (with bread). Restaurants can't charge you much for this humble fare. In order to jack up the price many establishments will assume that you desire a full-plate meal. You'll get mountains of meat, piles of potatoes, baskets of bread, and of course the waiter has also talked you into a Greek salad. Not only will you get a stiff bill, but you'll be wasting a lot. We have never seen anybody polish off an entire suvlaki plate. We heard of a German tourist who did it once. But we're sure it's only a tale. Remember: **me pita**. Then you'll still have room for that Greek salad. (See also Suvlaki & Yiros in the Staples & Specialities chapter.)

Carving pork yiros in Aristotelous Square, Thessaloniki, Macedonia

Taverna

The traditional, quintessential public eating house of Greece is the taverna. This is Zorba the Greek, Henry Miller and Lawrence Durrell type dining. This is what amounts to an extension of the Greek home table, offered forth to the community. Indeed it is believed that this is the origin of the taverna. There had always been inns in Greece. Since ancient times private homes along the road opened their doors to the passing public. There the traveller could get a simple meal, a bed and a bed companion. It was not until the late Byzantine era that the inn began to lose its association with the brothel and slowly acquire a reputation as a place where quality cooking was the chief attraction.

Until recent decades a taverna was a homely affair, the communal living room of the village. Its suppliers were not national distributors of foodstuffs, but households next door. In the much smaller communities, ignored by the shiploads and busloads of package tourists, you can still sit and watch as the lady from down the street comes to deliver her freshly made yoghurt. The fishing caïque will tie up in front of you and the fisherman will haul the catch right past your table. You may follow him into the kitchen to inspect your lunch.

Nowadays almost any food service operation may call itself a taverna. And that is what most Greeks are comfortable with. They generally don't want to go to a place calling itself a brassiere, bistro or trattoria. Taverna equals comfort.

Outdoor dining in Nafplio, Peloponnese

WHERE TO EAT & DRINK

A couple of variations on the taverna include the **hasapotaverna**, a basic restaurant attached to a butcher in a market (see the Shopping & Markets chapter). Then there's the **biraria**, a newcomer to the scene. This is not a microbrewery. But with a growing interest in beer among Greeks this sort of taverna specialises in dishes that, hopefully, go particularly well with beer. These are not necessarily salty foods, though they are present. The beireria is a work in progress. Another taverna variant is the **psistarya**, which specialises in charcoal-grilled meat, or meat roasted on a spit. A **paradhosiaki psarotaverna** specialises in fish. You usually find them on the coast, or in the north where trout are found. Look out for the ones that have the day's catch swimming in a tank.

The café scene, Thessaloniki, Macedonia

TRENDY TRIPE

Patsas, a rich-textured soup made with the stomach of a young lamb, was once considered working-class food. But – as with fashion – things change. For a time **patsadhika** (places that sell patsas) were the only establishments permitted to be open after 2am. When the clubs and bars closed, people would flock to these patsas places to continue the evening. Bejewelled women in tight dresses and pretty boys from the discos sat next to butchers whose aprons were splattered with blood. Patsas became hip as all the young aristocrats from Kolonaki stood in line for their fill. Before long patsadhika popped up everywhere, cashing in on the trend for tripe.

Matt Barlett lives on the island of Lesvos and is the author of I Married a Lesbian

Almost all tavernas have dining within and dining without. And the without is definitely the most popular in all but the very worst weather. You can spot most tavernas from blocks away simply by glimpsing the seated patrons massed on the footpath out front. And it is delightful to take a seat at such a place. But caveat emptor! Athens is synonymous with pollution on a scale so vast as to endanger the living and preserve the dead. On bad days you can actually taste the Athenian air. Lest we appear to single out the ancient city of Pericles, we should say that all other cities in Greece have their various types of pollution as well. And there's one kind of pollution that you'll encounter in every city, every village, every hamlet, ancient ruin, fishing harbour, public park or beach resort. And it is something you'll want to take into account when selecting your dining venue. It is noise pollution.

Young Greek men are besotted with the noise made by their motorcycles. For a young man to have a bike between his legs and rev the engine to its noisiest best is an inexpressible pleasure. And he must share it with the town by riding up and down in front of the tavernas where his mates will envy him and the ladies, hopefully, will swoon for his decibels. To facilitate this he removes his muffler. This is an illegal act, but the young Greek male takes delight in non-violent illegal acts. He will roar up to a table full of pals and gals and, while holding the throttle open for maximum admiration, shout a few jaunty phrases, crack a joke, wink at a girl and be gone in a rrrroooaaarrr, leaving his friends and you in a cloud of blue-tinged gasoline smoke.

Furnos (Pie Shop & Bakery)

Quite possibly the most common sort of food vendor you'll see in Greece is the pie shop, selling such favourites as **tiropita** (cheese pie) and **spanakopita** (spinach pie). No matter where a Greek works there will be a pie shop along the way, and here the hungry commuter may pop in for a nibble to take on the way to work. Pie shops are everywhere. You can't get away from them. If you love pies you'll be in heaven. If you hate pies you'll be in hell. In every city in Greece at any time of day or night you'll see people walking down the street eating pies. Even if you don't see them you can find them as the filo dough used to make most pies is so flaky that all pie eaters leave flurries of flakes in their wakes.

Making crepes at a creperie, Athens

Kreperi (Creperie)

This place is popular with university students, artists and bohemian types. The fare is simple but tasty: savoury and sweet crepes, usually made by a crepe cook working in a window like a pizza tosser. The most common savouries are cheese with mushrooms, and the sweets are only limited by your imagination. As with any Greek gastronomic venue this is a place for talk as much as a place for food. People will spend half an evening or more in a creperie, and they might not even have a crepe. Perhaps they will simply order a bottle of wine, or even a series of cocktails, as the creperies usually have a fully stocked bar. Many creperies have sound systems from which popular music is banned. These can be excellent places to listen to classical, Broadway, jazz, **rebetika** (Greek rhythm & blues) and anything else other than the pop charts.

WHERE TO EAT & DRINK

Ouzeri

It seems ironic that the ouzeri is thought of as a place to eat. After all, its purpose is to sell ouzo. But the Greek tippler must be the Greek nibbler, lest he become a Greek tragedy. The origin of the ouzeri is in the private home. During the late Ottoman time householders were at liberty to make their own spirits (they still can today, though with limitations). Then the doors could be opened and all with a drachma could come in for a glass. To provide the necessary solid absorption material, the house cook made little dainties. These became many of the mezedhes that we know today.

The ouzeri became a place where both the libidinous Greek and the abstemious Turk could meet for drinks and a snack. They would often bring along their musical instruments and have a jam session. They would play backgammon or dominoes and smoke hookah pipes. They would tell stories. The service and fare eventually became somewhat codified; the traditional order is for a plate of mezedhes and a quarter litre of ouzo (the alcoholic equivalent of a bottle of wine).

In recent decades ouzeris have been expanding on their offerings. Some of them offer a proper meal. Some even have wine, beer and coffee. And few patrons now bring their buzuki. They are tavernas in all but name and have lost their link with the past. And of course tavernas now sell ouzo. And sometimes people bring their instruments. The cosy, convivial and homely ouzeri, a snug place to spend a mildly boozy evening of song and stories is disappearing. Our maps will show you a few that still cling to their tradition.

A taverna ouzeri in Ladadika, Thessaloniki, Macedonia

Estiatorio (Restaurant)

Estiatorio is the Greek word for restaurant. It's a recent innovation in the Greek culinary scene. How does it differ from the taverna? Sometimes it's hard to say. The easiest way to tell the difference is by what's covering the table. If it's paper it's a taverna, if it's cloth it's an estiatorio. But is that the only difference? Well, sometimes it is, if the board of fare is Greek. If they offer foreign viands it will almost always be called an estiatorio, paper, cloth or otherwise. But the biggest difference, for you, the traveller, between tavernas and estiatorio, is that you will pay more for the same dish in an estiatorio. And the waiter will expect a generous tip.

Estiatorios specialising in non-Greek food are quite rare. People in Athens will boast of the huge number of foreign restaurants that have recently opened in their fair city. But any number larger than one will be thought of as huge. In Athens there is a pan-Asian restaurant called Far East Restaurant. A recent influx of immigrants has resulted in a few curry joints. In Hania you'll find the contradictory Suki-Yaki Authentic Chinese Cuisine. And in Ioannina

Overlooking Barbati Beach, Corfu

you may be tempted by the Canadian Pizzeria. If you are watchful you may notice that every community of size has at least one Mexican restaurant. Iraklio has three, for example, all within walking distance of each other. Whence this interest in Mexican fare? Every other man in Greece has served in the merchant marine. Most of the proprietors of these restaurants have made many a call on Mexican ports and acquired a taste for tortillas. Unfortunately they did not acquire a taste for chilli peppers and the food is uniformly tame. Bring your own hot sauce.

Fastfundadhiko (Fast-Food)

Suvlaki used to be the fast-food of Greece. But now fast-food is the fast-food of Greece. This situation didn't start with the American cultural imperialists, the first assault upon the culinary ramparts of Greece was made by native-bred troops. Despite their nativity, however, fast-food is an American instrument of conquest, and so the first fast-food battalions had to have English-sounding names. Enter Goody's and Everest. Let their names strike fear!

Goody's, the more fiendish of the twain, is a slavish imitator of the standard burgers-and-fries joint. In fairness we will say that the odour emitted by a Goody's is goodier than the effluent of those it emulates. This is not praise, though, only fairness.

Everest is the more insidious of this unholy alliance. It offers an array of Greek **pites** (pies) both savoury and sweet. It also offers ready-made sandwiches that incorporate what looks like respectable bread. And they offer a lot of junk as well.

So much for the initial landings of the fast-food invasion. Now the big guns are moving in. We could list every victory and defeat, tell you who holds what territory and what is still up for grabs. But it will be enough to tell you that you may now enjoy your Big Mac and a view of the Parthenon at the same time.

Everest, a Greek fast-food chain

Tuckedaway

This is a category of eatery that no guide book to Greece has ever mentioned. And perhaps even the Greeks are not aware of it. Or if they are aware, they are not aware that they are aware. All over Greece there are tavernas, ouzeris, and even estiatorios that are small, deliciously cosy, off the path, tucked away into some hidden corner or basement, or just in a place that's hard to find. We find that finding a place that's hard to find in a country for which the first guide book was written 2000 years ago is quite a find. The tuckedaway, as we call it, is one of Greece's gastronomic treasures. We have made sure to put many on our maps.

A roofless restaurant, Hania, Crete

Roofless Restaurant

The weather is fine in most of Greece most of the year, and this has given rise to what we call the roofless restaurant. It is usually of the taverna type, though operated by younger, artistic sorts who want to push the envelope without punching through it. All over Greece there are buildings with roofs that have fallen in, mostly due to age but also to earthquakes and even wartime bombing. The still-standing walls provide protection from chilly breezes, yet the sky is yours for the gazing.

An interesting variation on this theme is the outdoor movie theatre. Again, it's a roofless four walls, but you get to see current, or sometimes old classic, movies. Some people bring a picnic. Others purchase pies and other finger foods, as well as beer, wine, water, even ouzo at the theatre's kiosk. These were once a very common thing in all the cities, rather like drive-in movies of the US. And like the drive-ins, they began to disappear, victims of expensive real estate. But unlike the drive-ins, people here protested about their loss. Now many are under one sort of protection or another. So you're just in time for dinner and a show.

Men doing what they do best, Thessaloniki, Macedonia

Kafenion

This is one of the oldest gastronomic institutions in Greece. A product of the Ottoman occupation, it is the original coffee shop. You'll see these everywhere, and you may wonder why they exist. Their decor is, well, nonexistent. A suburban garage has more to commend itself to the eye. Traditionally kafenia serve Greek coffee and little else. And traditionally only men above a certain age patronise them. They are full of tobacco smoke. And yet they, the men and the kafenia, refuse to die. This is because they are undemanding places. One may go to the kafenion and play checkers with friends, or simply sit alone with one's thoughts. You can strike up a conversation, or be left alone. Nowadays you may have beer or ouzo, as well as gritty Greek coffee. Women may go to the kafenion. Always could. There was never any law prohibiting it. But in the past women simply would not care to be seen there, lounging with the drones. But we see them nowadays, chatting, smoking, and having a cuppa. The kafenion is so undemanding, so relaxed, that it is an island of respite in an increasingly demanding world. Nevertheless the kafenion is slowly disappearing. Get it while you can. Can't find a kafenion? Almost every parish church has one sidling alongside.

Children are welcomed everywhere

Kafeteria (Cafeteria)
This is the place to come for hot and cold drinks, mid-morning snacks, toasted sandwiches, omelettes and ice creams. Unlike a snack bar, you are expected to sit at a table, rather than have a takeaway meal. Kafeterias are usually located around the main square or along the harbour front.

Nihterino Kendro
This is where Greeks have a night out: dine, smash plates and dance to live music. They can be expensive, depending on the calibre of the artists they attract. Watch for richly bejewelled men setting fire to bank notes to show their largesse.

Zaharoplastio (Patisserie or Sweet Shop)
A zacharoplastio provides tables where you can sit and enjoy a piece of cake and a coffee. This is where you'll find Greeks in the late afternoon, especially on summer evenings.

Hanging out in Pyrgi, Chios, North-Eastern Aegean

THE ICONOCLASTS – Faces of Gastronomy

It is fitting that Thanasis and Donna Kritikos are Salonican (from Thessaloniki). Salonicans have a reputation for being the most cosmopolitan of Greeks. And for being the most demanding in quality of goods and lifestyle. At least that's what any Salonican will tell you. Donna and Thanasis are the son and daughter of the late Yorgos Kritikos, perhaps the most celebrated restaurateur in the city. He established Taverna Krikelas in 1938. Anybody who would establish such a risky business as a restaurant on the eve of war has got to be one who thinks outside the box. This trait he apparently passed down to his children, because Donna and her brother are blazing new gastronomic trails.

Their father's operation, seemingly mad opening notwithstanding, hewed strictly to Greek traditions. But when he opened yet another restaurant in 1965, in a century-old nut warehouse, the kids were already thinking ahead. They try to maintain the soul of Greek cuisine while looking for ways not so much to change it, but simply to build upon it. They know that the present day Greek kitchen muse did not, like Athena from the head of Zeus, burst forth fully formed in an instant. It developed over centuries and generations. As travellers, traders and conquerors came through Greece they brought with them new products and processes. The Greeks took from them what they thought was good and incorporated them into their diet. This is the process Donna and Thanasis carry on. They just do it faster. And they do it well. We have seen others try this and fail.

The elegant interior of Taverna Krikelas, the starched tablecloths, the crystal and silver, the skilful lighting and the panelled walls all suggest that you are somewhere far from Greece. And the staff in dazzling white shirts and neatly tied neckwear reinforce the illusion. But you are immediately brought back to Greece by their native charm and friendliness. The warm smiles tell you that you are going to taste something Greek tonight, and yet still something different.

There is salmon on the menu – a rare thing in Greece – yet it's cooked in a way that suggests salmon has always been on the Greek table. Spinach is cooked in the water in which the salmon is poached. The penchant among western Europeans for buttered bread never found favour with the Kritikos family (nor anyone else in Greece), yet they have found a way to please both locals and visitors. The bread comes not with oil, but with a beguiling blend of butter and feta seasoned with peppercorns. Brother and sister practice many techniques straight from the French kitchen, like sauce reduction, yet nothing tastes French. Things seem to taste intensely Greek, yet new and different. They both travel in Europe once a year to keep track of trends and ideas. But they only use those that will complement their native fare. Still, there are Greeks who would not set foot in Taverna Krikelas. Not as long as there is cloth on the table. The paper covering is one icon they won't stand breaking.

Vegetarians & Vegans

Wherever you call home, no matter how granola-and-tofu friendly it is, it's easier and tastier to go vegetarian in Greece. This is ironic since no Greek would claim to be a vegetarian, at least none of our acquaintance.

It would be almost impossible, and certainly unthinkable, to observe the Greek Orthodox faith without the paschal lamb at Easter. And Christmas without roast pork would be just another day. Sunday without some kind of meat in the pot just wouldn't be worth waking up to. And a diet without fish simply would not be Greek. But that same Orthodox faith that calls for flesh also calls for fasting (see the Celebrating chapter). Not necessarily the hard fasting of refusing all food, but the soft fasting of refusing meat, and sometimes all animal products, which regularly makes the Greeks accidental vegans. Wednesdays and Fridays are traditional fast days and some village tavernas serve only vegetarian fare. Others are always prepared to accommodate the observant. During Lent and the 40 days before Christmas people fast. Individuals, especially clergy, can be on personal fasts at any time and taverna keepers know this.

Fasting aside, the Greeks just love their vegetables. On any day most tavernas will offer **yemista** (stuffed vegetables). In the north, vegetable pilafs are common. Virtually all commercial kitchens offer beans or other pulses. Vegetable casseroles are sta-ples, such as okra with tomato, or green beans with onions. No menu lacks **horta** (wild greens). Of course the bread is magic, pasta is often meatless and potatoes are in abun-dance. A range of salads is always available everywhere. And mezed-hes are as often vegetarian as not. In short, you're on your way to vege-tarian heaven. And to guide you to your no-meat nirvana are the priests of the Orthodox church. You will see them everywhere in their black robes and distinctive stovepipe hats. Priests will fast for as much as nine months of the year, yet they still eat well. So wherever you see priests eating, it's a near guarantee of good vegetarian food. And if they are fat priests, it's even better.

Greek salad and tzatziki, Taverna Kokkalis, Stamata near Kifissis, Athens

Travelling with Kids

Greeks love children, and if you bring yours you'll probably end up having to share them. All tavernas are child friendly. And if your child is a cute little girl the waiters may make such a fuss over her that she will not want to go home with you. There is no such thing as a children's menu. Kids eat what their parents eat, often just sharing what's on their plates. The only real concern about children is the weather. Dining outdoors on a blisteringly hot day can be too much for the little ones.

Enjoying a large morning snack, Athens Central Market, Athens

Understanding the Menu

If you are in a tourist resort, the menu and ordering process are simple, straightforward, in English and just like at home. They will even bring you ketchup, Worcestershire or HP sauce. But you are reading this book and so will be seeking things that are not just like at home.

Step into the taverna with fish in mind and simply tell the responsible person that you want to see the day's catch. You will not take them by surprise, unless they are surprised by your gastronomic sagacity, for this is the custom. They will gladly lead you into the kitchen or pantry and proudly display the excellent bream, fresh mullet, carp and kalamari. If you're in Epiros they may also have trout, snails and frogs. Always do this when seeking fish for dinner. The menu cannot reflect a catch that may change more than once a day. You'll be assured of what you're getting, you'll get the size you desire, and the variety. You'll know by the clear eyes and the firm flesh that it's fresh. If you're staying on an island

Menu in Greek, Paros

or small seaside resort, you can meet the fishing boats as they come into the port in the morning. There you can do as locals: haggle with the fisherman for what you desire. Watch the locals first to see what the going rates are. Then you can take your catch to your digs if you've got a stove, or you can take it to your regular taverna and ask them to cook it for you. Unless you're in one of those soulless resorts they'll be glad to accommodate you, and you'll get a break on the price. And when they bring that perfectly prepared fish to your table, do as any good Greek. Eat the head and suck out the eyes. Mmmmm, gooood. Really.

In any other traditional or small town situation the procedure is similar. If you ask for the menu the waiter is likely to say "I am the menu", and proceed to tell you what is on offer today. The waiter may gesture to the counter where the food, both pre-cooked and uncooked, is on display. Just point to what you like, then take your seat. Then again, in many smaller establishments the waiter will bring you a tray of the day's selections and you can simply take your desire then and there. Greeks are not fond of fuss. Learn to say **nero** (water) and **krasi** (wine) and you're ready to dine.

LADIES ONLY – The Greek Waiter Syndrome

Perplexed? Wondering why you just turned into the most desirable object on the planet? Why roses are coming your way? Then perhaps you have just had a close encounter with a Greek waiter. Take a long hard look at this waiter (or bartender) and see which of the following categories he fits.

Yorgos the Undernourished
Characterised by Albanian-style haircut (of a time before hairdressers and styling), non-existent bum and very skinny limbs. Desperate for sex with anything. Underpaid, exploited and shunned by Greek women, his only hope is to pull a tourist. Works long hours and will not have much to contribute to your understanding of Greek people and lifestyle.

Petros the Patriarch
Biggish, fattish, greyish, smiley and, all too often, leery. Usually comes with all the fixtures: wife, children, belly, moustache, bald spot and desire for romance with tourists. Will happily woo you with flowers and ice cream. Assumes that as a tourist the only reason you are in Greece is for sex with middle-aged waiters. You are a woman and as you are either on your own, or are with a north-European man who is bound to be gay, it is his duty to offer you sex.

Costa the Adolescent
Like many Greek men, Costa will only grow up when his father dies. He lives with his parents and will be mothered until he marries at 35. Consequently he has limited understanding about women and hormones. Tourists are seen as a way for proving his virility and manhood without the complications of marriage and babies.

Tassos the Tour Guide
Friendly soul, greets you with a smile and takes his time in asking you out. Often chats about the places to see and more of a flirt meister than sex machine. For the most part, being nice to you is part of his job. In fact his job may depend on his ability to flirt with tourists and keep them sweet.

Manos the Manager
He'll offer you free brandy or wine, plates of fruit and other titbits. He's doing his job well, however, so we advise you to always check your bill on subsequent visits.

All of them think that staring at you is OK, in fact when they stare at you, they are asking you if you want sex. If you are interested, you're supposed to look back. The longer they stare, the more interested they are in having sex. A friend of mine who is very blond (which, as far as the men are concerned, means she is desperate for sex) finds something on them that's not quite as it should be, such as dirty shoes or a stain on their trousers. She then stares at it very pointedly. Works a treat. They shuffle off pronto.

Tourist hot spots are full of men who think they are God's gift to tourists. The Plaka in the centre of Athens is particularly bad; every Greek boy/man has, I think, gone there at some time to try his hand at the ritual of picking up foreign women.

Nevertheless most Greek men are very hospitable and friendly, and not every overture is to do with ulterior motives. For example, on arriving in Samos, tired and weary, I went looking for apartments where they wouldn't mind my dog. Needless to say they turned out to be non-existent, so I went for a coffee in a nearby taverna. The owner came and chatted to me, and on discovering it was my birthday cooked me my favourite food and wouldn't let me pay a penny. But I will let the Greek waiters themselves have the last words on the subject, in the form of one of their most popular songs. I call it the Greek waiter song:

The Greek waiter song
The best waiter am I,
With a good mood I serve everybody,
I give the jugs of wine very fast,
They look at me and everyone gets drunk,
Then I give the food fast and
Everyone is happy and give me tips
They are so drunk they are like rags
She makes the bills very high but nobody notices
Because they are so busy looking at me.
The best waiter am I.

Pamela Washington teaches English in Athens

In a joint with a printed menu the format is fairly standard. It will lead with mezedhes or **orektika** (appetisers) and **salatas** (salads). Some menus will follow this with **dhiafora**, often translated as 'variety of dishes'. These include pies, meatballs, sausages, pasta dishes and musaka. Virtually all menus will offer **ladheros**, dishes cooked in oil. These are almost always vegetable dishes such as **yemista** (stuffed vegetables). **Kreatika** means meat dishes, mostly roasted or stewed. Some tavernas will offer **tisoras**, dishes cooked to order, such as steaks or chops. **Supa** (soup) usually follows meat on the menu. Beverages come next. Beer, wine and coffee are easy, but be aware that **pota** (drinks) usually means spirits. **Anapsihtika** refers to soft drinks. At the end of the menu you'll find **ghlyka** (desserts or sweets).

Menu in English, Hania, Crete

Where to Drink

Nightclubs, bouzouki clubs and discos aside, you may drink wherever Greeks eat. Most Greeks are uneasy about drinking by itself. They must have something to eat to help offset the effects of alcohol. As much as they love to eat, drink, sing, dance, get down and boogie, they don't like to get drunk. And they don't like to be seen as, or be thought of as, drunk. This is not to say that Greeks never get drunk, they just won't admit to it. This is not a pub or saloon culture. They'll spend hours over frappe but not over beer (sigh). They'll sit and guzzle water or Greek coffee till their teeth float but they won't do the same with wine. Even at an establishment with a huge neon sign proclaiming BAR, they will spend most of their hours there nursing the damnable frappe.

There are, however, places dedicated to the enjoyment of drink for its own sake. These tend to fall into three categories. The tourist bar is just that, and there are plenty of them in the resorts. All staff speak English, they won't make snide remarks if you wear your wrap-around sunglasses at night, they will compliment you on your nose ring, and they will sell you drinks with names like Sex on the Beach, Screaming Orgasm, Purple Passion, Reluctant Virgin. They might not really know how to make those drinks, but they will put stuff in a shaker and shake it. It will be colourful and costly. They will facilitate your desire to drink till you drop should you so desire. If you're there for more than a week you'll be able to participate in the weekly raffle and maybe win a T-shirt that says: I puked on Paros.

Artists, writers, students and unemployed Greek youths congregate in places called bar or cafe or cafe bar. Many Greek youths are unemployed, and this is not a criticism as the unemployment rate is high in Greece. It is not uncommon for Greeks to live with their parents and draw an allowance up to the age of 30, or until they marry. And even then they often continue to live with the parents of one spouse or the other, renovating the house to accommodate the newlyweds. But before that they may attend university, and hang out at the bar, cafe or cafe bar. This is the kind of place that looks like a saloon or cocktail lounge. There's a long bar, beer on tap, bottles of booze arrayed on shelves, even a brass rail to set your foot on as you belly up. And there will be Greek youths nursing frappe all day. They won't start drinking until about 10pm. But you can drink any time, and these are often very pleasant places to strike up a conversation. On the islands and coastal towns you'll find these places on the waterfronts. In the mainland cities they are wherever universities are located, such as Exharia in Athens. You'll also find expensive versions of these in the wealthy sections of town, such as Kolonaki in Athens, or Ladadika in Thessaloniki, but they are rather snooty places. And the down-to-earth Greeks don't do snooty very well.

Lastly there is the sleazy bar. Some of them are strip clubs, complete with touts who wander up and down the street enticing gentlemen (they never seem to entice the ladies) with promises of a free drink and other inducements. Abandon all hope, ye who enter. And if you should find yourself in a cosy, dimly lit place staffed by women who are bewigged and heavily made up and speak with foreign accents, get the hell out, partner. And mind your wallet.

a greek
banquet

So now you've been to Greece and can't wait to share your culinary discoveries with your friends. Good for you. We applaud your efforts to broaden the minds and palates of others. Hopefully you have brought home some Greek olive oil for the purpose, and maybe some honey, ouzo or wine. There are simply no substitutes.

We suggest that you take one of two approaches to the perfect Greek meal: indoor or outdoor. The outdoor meal will approximate the Easter feast. You need to be in an area where a whole spring lamb can be had, and of course you need the real estate in which to prepare it, either your backyard or a friend's maybe. You'll want to arrange for the lamb some days ahead of time, as you would in Greece. And you must plan the shape, size and depth of your fire pit. Electrically powered spits, as well as hand-driven ones, are available at rental stores. It will take anywhere from four to six hours to roast the little beastie. Your butcher can advise you.

Arni Ofto (Roast Lamb on the Spit)

Ingredients

1	lamb prepared for the spit
1-2	lemons
1 cup	olive oil
1 Tbs	oregano

Rub the lamb generously with lemon juice and olive oil, and sprinkle with organo. Skewer it onto the spit. When your fire has reduced to a bed of glowing coals, position the lamb about 25cm (10 inches) above it. Be prepared to adjust the hight if the lamb cooks to fast or too slow. Turn the spit and from time to time baste the meat with oil and lemon (you'll also need to replenish your fire every 30 minutes or so). For an added touch, throw fresh rosemary on the fire and let its aroma rise to the meat.

Serves a small army.

Time the arrival of your guests so that the air is thick with the aroma of roasting lamb. Give them wine and very small mezedhes, just enough to tease them. But give them no satisfaction. If any of them beg on bended knee, carve off a slice of the outer meat and let them eat it with their fingers. Retsina, if you can get it, is the best thing with which to grease the wheels at this point. If not, some dry white wine, a pale beer or water will do to keep folk refreshed. When the lamb is done and the people ravenous, just start hacking away at it. There is no particular Greek method of carving. Try to see that each guest gets something well done from the outside and something rare from the inside. Serve this with salad, bread and more wine.

Ah, but now you want to give a fine sit down supper that all will say was a lovely affair and that you were the perfect host. But let's start with the Holy Trinity of bread, olives and wine. Be sure to find some superior bread,

---

THE TRUTH OF THE MATTER

We may live without poetry music or art.
We may live without conscience, or live without heart.
We may live without friends, we may live without books.
But civilised man cannot live without cooks.

He may live without books – what is knowledge but grieving?
He may live without hope – what is hope but deceiving?
He may live without love – what is passion but pining?
But where is the man who can live without dining?

Athenaeus, The Deipnosophists, *circa AD 200*

---

even if it isn't Greek. Spermo, the grainy granddaughter of Dionysus, will appreciate your efforts. You might want to stand outside as the guests arrive touting the place and its low prices. Flirt with the females. Greet your guests with retsina, white wine or ouzo, or all three, and jugs of water. Dolmadhes are an easy way to start things off, or **skordhalya** (garlic sauce) used as a dip (see the recipe). **Selinosalata** (parsley salad) and **skumbri se klimatofila** (mackerel in vine leaves) are easily made and you should have no trouble finding the ingredients (see the recipes). Slabs of feta are almost universally available, though the cheese may come from the Netherlands or Israel (ssshh). Slather it with oil and serve it with onions. Or make your guests' eyes boggle with **htapodhi sta karvuna** (grilled octopus; see the recipe). For maximum taste with minimum effort, nothing beats plain olives. And for that genuine taverna feel, cover the table with butcher's paper.

Always be sure to include vegetables in any Greek meal. **Kukya me aghriangginares** (broad beans with artichokes) look and taste delicious, and are easy to prepare (see the recipe). For the very homey touch, a stew of some sort is called for. **Laghoto** is a good option (see the recipe).

Of course there's always seafood. Fish cookery is usually simple and so easy for the host. Fish + oil + lemon + garlic = success (see the recipe Red Mullet on a Bed of Dill). Fried potatoes can be a pain to make in the home kitchen, even though they are de rigeur in the taverna. You must use olive oil, there is no substitute. Or just give them more bread. Be sure to give your guests salad or greens dressed with oil and lemon. And make sure the wine flows.

At the end serve baklava, which you have made two days before and have let sit to soak up the goodness of its honey and spice. People may argue about the origin of lukumi (Greek/Turkish delight) but that's because they want it as their own (see the recipe). Fresh fruit should also grace the table. Use your Greek coffee set to serve, well, whatever kind of coffee you like. And follow with brandy, water, and more wine. Never let the wine stop flowing. Never let Dionysus die. Yammas!

Htapodhi sta Karvuna (Grilled Octopus)

This is one of the great constants throughout the Aegean. Every seaside taverna will offer it. It is best when grilled over hot coals.

Ingredients

1	whole octopus, cleaned
¼ cup	olive oil
1 tsp	oregano or thyme
2 Tbs	red wine vinegar

Mix the oil, vinegar and herbs. Brush the octopus with the marinade and grill it whole about 4 inches above the coals until it can be pierced with a fork (about 15 minutes per side). Brush with the marinade at each turning. Cut into small pieces and drizzle over the remaining marinade.

Serves a whole party as a meze

Laghoto (Kefallonian Ragout of Hare)

Traditionally this dish called for hare or other game because other meats were expensive. But game was in abundance in the islands and one could always catch something with a simple snare. Nowadays things are reversed. Game is rare and meat such as lamb is relatively cheap. So this dish will now be most commonly made with rabbit, chicken or even lamb. The combining of lemon with tomato is unusual in Greece, as are many things in the Ionian Islands.

Ingredients

1kg (2lb)	hare, rabbit, chicken or lamb
¼ cup	olive oil
2	heads garlic, peeled
4	tomatoes, peeled, seeded and chopped
	juice of one lemon
	salt and pepper to taste

In a large skillet brown the meat then set it aside. Simmer the garlic cloves in just enough water to cover until tender. Combine all the ingredients and simmer in the pan until the meat is tender.

Serves 6-8

eat your words
language guide

Pronunciation
Syllables, stress, phrase-words
All syllables in Greek should be fully articulated (diphthongs are written as single syllables). Stressed syllables (in bold type) are pronounced with more emphasis. The rhythm of Greek can be quite mechanical.

Some short words join in speech with the word before or after, sometimes with vowel loss between words and/or the creation of a second stress.

Aspiration
Greek sounds generally involve less air than English, and there is no puff of air after Greek **k, p, t, g, b, d**. Take a breath, then hold your diaphragm a little so as to exhale less while you speak. After a while it comes naturally!

Vowels
English speakers need to exaggerate mouth and lip positions for the five 'pure' Greek vowels:

a	as the 'a' in 'art' (sound produced at back of mouth, mouth open wide).
e	as the 'e' in 'bet' (middle of mouth, lips half stretched sideways).
i	as the 'ea' in 'flea' (just behind teeth, lips fully stretched sideways).
o	as the 'o' in 'hot' (middle of mouth, lips rounded).
u	as the 'oo' in 'fool' (just behind teeth, lips shaped into a small, tight circle).

An 'i' sound before another vowel often converts to a 'y' sound.

Gutturals
Four light guttural sounds are represented by **k, g, h, gh**. Greek **k** (voiceless) and **g** (voiced) explode further back in the mouth than the English sounds. **h, gh** are made in the same position but their sound continues: the **h** is a bit like clearing your throat, while **gh** represents the voiced version. Practice making these four sounds in the same position, alternately stopping the air and/or the vocal cords. Before the front vowels **e, i** they move forward in the mouth and sound closer to English **k, g, hy, y**.

Consonants
Greek **b, d, f, m, n, p, t, v** are not very different from English (though less aspirated).

dh	as the 'th' in 'then' (tip rather than middle of tongue)
g	as the 'g' in 'guard' but further back in the mouth
gh	as the 'y' in 'yard' but more throaty
h	as the 'h' in 'hard' but more throaty
k	as the 'c' in 'card' but further back in the mouth
l	as the 'l' in 'slip' (tip rather than back of tongue)
ng	as the 'n' in 'ink'
r	as the 'r' in 'print', but with tip of tongue and lightly rolled
s	as the 's' in 'see', but teeth slightly further apart
th	as the 'th' in 'thin' (tip rather than middle of tongue)
y	as the 'y' in 'yield'
z	as the 'z' in 'zoo', but teeth slightly further apart

Useful Phrases
Eating Out

restaurant	to e-sti-a-**to**-ri-o	το εστιατόριο
cheap restaurant	to fti-**no** e-sti-a-**to**-ri-o	το φτηνό εστιατόριο
taverna	i ta-**ver**-na	η ταβέρνα

I want to make a reservation for this evening.
   the-lo na **kli**-so e-na   Θέλω να κλείσω ένα
   tra-**pe**-zi ya a-**po**-pse   τραπέζι για απόψε.
Do you speak English?
   mi-**las** ang-gli-**ka**?   Μιλάς Αγγλικά;
Table for ..., please.
   e-na tra-**pe**-zi ya ... ,   Ένα τραπέζι για ...,
   pa-ra-ka-**lo**   παρακαλώ.
Do you accept credit cards?
   dhe-he-ste pi-sto-ti-**kes kar**-tes?   Δέχεστε πιστωτικές κάρτες;
Do you have a highchair for the baby?
   e-he-te ka-**re**-kla ya to mo-**ro**?   Έχετε καρέκλα για το μωρό;
Can I smoke here?
   bo-**ro** na ka-**pni**-zo e-**dho**?   Μπορώ να καπνίσω εδώ;
Can I pay by credit card?
   bo-**ro** na pli-**ro**-so   Μπορώ να πληρώσω
   me pi-sto-ti-**ki kar**-ta?   με πιστωτική κάρτα;
Just a cup of coffee, please.
   mo-no e-na ka-**fe**, pa-ra-ka-**lo**   Μόνο ένα καφέ, παρακαλώ.
I just want a snack.
   the-lo ka-ti e-la-**fri**   Θέλω κάτι ελαφρύ.
Do you serve breakfast?
   ser-**vi**-re-te pro-i-**no**?   Σερβίρετε πρωινό;
Are you open for lunch/dinner
on (Saturday)?
   i-ste a-ni-**hti** ya me-si-me-ri-an-**no**/   Είστε ανοιχτοί για μεσημεριανό/
   vra-dhi-**no** to (**sa**-va-to)?   βραδινό το (Σάββατο);
Can we have a table ...?
   bo-**ru**-me na **e**-hu-me   Μπορούμε να έχουμε
   e-na tra-**pe**-zi ...?   ένα τραπέζι ...;

by the window	**dhi**-pla sto pa-**ra**-thi-ro	δίπλα στο παράθυρο
on the sand	sti-**na**-mo	στην άμμο
in a shady spot	sti-**skya**	στη σκιά
by the fire	**dhi**-pla sti fo-**tya**	δίπλα στη φωτιά

Can we sit ...?	bo-**ru**-me na ka-**thi**-su-me ...?	Μπορούμε να καθήσουμε ...;
under the grapevines	**ka**-to a-**po** tin kli-ma-tar-**ya**	κάτω από την κληματαριά
in the courtyard	stin a-**vli**	στην αυλή
by the sea	kon-**da** sti **tha**-la-sa	κοντά στη θάλασσα

Just Try It!

What's the speciality of this region?
  ti **i**-ne i spe-si-a-li-**te**
  tis pe-ri-o-**hyis**?
Τι είναι η σπεσιαλιτέ
της περιοχής;

What's the speciality here?
  ti **i**-ne i spe-si-a-li-**te** sas?
Τι είναι η σπεσιαλιτέ σας;

What's that?   ti **i**-ne a-**fto**?   Τι είναι αυτό;
What do you recommend? ti tha pro-**ti**-na-te?   Τι θα προτείνατε;
What are they eating? ti **i**-ne a-**fto** pu **tro**-ne? Τι είναι αυτό που τρώνε;

Bring us the best of what you have!
  fe-re mas **o**-ti ka-**li**-te-ro **e**-hyis!
Φέρε μας ό,τι καλύτερο έχεις!

The Menu

May I see the menu please?
  bo-**ro** na dho ton ka-**ta**-lo-gho
  pa-ra-ka-**lo**?
Μπορώ να δω τον κατάλογο
παρακαλώ;

Do you have a menu in English?
  e-hye-te to me-**nu** stang-gli-**ka**?
Έχετε το μενού στα αγγλικά;

What are today's specials?
  ti **i**-ne i si-me-ri-**nes** sas
  spe-si-a-li-**te**?
Τι είναι οι σημερινές σας
σπεσιαλιτέ;

Can I have a look in the kitchen?
(in order to choose your meal)
  bo-**ro** na **ri**-kso mya ma-**tya**
  stin ku-**zi**-na?
Μπορώ να ρίξω μια ματιά
στην κουζίνα;

I'd like ...
  tha **i**-the-la ...
Θα ήθελα ...

I'd like the set lunch, please.
  tha **i**-the-la to ka-tho-ri-**zme**-no
  me-si-me-ri-a-**no** me-**nu**, pa-ra-ka-**lo**
Θα ήθελα το καθορισμένο
μεσημεριανό μενού παρακαλώ.

Is service included in the bill?
  sim-be-ri-lam-**va**-ne-te to
  ser-vis sto lo-ghar-ya-**zmo**?
Συμπεριλαμβάνεται το σέρβις
στο λογαριασμό;

Does it come with salad?
  ser-**vi**-re-te me sa-**la**-ta?
Σερβίρεται με σαλάτα;

What's the soup of the day?
  pya **i**-ne i **su**-pa tis i-**me**-ras?
Ποια είναι η σούπα της ημέρας;

Do you happen to have ...?
  mi-pos **e**-hye-te ...?
Μήπως έχετε ...;

Throughout the Meal

What's in this dish?
  ti **i**-ne sa-**fto** to fa-yi-**to**?
Τι είναι σε αυτό το φαγητό;

Do you have sauce?
  e-hye-te sal-**tsa**?
Έχετε σάλτσα;

Not too spicy, please.
  o-hyi po-**li** pi-**kan**-di-ko, pa-ra-ka-**lo**   Οχι πολύ πικάντικο παρακαλώ.
Is that dish spicy?
  a-**fto** to fa-yi-**to i**-ne pi-**kan**-di-ko?   Αυτό το φαγητό είναι πικάντικο;
I like it hot and spicy.
  mu a-**re**-si na **i**-ne   Μου αρέσει να είναι καυτερό
  ka-fte-**ro** ke pi-**kan**-di-ko   και πικάντικο.
It's not hot. [temperature]
  dhen **i**-ne ze-**sto**   Δεν είναι ζεστό.
I didn't order this.
  dhen pa-**rang**-gi-la a-**fto**   Δεν παράγγειλα αυτό.

Please bring me ...	mu **fer**-ne-te ... pa-ra-ka-**lo**	Μου φέρνετε ... παρακαλώ
an ashtray	**e**-na sta-hto-dho-**hyi**-o	ένα σταχτοδοχείο
some/more	**li**-gho/pe-ri-**so**-te-ro	λίγο/περισσότερο
bread	pso-**mi**	ψωμί
a cup	fli-**dza**-ni	φλιτζάνι
a fork	pi-**ru**-ni	πιρούνι
a glass	po-**ti**-ri	ποτήρι
a wine glass	po-**ti**-ri tu kra-**syu**	ποτήρι του κρασιού
a knife	ma-**hye**-ri	μαχαίρι
a napkin	pe-**tse**-ta	πετσέτα
some pepper	**li**-gho pi-**pe**-ri	λίγο πιπέρι
a plate	**pya**-to	πιάτο
some salt	**li**-gho a-**la**-ti	λίγο αλάτι
some butter	**li**-gho **vu**-ti-ro	λίγο βούτυρο
a spoon	ku-**ta**-li	κουτάλι
a teaspoon	mi-**kro** ku-ta-**la**-ki	μικρό κουταλάκι
some water	**li**-gho ne-**ro**	λίγο νερό
some wine	**li**-gho kra-**si**	λίγο κρασί

I'd like something to drink.
  tha **i**-the-la **ka**-ti na pyo   Θα ήθελα κάτι να πιω.
Can I have a (beer), please?
  bo-**ro** na **e**-ho mya (**bi**-ra)   Μπορώ να έχω μια (μπίρα)
  pa-ra-ka-**lo**?   παρακαλώ;
It's taking a long time, please hurry up.
  per-ni po-**li o**-ra, pa-ra-ka-**lo**   Παίρνει πολλή ώρα, παρακαλώ
  ka-ne-te pyo **ghri**-go-ra   κάνετε πιο γρήγορα.
Will the food be much longer?
  thar-**yi**-si a-**ko**-ma to fa-yi-**to**?   Θα αργήσει ακόμα το φαγητό;
Can I have a clean (glass)?
  bo-**ro** na **e**-ho ka-tha-**ro** (po-**ti**-ri)?   Μπορώ να έχω καθαρό (ποτήρι);
We would like to move to another table.
  tha **the**-la-me na me-ta-ki-**ni**-su-me   Θα θέλαμε να μετακινήσουμε
  se **a**-lo tra-**pe**-zi   σε άλλο τραπέζι.

Please open the window.
bo-**ri**-te na-**ni**-kse-te to pa-ra-thi-ro   Μπορείτε να ανοίξετε το παράθυρο.

This food is ...	to fa-yi-**to i**-ne ...	Το φαγητό είναι ...
cold	**kri**-o	κρύο
brilliant/delicious	no-sti-**mo**-ta-to/thav-**ma**-si-o	νοστιμότατο/θαυμάσιο
burnt	ka-**me**-no	καμένο
spoiled	ha-la-**zme**-no	χαλασμένο
stale	ba-**ya**-ti-ko	μπαγιάτικο
undercooked	dhen i-ne psi-**me**-no ar-ke-**ta**	δεν είναι ψημένο αρκετά
overcooked	po-**li** psi-**me**-no	πολύ ψημένο
very oily	po-**li** la-dhe-**ro**	πολύ λαδερό
too salty	po-**li** al-mi-**ro**	πολύ αλμυρό

Thank you, that was delicious.
e-fha-ri-**sto**, **i**-tan no-sti-**mo**-ta-tos   Ευχαριστώ, ήταν νοστιμότατος.
The meal was excellent, thank you
to fa-yi-**to i**-tan thav-**ma**-si-o,   Το φαγητό ήταν θαυμάσιο,
e-fha-ri-**stu**-me   ευχαριστούμε
The bill, please.
to lo-ghar-ya-**zmo**, pa-ra-ka-**lo**   Το λογαριασμό, παρακαλώ.
It's not hot (spicy).
dhen i-ne ka-fte-**ro** (pi-**kan**-di-ko)   Δεν είναι καυτερό (πικάντικο).
Can you please bring me some/more ...?
bo-**ri**-te na mu **fe**-re-te   Μπορείτε να μου φέρετε
li-gho/a-**ko**-ma ...?   λίγο/ακόμα ...;

I'd like ...	tha **i**-the-la	Θα ήθελα ...
I'd like another ...	tha **i**-the-la a-lo e-na ...	Θα ήθελα άλλο ένα ...
I didn't order this.	dhen pa-**rang**-gi-la a-**fto**	Δεν παράγγειλα αυτό.
Waiter!	gar-**son**!	Γκαρσόν!

I'd like something to drink.
tha mu **a**-re-se **ka**-ti na pyo   Θα μου άρεσε κάτι να πιω.
Is the water filtered?
i-ne to **ne**-ro fil-tra-ri-**zme**-no?   Είναι το νερό φιλτραρισμένο;
May I have some more ...?
bo-**ro** na **e**-ho a-**ko**-ma **li**-gho?   Μπορώ να έχω ακόμα λίγο;

At the Mezedhopolion (snack bar serving alcohol and mezedhes)
Can you recommend a selection of dishes?
bo-**ri**-te na pro-**ti**-ne-te mya   Μπορείτε να προτείνετε μια
pi-ki-**li**-a a-po me-**ze**-dhes?   ποικιλία από μεζέδες;
What is this/that one?
ti **i**-ne a-**fto**?   Τι είναι αυτό;
Can I try this one?
bo-**ro** na dho-ki-**ma**-so a-**fto**?   Μπορώ να δοκιμάσω αυτό;
These are delicious!
a-**fta i**-ne i-**pe**-ro-ha!   Αυτά είναι υπέροχα!

I'd like two meat, two seafood,
two vegetable.
  tha **i**-the-la **dhi**-o fa-yi-**ta** me
    kre-as, **dhi**-o me tha-la-si-**na**
  ke **dhi**-o me la-ha-ni-**ka**

Θα ήθελα δύο φαγητά με
κρέας, δύο με θαλασσινά
και δύο με λαχανικά.

What size are your serves?
  po-so me-**gha**-les **i**-ne i me-**ri**-dhes?

Πόσο μεγάλες είναι οι μερίδες;

Another one of these, please.
  a-lo **e**-na a-pa-**fto**, pa-ra-ka-**lo**

Άλλο ένα από αυτό, παρακαλώ.

At the Zaharoplastion (sitdown and take away pastry and cake shop)
I want to buy some cakes.
  tha **i**-the-la na a-gho-**ra**-so
    li-gha ghli-**ka**

Θα ήθελα να αγοράσω
λίγα γλυκά.

What are these pastries called?
  pos ta **le**-ne a-**fta**?

Πώς τα λένε αυτά;

What's a traditional Greek cake/
pastry/biscuit?
  pya i-ne ta pa-ra-dho-si-a-**ka**
    e-li-ni-**ka** ghli-**ka**?

Ποια είναι τα παραδοσιακά
Ελληνικά γλυκά;

Do you have any cakes with/
without nuts/cream/honey?
  e-hye-te ghli-**ka** me/ho-**ris** ksi-**rus**
    kar-**pus/kre**-ma **gha**-la-ktos/**me**-li?

Έχετε γλυκά με/χωρίς ξηρούς
καρπούς/κρέμα γάλακτος/μέλι;

Do you serve coffee and cakes?
  bo-**ru**-me na ka-**thi**-su-me
    ya ka-**fe** ke ghli-**ko**?

Μπορούμε να καθήσουμε
για καφέ και γλυκό;

You May Hear
o-**ri**-ste, ti tha **pa**-re-te?	Ορίστε, τι θα πάρετε;	Yes, what is it you want?
a-**me**-sos	Αμέσως.	Directly/Immediately.
e-na le-**pto**	Ένα λεπτό.	Just a minute.
ti tha **fa**-te/**pyi**-te?	Τι θα φάτε/πιείτε;	What will you eat/drink?
ti-po-ta a-**lo**?	Τίποτα άλλο;	Anything else?
dhen **e**-hu-me ... **si**-me-ra	Δεν έχουμε ... σήμερα.	We have no ... today.
the-le-te ...?	Θέλετε ...;	Would you like ...?
o-**ri**-ste	Ορίστε.	Here you are.

the-le-te na **pyi**-te **ka**-ti?
  Θέλετε να πιείτε κάτι;   Do you want anything to drink?
ka-**li** o-re-ksi!
  Καλή όρεξη!   Enjoy your meal! (Good appetite!)

Family Meals
Can I bring anything?   bo-**ro** na **fe**-ro **ka**-ti?   Μπορώ να φέρω κάτι;
Let me help you.   na se vo-i-**thi**-so   Να σε βοηθήσω.

Can I watch you make this?
  bo-**ro** na dho **pos** to **ka**-nis a-**fto**?   Μπορώ να δω πώς το κάνεις αυτό;

You're a great cook!
   i-se thav-**ma**-si-os **ma**-yi-ras!   Είσαι θαυμάσιος μάγειρας!
This is magnificent/brilliant!
   i-ne i-**pe**-ro-ho/e-kse-re-ti-**ko**!   Είναι υπέροχο/εξαιρετικό!
This is very tasty.
   a-**fto i**-ne po-**li no**-sti-mo   Αυτό είναι πολύ νόστιμο.
Do you have the recipe for this?
   e-hyis ti sin-da-**yi** ya-**fto**?   Έχεις τη συνταγή για αυτό;
Is this a family recipe?
   i-ne i-ko-ye-ni-a-**ki** sin-da-**yi**?   Είναι οικογενειακή συνταγή;
Are the ingredients local?
   i-ne ta si-sta-ti-**ka do**-pya?   Είναι τα συστατικά ντόπια;
How do you make this?
   pos to **ftya**-hnis a-**fto**?   Πώς το φτιάχνεις αυτό;
I've never eaten food like this before.
   dhen **e**-ho ksa-na-**fai**   Δεν έχω ξαναφάει
   fa-yi-**to** sa-na-**fto**   φαγητό σαν αυτό.

If you ever come to (Australia)
I'll cook you a local dish.
   an **er**-this stin (af-stra-**li**-a) tha su   Αν έρθεις στην (Αυστραλία) θα σου
   ma-yi-**re**-pso to-pi-**ko** fa-yi-**to**   μαγειρέψω τοπικό φαγητό
Could you pass the (salt) please?
   mu **dhi**-nis to (a-**la**-ti) pa-ra-ka-**lo**?   Μου δίνεις το (αλάτι) παρακαλώ;
One is enough, thank you.
   e-na ar-**ki**, e-fha-ri-**sto**   Ένα αρκεί, ευχαριστώ.
Do you use ... in this?
   hri-si-mo-pi-**is** ... sa-**fto**?   Χρησιμοποιείς ... σε αυτό;

No thank you, I'm full. [male]
   o-hyi e-fha-ri-**sto**, **i**-me hor-**ta**-tos   Όχι ευχαριστώ, είμαι χορτάτος.
No thank you, I'm full. [female]
   o-hyi e-fha-ri-**sto**, **i**-me hor-**ta**-ti   Όχι ευχαριστώ, είμαι χορτάτη.

I've already eaten.
   e-ho **fai i**-dhi   Έχω φάει ήδη.
Thanks very much for the meal.
   e-fha-ri-**sto** po-**li** ya to fa-yi-**to**   Ευχαριστώ πολύ για το φαγητό.
I really appreciated it.
   e-fha-ri-**sti**-thi-ka to fa-yi-**to**   Ευχαριστήθηκα το φαγητό.

Vegetarian & Special Meals
I'm a vegetarian.   **i**-me hor-to-**fa**-ghos   Είμαι χορτοφάγος.

I don't eat meat or dairy products.
   dhen **tro**-o **kre**-as i gha-la-kto-   Δε τρώω κρέας ή
   ko-mi-**ka** pro-i-**on**-da   γαλακτοκομικά προϊόντα.

Is it cooked with pork lard or
chicken stock?
  i-ne psi-**me**-no me hyi-ri-**no**
  li-pos i zo-**mo** ko-tas?

Είναι ψημένο με χοιρινό λίπος
ή ζωμό κότας;

I only eat vegetables.
  tro-o **mo**-no la-ha-ni-**ka**

Τρώω μόνο λαχανικά.

What are your vegetable dishes?
  ti fa-yi-**ta e**-hye-te a-**po** la-ha-ni-**ka**?

Τι φαγητά έχετε από λαχανικά;

Can you recommend a vegetable dish?
  bo-**ri**-te na pro-**ti**-ne-te fa-yi-**to**
  me la-ha-ni-**ka**?

Μπορείτε να προτείνετε
φαγητό με λαχανικά;

I don't want any meat at all.
  dhe **the**-lo ka-**tho**-lu **kre**-as

Δε θέλω καθόλου κρέας.

Don't add egg.   **mi va**-le-te a-**vgo**   Μη βάλετε αυγό.

I don't eat ...	dhen **tro**-o ...	Δεν τρώω ...
chicken	ko-**to**-pu-lo	κοτόπουλο
cured/processed meats	a-lan-di-**ka**	αλλαντικά
fish	**psa**-ri	ψάρι
meat	**kre**-as	κρέας
pork	hyi-ri-**no**	χοιρινό
poultry	pu-le-ri-**ka**	πουλερικά
seafood	tha-la-si-**na**	θαλασσινά

Do you have any vegetarian dishes?
  e-hye-te fa-yi-**ta** ya hor-to-**fa**-ghus?

Εχετε φαγητά για χορτοφάγους;

Can you recommend a vegetarian
dish, please?
  bo-**ri**-te na pro-**ti**-ne-te **e**-na
  fa-yi-**to** ya hor-to-**fa**-ghus?

Μπορείτε να προτείνετε ένα
φαγητό για χορτοφάγους;

Does this dish have meat?
  e-hyi a-**fto** to fa-yi-**to kre**-as?

Εχει αυτό το φαγητό κρέας;

Can I get this without the meat?
  bo-**ro** na **e**-ho a-**fto** ho-**ris kre**-as?

Μπορώ να έχω αυτό χωρίς κρέας;

Does it contain eggs/dairy products?
  pe-ri-**e**-hyi a-**vgha**/gha-la-kto-ko-mi-**ka**
  pro-i-**on**-da?

Περιέχει αυγά/γαλακτοκομικά
προϊόντα;

Does this dish have gelatine?
  e-hyi to fa-yi-**to** ze-la-**ti**-ni?

Εχει το φαγητό ζελατίνη;

I'm allergic to ... (peanuts) [male]
  i-me a-ler-yi-**kos** ya ... (fi-**sti**-ki-a)

Είμαι αλλεργικός για ... (φιστίκια)

I'm allergic to ... (peanuts) [female]
  i-me a-ler-yi-**ki** ya ... (fi-**sti**-ki-a)

Είμαι αλλεργική για ... (φιστίκια)

I follow a particular diet.
  a-ko-lu-**tho** sing-ge-kri-**me**-ni **dhi**-e-ta

Ακολουθώ συγκεκριμένη δίαιτα.

I follow a ... diet	a-ko-lu-**tho** mya ... **dhi**-e-ta	Ακολουθώ μια ... δίαιτα
carbohydrate	i-dha-**tan**-thra-kas	υδατάνθρακας
fat	**li**-pos	λίπος
high-fibre	po-**les** fi-ti-**kes** i-nes	πολλές φυτικές ίνες
low-fat	ha-mi-**lo** se li-pa-**ra**	χαμηλό σε λιπαρά

Is it ...?	**i**-ne ... ?	Είναι ...;
gluten-free	ho-**ris** ghlu-**te**-ni	χωρίς γλουτένη
lactose-free	ho-**ris** la-**kto**-zi	χωρίς λακτόζη
salt-free	ho-**ris** a-**la**-ti	χωρίς αλάτι
sugar-free	ho-**ris** **za**-ha-ri	χωρίς ζάχαρη
wheat-free	ho-**ris** si-**ta**-ri	χωρίς σιτάρι
yeast-free	ho-**ris** ma-**ya**	χωρίς μαγιά
Is this organic?	**i**-ne or-gha-ni-**ko**?	Είναι οργανικό;
organically grown produce	or-gha-ni-**ka** ka-li-er-yi-**me**-na pro-i-**on**-da	οργανικά καλλιεργημένα προϊόντα

| I'm a diabetic | **i**-me di-a-vi-ti-**kos** | Είμαι διαβητικός |

At the Market & Self-Catering

Where's the nearest (market)?
  pu i-ne to pli-si-**e**-ste-ro (a-gho-**ra**)?   Πού είναι το πλησιέστερο (αγορά);
Where can I find (the sugar)?
  pu bo-**ro** na vro (ti **za**-ha-ri)?   Πού μπορώ να βρω (τη ζάχαρη);

Can I have a ...?	bo-**ro** na **e**-ho ...?	Μπορώ να εχώ ...;
bottle	bu-**ka**-li	μπουκάλι
box	ku-**ti**	κουτί
can	kon-**ser**-va	κονσέρβα
packet	pa-**ke**-to	πακέτο
sachet/bag	**tsan**-da	τσάντα
tin of ...	kon-**ser**-va me ...	κονσέρβα με ...

| How much? | **po**-so **ka**-ni | Πόσο κάνει; |

How much is (a kilo of cheese)?
  po-so **ka**-ni (**e**-na ki-**lo** ti-**ri**)?   Πόσο κάνει (ένα κιλό τυρί);
How much altogether?
  po-so **ka**-nun **o**-la ma-**zi**?   Πόσο κάνουν όλα μαζί;

How much (for) ...?	**po**-so **ka**-ni (a-**fto**) ...?	Πόσο κάνει (αυτό) ...;
both	ke ta **dhi**-o	Και τα δύο
per fruit	to **ka**-the **fru**-to	το κάθε φρούτο
per piece	to ko-**ma**-ti	το κομμάτι
this	a-**fto**	αυτό

This is (too) expensive.
  i-ne (po-**li**) a-kri-**vo**   Είναι (πολύ) ακριβό.

Do you have anything cheaper?
   e-hye-te **ti**-po-ta fti-**no**-te-ro?   Έχετε τίποτα φτηνότερο;
Give me half/a kilo, please.
   mu **dhi**-ne-te mi-**so**/e-na ki-**lo**,   Μου δίνετε μισό/ένα
   pa-ra-ka-**lo**   κιλό, παρακαλώ.
I'd like (six) slices of (ham).
   tha **i**-the-la (e-ksi) **fe**-tes (zam-**bon**)   Θα ήθελα (έξι) φέτες (ζαμπόν).
I don't want to buy anything.
   dhe **the**-lo na a-gho-ra-so ti-po-ta   Δε θέλω να αγοράσω τίποτα.

I'm just looking.	a-**plos** ki-**ta**-zo	Απλώς κοιτάζω.
No!	o-**hyi**!	Όχι!
Who's next?	**pyos e**-hyi si-**ra**?	Ποιος έχει σειρά;
I'd like some ...	tha **i**-the-la **li**-gho ...	Θα ήθελα λίγο ...

I'd like to buy ...
   tha **i**-the-la na a-gho-**ra**-so ...   Θα ήθελα να αγοράσω ...
Where can I buy ...?
   pu bo-**ro** na a-gho-**ra**-so ... ?   Πού μπορώ να αγοράσω ...;

I'd like (some) ...	tha **i**-the-la ...	Θα ήθελα
bread	(**li**-gho) pso-**mi**	(λίγο) ψωμί
butter	(**li**-gho) **vu**-ti-ro	(λίγο) βούτυρο
cheese	(**li**-gho) ti-**ri**	(λίγο) τυρί
chocolate	(**li**-yi) so-ko-**la**-ta	(λίγη) σοκολάτα
eggs	(**li**-gha) a-**vga**	(λίγα) αυγά
flour	(**li**-gho) a-**le**-vri	(λίγο) αλεύρι
fruit &	(**li**-gha) **fru**-ta ke	(λίγα) φρούτα και
vegetables	la-ha-ni-**ka**	λαχανικά
ham	(**li**-gho) zam-**bon**	(λίγο) ζαμπόν
honey	(**li**-gho) **me**-li	(λίγο) μέλι
jam	(**li**-yi) mar-me-**la**-dha	(λίγη) μαρμελάδα
margarine	(**li**-yi) mar-gha-**ri**-ni	(λίγη) μαργαρίνη
marmalade	(**li**-yi) mar-me-**la**-dha	(λίγη) μαρμελάδα από
	a-**po** e-spe-ri-dho-i-**dhi**	εσπεριδοειδή
milk	(**li**-gho) **gha**-la	(λίγο) γάλα
olive oil	(**li**-gho) e-le-**o**-la-dho	(λίγο) ελαιόλαδο
pasta	(**li**-gha) ma-ka-**ro**-nya	(λίγα) μακαρόνια
pepper	(**li**-gho) pi-**pe**-ri	(λίγο) πιπέρι
rice	(**li**-gho) **ri**-zi	(λίγο) ρύζι
salt	(**li**-gho) a-**la**-ti	(λίγο) αλάτι
sugar	(**li**-yi) **za**-ha-ri	(λίγη) ζάχαρη
yoghurt	(**li**-gho) ya-**ur**-ti	(λίγο) γιαούρτι
olives	(**li**-yes) e-**lyes**	(λίγες) ελιές
black olives	(**li**-yes) e-**lyes ma**-vres	(λίγες) ελιές μαύρες
green olives	(**li**-yes) e-**lyes pra**-si-nes	(λίγες) ελιές πράσινες
stuffed olives	(**li**-yes) e-**lyes** ye-mi-**stes**	(λίγες) ελιές γεμιστές

This is a present for someone.
  a-**fto** i-ne **dho**-ro ya **ka**-pyon
  Αυτό είναι δώρο για κάποιον.
Best before ...
  i-me-ro-mi-**ni**-a **li**-kse-os ...
  Ημερομηνία λήξεως ...
Can I taste it?
  bo-**ro** na to dho-ki-**ma**-so?
  Μπορώ να το δοκιμάσω;
Will this keep in the fridge?
  tha kra-**ti**-si sto psi-**yi**-o?
  Θα κρατήσει στο ψυγείο;
Do you have anything better?
  e-hye-te **ti**-po-ta ka-**li**-te-ro?
  Εχετε τίποτα καλύτερο;
What's the local speciality?
  pya i-ne i to-pi-**ki** spe-si-a-li-**te**?
  Ποια είναι η τοπική σπεσιαλιτέ;
Where/what is the expiry date?
  pu/pya i-ne i i-me-ro-mi-**ni**-a
  li-kse-os?
  Πού/Ποια είναι η ημερομηνία
  λήξεως;
Can you give me a discount?
  bo-**ri**-te na mu **ka**-ne-te **ek**-pto-si?
  Μπορείτε να μου κάνετε έκπτωση;
The ingredients of this recipe are ...
  ta si-sta-ti-**ka** tis sin-da-**yis** i-ne ...
  Τα συστατικά της συνταγής είναι ...
When does this shop open?
  po-te a-**ni**-yi a-**fto** to ma-gha-**zi**?
  Πότε ανοίγει αυτό το μαγαζί;

I am looking for ...   **psa**-hno na vro ...
  Ψάχνω να βρω ...
Where can I find?   **pu** bo-**ro** na vro?
  Πού μπορώ να βρω;

At the Bar
Shall we go for a drink?
  the-le-te na **pa**-me ya **e**-na po-**to**?
  Θέλετε να πάμε για ένα ποτό;
I'll buy you a drink.
  tha su a-gho-**ra**-so **e**-na po-**to**
  Θα σου αγοράσω ένα ποτό.
Thanks, but I don't feel like it.
  e-fha-ri-**sto** a-**la** dhen **ka**-no ke-**fi**
  Ευχαριστώ αλλά δεν κάνω κέφι.
I don't drink (alcohol).
  dhen **pi**-no (i-no-pnev-ma-to-dhi
  po-**ta**)
  Δεν πίνω (οινοπνευματώδη ποτά).
What would you like?
  ti tha **the**-la-te?
  Τι θα θέλατε;
You can get the next one.
  bo-**ris** na **pa**-ris to e-**po**-me-no
  Μπορείς να πάρεις το επόμενο.

I'll have ...   tha **pa**-ro ...
  θα πάρω ...
It's on me.   e-**gho** ker-**na**-o
  Εγώ κερνάω.
It's my round.   **i**-ne i si-**ra** mu
  Είναι η σειρά μου.
OK.   en-**da**-ksi
  Εντάξει

Can I buy you a coffee?
  bo-**ro** na su a-gho-**ra**-so
  e-nan ka-**fe**?
  Μπορώ να σου αγοράσω έναν καφέ;
I think I've had one too many.
  no-**mi**-zo **e**-ho pyi ar-ke-**ta**
  Νομίζω έχω πιει αρκετά.

One more and I'll be under the table.
    e-na a-**ko**-ma ke tha **yi**-no **fe**-si   ήνα ακόμα και θα γίνω φέσι.
I'm never, ever drinking again.
    dhen tha ksa-na-**pi**-no po-**te**   Δεν θα ξαναπίνω ποτέ.

I'm next.	e-**gho** e-ho si-**ra**	Εγώ έχω σειρά.
Excuse me.	me sing-ho-**ris**	Με συγχωρείς.

I was here before this lady.
    i-mun e-**dho** prin a-**po** tin ki-**ri**-a   Ημουν εδώ πριν από την κυρία.
I was here before this gentleman.
    i-**mun** e-**dho** prin a-**po** ton **ki**-ri-o   Ημουν εδώ πριν από τον κύριο.

I'll have a [one] ...	tha **pa**-ro	Θα πάρω ...
beer	mya **bi**-ra	μια μπίρα
brandy	e-na kon-**yak**	ένα κονιάκ
cider	mya mi-**li**-ti	μια μηλίτη
cocktail	e-na ko-**kte**-il	ένα κοκτέιλ
liqueur	e-na li-**ker**	ένα λικέρ
whisky	e-na u-**i**-ski	ένα ουίσκι

Cheers!	i-si-**yi**-a!	Εις υγεία!
No ice.	ho-**ris pa**-gho	Χωρίς πάγο.

Can I have ice, please?
    bo-**ro** na e-ho **pa**-gho,   Μπορώ να έχω πάγο,
    se pa-ra-ka-**lo**?   σε παρακαλώ;

Same again, please.	to **i**-di-o, pa-ra-ka-**lo**	Το ίδιο παρακαλώ.
Good health!	sti-ni-**ya**-su!	Στην υγειά σου!
Is food available here?	i-**par**-hyi fa-yi-**to** e-**dho**?	Υπάρχει φαγητό εδώ;
Where's the toilet?	**pu i**-ne i tu-a-**le**-ta?	Πού είναι η τουαλέτα;

I'm a bit tired, I'd better get
home. [male]
    i-me **li**-gho ku-ra-**zme**-nos,   Είμαι λίγο κουρασμένος
    ka-**lu**-te-ra na **pa**-o **spi**-ti   καλύτερα να πάω σπίτι.
I'm a bit tired, I'd better get
home. [female]
    i-me **li**-gho ku-ra-**zme**-ni,   Είμαι λίγο κουρασμένη,
    ka-**lu**-te-ra na **pa**-o **spi**-ti   καλύτερα να πάω σπίτι.

I'm pissed.	i-me **fe**-si	Είμαι φέσι.
I feel ill.	dhen e-**stha**-no-me ka-**la**	Δεν αισθάνομαι καλά.

I want to throw up.
    mur-hye-te na **ka**-no e-me-**to**   Μου 'ρχεται να κάνω εμετό.
I'm hung over. (have a headache)
    e-ho po-no-**ke**-fa-lo   έχω πονοκέφαλο.
So, do you come here often?
    li-**pon**, er-hye-se e-**dho** si-**hna**?   Λοιπόν, έρχεσαι εδώ συχνά;

I really, really love you.
   sa-gha-**po** pa-ra **pa**-ra po-**li**   Σε αγαπώ πάρα πάρα πολύ.
What did I do last night?
   ti **e**-ka-na htes to **vra**-dhi?   Τι έκανα χτες το βράδυ;

Wine

May I see the wine list, please?
   bo-**ro** na dho ton ka-**ta**-lo-gho   Μπορώ να δω τον κατάλογο
   ton kra-**syon**, se pa-ra-ka-**lo**?   των κρασιών, σε παρακαλώ;
What is a good year?
   pya i-ne ka-**li** hro-**nya**?   Ποια είναι καλή χρονιά;
Can you recommend a good
local wine?
   bo-**ri**-te na pro-**ti**-ne-te   Μπορείτε να προτείνετε
   e-na ka-**lo** to-pi-**ko** kra-**si**?   ένα καλό τοπικό κρασί;
May I taste it?
   bo-**ro** na to dho-ki-**ma**-so?   Μπορώ να το δοκιμάσω;
Which wine would you recommend
with this dish?
   pyo kra-**si** tha pro-**ti**-na-te   Ποιο κρασί θα προτείνατε
   ma-**fto** to fa-yi-**to**?   με αυτό το φαγητό;
I'd like a glass/bottle of ... wine.
   tha **i**-th-la **e**-na po-**ti**-ri/   Θα ήθελα ένα ποτήρι/
   bu-**ka**-li ... kra-**si**   μπουκάλι ... κρασί.

red	**ko**-ki-no	κόκκινο
rosé	ro-**ze**	ροζέ
white	**a**-spro	άσπρο
house	to dhi-**ko** sas	το δικό σας
local	**do**-pyo	ντόπιο
barrel	**hyi**-ma	χύμα

I'd like half/one kilo of ... wine
   tha **i**-th-la mi-**so**/e-na ki-**lo** ... kra-**si**   Θα ήθελα μισό/ένα κιλό ... κρασί

This wine has a nice/bad taste.
   a-**fto** to kra-**si** e-**hyi** o-**re**-a/   Αυτό το κρασί έχει ωραία/
   a-**shi**-mi **yef**-si   άσχημη γεύση.
This wine is corked.
   a-**fto** to kra-**si** i-ne ha-la-**zme**-no   Αυτό το κρασί είναι χαλασμένο.

Children

Are children allowed?
   ta pe-**dhya** e-pi-**tre**-pon-de?   Τα παιδιά επιτρέπονται;
Is there a children's menu?
   ipar-hyi ka-**ta**-lo-ghos ya ta pe-**dhya**?   Υπάρχει κατάλογος για τα παιδιά;

English – Greek Glossary

In Greek, the definite article is used with the names of people and places and when referring to specific things ('the book'), things as a class ('books'), and abstract ideas ('democracy'). Nouns belong to one of three genders – masculine, feminine, neuter. Each gender has its own article: o, i, to (ο, η, το); the plurals are i, i, ta (οι, οι, τα).

Stress in Greek words is restricted to the last three syllables. The stressed vowel has an accent (´) written on it. Isolated verbs are given in their 'I cook/do cook/am cooking' form. Sub-groups of a word are preceded by a dash e.g., **-yemistes** for stuffed peppers. Articles are sometimes pronounced as a single word with their nouns.

A

alcohol	*to al-ko-**ol***	to alkool	το αλκοόλ
alcoholic spirits	*ta i-no-pnev-ma-to-dhi*	ta inopnevmatodhi	τα οινοπνευματώδη
allspice	*to ba-ha-ri*	to bahari	το μπαχάρι
almonds	*ta-mi-ghdha-la*	ta amighdhala	τα αμύγδαλα
amaranth	*ta vli-ta*	ta vlita	τα βλίτα
amount	*i po-so-ti-ta (to po-so)*	i posotita (to poso)	η ποσότητα (το ποσό)
anchovy	*o **gha**-vros*	o ghavros	ο γαύρος
anemone, sea	*i gha-li-pes*	i ghalipes	οι γαλύπες
aniseed	*to ghli-**ka**-ni-so*	to ghlikaniso	το γλυκάνισο
appetiser	*to o-re-kti-**ko***	to orektiko	το ορεκτικό
apple	*to **mi**-lo*	to milo	το μήλο
apricot	*to ve-ri-ko-ko*	to verikoko	το βερίκοκο
artichoke	*i ang-gi-**na**-ra*	i angginara	η αγγινάρα
asparagus	*ta spa-**rang**-gi-a*	ta sparanggia	τα σπαράγγια
assortment	*ta dhi-a-fo-ra*	ta dhiafora	τα διάφορα
avocado	*to a-vo-**ka**-do*	to avokado	το αβοκάντο

B

bacon	*to **be**-i-kon*	to beikon	το μπέικον
bake	*psi-no*	psino	ψήνω
baked	*sto **fur**-no*	sto furno	στο φούρνο
bakery	*o **fur**-nos*	o furnos	ο φούρνος
baking powder	*to **be**-i-kin pa-u-der*	to beikin pauder	το μπέικιν πάουντερ
baklava	*o ba-kla-**vas***	o baklavas	ο μπακλαβάς
banana	*i ba-**na**-na*	i banana	η μπανάνα
barbecued	*sta **kar**-vu-na*	sta karvuna	στα κάρβουνα
barley	*to kri-**tha**-ri*	to krithari	το κριθάρι
bass, sea	*to la-**vra**-ki*	to lavraki	το λαβράκι
batter	*to kur-**ku**-ti*	to kurkuti	το κουρκούτι
bay leaf	*i **dhaf**-ni*	i dhafni	η δάφνη

beans			
–black-eyed peas	ta lu-vya	ta luvya	τα λουβιά
–broad	ta ku-kya	ta kukya	τα κουκιά
–dried	ta fa-so-li-a	ta fasolia	τα φασόλια
–green	ta fa-so-la-kya	ta fasolakya	τα φασολάκια
–haricot	ta fa-so-li-a	ta fasolia	τα φασόλια
–lima	ta fa-so-li-a	ta fasolia	τα φασόλια
–red kidney	to ko-ki-no fa-so-li	to kokino fasoli	το κόκκινο φασόλι
bechamel sauce	i be-sa-mel	i besamel	η μπεσαμέλ
beef	to vo-dhi-no	to vodhino	το βοδινό
–corned	to korn-be-if	to kornbeif	το κορνμπέιφ
beer	i bi-ra	i bira	η μπίρα
beetroot	to pan-dza-ri	to pandzari	το παντζάρι
berry	to mu-ro	to muro	το μούρο
–blackberry	to va-to-mu-ro	to vatomuro	το βατόμουρο
bill	o lo-ghar-yaz-mos	o logharyazmos	ο λογαριασμός
bird	to pu-li	to puli	το πουλί
biscuit	to bi-sko-to/ku-lu-ra-ki	to biskoto/kuluraki	το μπισκότο/κουλουράκι
bitter	pi-kros	pikros	πικρός
bitters	i bi-ters	i biters	η μπίττερς
blackberry	to va-to-mu-ro	to vatomuro	το βατόμουρο
black-eyed peas	ta lu-vya	ta luvya	τα λουβιά
blender	to blen-der	to blender	το μπλέντερ
boar, wild	o ka-pros	o kapros	ο κάπρος
boil	vra-zo	vrazo	βράζω
boiled	vra-stos/vra-zme-nos	vrastos/vrazmenos	βραστός/βρασμένος
borage	i pu-ran-dza	i purandza	η πουράντζα
bottle	to bu-ka-li	to bukali	το μπουκάλι
bottled water	to ne-ro em-fi-a-lo-me-no	to nero emfialomeno	το νερό εμφιαλωμένο
bowl	to ki-pe-lo	to kipelo	το κύπελλο
–mixing	to bol ya a-na-mi-ksi i-li-kon	to bol ya anamiksi ilikon	το μπωλ για ανάμειξη υλικών
–salad	i sa-la-ti-e-ra	i salatiera	η σαλατιέρα
brains	ta mya-la	ta myala	τα μυαλά
braise	psi-no stin ka-tsa-ro-la	psino stin katsarola	ψήνω στην κατσαρόλα
bran	to pi-tu-ro	to pituro	το πίτουρο
brandy	to kon-yak	to konyak	το κονιάκ
bread	to pso-mi	to psomi	το ψωμί
–church-offering	to pros-fo-ro	to prosforo	το πρόσφορο
–olive	to e-le-o-pso-mo	to eleopsomo	το ελαιόψωμο
breakfast	to pro-i-no	to proino	το πρωινό

bream, gilt head	*i tsi-pu-ra*	i tsipura	η τσιπούρα
bream, sea	*to fa-ghri/li-thri-ni/ me-la-nu-ri*	to faghri/lithrini/ melanuri	το φαγρί/λιθρίνι/ μελανούρι
breast	*to sti-thos*	to stithos	το στήθος
broccoli	*to bro-ko-lo*	to brokolo	το μπρόκολο
broth	*o zo-mos*	o zomos	ο ζωμός
buns	*ta ku-lu-ra-ki*	ta kulurakya	τα κουλουράκια
burghul	*to pli-ghu-ri*	to plighuri	το πλιγούρι
butter	*to vu-ti-ro*	to vutiro	το βούτυρο
butter knife	*to ma-hye-ri vu-ti-ru*	to mahyeri vutiru	το μαχαίρι βουτύρου
buttermilk	*to vu-ti-ro-ga-lo*	to vutirogalo	το βουτυρόγαλο

C

cabbage	*to la-ha-no*	to lahano	το λάχανο
–red	*to ko-ki-no la-ha-no*	to kokino lahano	το κόκκινο λάχανο
–white	*to a-spro la-ha-no*	to aspro lahano	το άσπρο λάχανο
cake	*to ghli-ki-zma/ke-ik*	to ghlikizma/keik	το γλύκισμα/κέικ
–fruit	*me fru-ta*	to keik me fruta	το κέικ με φρούτα
can	*i kon-ser-va*	i konserva	η κονσέρβα
candy	*i ka-ra-me-la*	i karamela	η καραμέλα
canned	*tu ku-tyu*	tu kutyu	του κουτιού
canteen	*i kan-ti-na*	i kantina	η καντίνα
canteloupe	*to pe-po-ni*	to peponi	το πεπόνι
caper	*i ka-pa-ri*	i kapari	η κάππαρη
capon	*to ka-po-ni*	to kaponi	το καπόνι
capsicum	*i pi-per-ya*	i piperya	οι πιπεριά
–red	*i ko-ki-ni pi-per-ya*	i kokini piperya	η κόκκινη πιπεριά
–yellow	*i ki-tri-ni pi-per-ya*	i kitrini piperya	η κίτρινη πιπεριά
carafe	*i ka-ra-fa*	i karafa	η καράφα
caramel	*i ka-ra-me-la*	i karamela	η καραμέλα
cardamom	*to kar-dha-mo*	to kardhamo	το κάρδαμο
carrot	*to ka-ro-to*	to karoto	το καρότο
cauliflower	*to ku-nu-pi-dhi*	to kunupidhi	το κουνουπίδι
caviar	*to ha-vya-ri*	to havyari	το χαβιάρι
cayenne	*to ko-ki-no-pi-pe-ro*	to kokinopipero	το κοκκινοπίπερο
celeriac	*i se-li-no-ri-za*	i selinoriza	η σελινόριζα
celery	*to se-li-no*	to selino	το σέλινο
cereal	*ta dhi-mi-tri-a-ka*	ta dhimitriaka	τα δημητριακά
chamomile	*to ha-mo-mi-li*	to hamomili	το χαμομήλι
champagne	*i sam-pa-nya*	i sampanya	η σαμπάνια
chargrilled	*sta kar-vu-na*	sta karvuna	στα κάρβουνα
charlock	*i vru-va*	i vruva	η βρούβα
cheese	*to ti-ri*	to tiri	το τυρί
–blue	*ble*	ble	μπλε
–cottage	*ma-la-ki mi-zi-thra*	malaki mizithra	μαλακή μυζήθρα

–cream	kre-mo-dhes	kremodhes	κρεμώδες
–feta	i fe-ta	i feta	η φέτα
–hard	skli-ro	skliro	σκληρό
–semi-firm	i-mi-skli-ro	imiskliro	ημίσκληρο
–soft	ma-la-ko	malako	μαλακό
chef	o ma-yi-ras	o mayiras	ο μάγειρας
cherry	to ke-ra-si	to kerasi	το κεράσι
–morello	to vi-si-no	to visino	το βύσσινο
chewing gum	i tsi-hla	i tsihla	η τσίχλα
chicken	to ko-to-pu-lo	to kotopulo	το κοτόπουλο
chickpea	ta re-vi-thi-a	to revithi	τα ρεβίθι
chicory	ta ki-ho-rya	ta kihorya	τα κιχώρια
chilli	i ka-fte-ri pi-per-ya	i kafteri piperya	η καυτερή πιπεριά
chips, potato	ta tsips	ta tsips	τα τσιπς
chive	to tsa-iv	to tsaiv	το τσάιβ
chocolate	i so-ko-la-ta	i sokolata	η σοκολάτα
–hot drink	gha-la	i sokolata ghala	η σοκολάτα γάλα
chopping board	to sa-ni-dhi ya te-ma-hi-zmo/ ko-psi-mo	to sanidhi ya temahizmo/ kopsimo	το σανίδι για τεμαχισμό/ κόψιμο
chop (steak)	i bri-zo-la	i brizola	η μπριζόλα
–pork	i hyi-ri-ni bri-zo-la	i hyirini brizola	η χοιρινή μπριζόλα
cider	o mi-li-tis i-nos	o militis inos	ο μηλίτης οίνος
cinnamon	i ka-ne-la	i kanela	η κανέλα
citrus	to e-spe-ri-dho-i-dhes	to esperidhoidhes	το εσπεριδοειδές
clam	i a-hyi-va-dha	i ahyivadha	η αχηβάδα
clotted cream	to ka-i-ma-ki pigh-me-no	to kaimaki pighmeno	το καϊμάκι πηγμένο
cloves	ta gha-ri-fa-la	ta gharifala	τα γαρίφαλα
cockles	ta ki-dho-nya	ta kidhonya	τα κυδώνια
cocktail	to ko-kte-il	to kokteil	το κοκτέιλ
cocoa	to ka-ka-o	to kakao	το κακάο
coconut	i ka-ri-dha	i karidha	η καρύδα
cod, dried salt	o ba-ka-lya-ros	o bakalyaros	ο μπακαλιάρος
coffee	o ka-fes	o kafes	ο καφές
–beans	i ko-ki ka-fe	i koki kafe	οι κόκκοι καφέ
–cold	o fra-pes	o frapes	ο φραπές
–Greek	e-li-ni-kos	o kafes elinikos	καφές Ελληνικός
–grinder	o mi-los tu ka-fe	o milos tu kafe	ο μύλος του καφέ
–instant	o nes ka-fes	o nes kafes	ο Νες Καφές
–shop	to ka-fe-ni-o	to kafenio	το καφενείο
cognac	to kon-yak	to konyak	το κονιάκ
compote	i kom-po-sta	i komposta	η κομπόστα

condiments	ta ka-ri-**kev**-ma-ta	ta karikevmata	τα καρυκεύματα
conserve	i mar-me-**la**-dha	i marmeladha	η μαρμελάδα
consomme	to kon-so-**me**	to konsome	το κονσομέ
cookies	ta bi-**sko**-ta/	ta biskota/	τα μπισκότα/
	ku-lu-ra-kiya	kulurakiya	κουλουράκια
coriander	to **ko**-lyan-dros	to kolyandros	το κόλιαντρος
corn	to ka-la-**mbo**-ki	to kalamboki	το καλαμπόκι
corned beef	to korn-**be**-if	to kornbeif	το κορνμπέιφ
cottage cheese	ma-la-ki mi-**zi**-thra	malaki mizithra	μαλακή μυζήθρα
course, first	to **pro**-to **pya**-to	to proto pyato	το πρώτο πιάτο
course, main	to **ki**-ri-o fa-**yi**-to	to kirio fayito	το κύριο φαγητό
cover charge	to ku-**ver**	to kuver	το κουβέρ
crab	to ka-**vu**-ri	to kavuri	το καβούρι
cracked wheat	to pli-**ghu**-ri	to plighuri	το πλιγούρι
crayfish	i ka-ra-**vi**-dha	i karavidha	η καραβίδα
cream	i **kre**-ma	i krema	η κρέμα
–cheese	to ti-ri kre-**mo**-dhes	to tiri kremodhes	το τυρί κρεμώδες
–clotted	to ka-i-**ma**-ki	to kaimaki	το καϊμάκι πηγμένο
	pigh-**me**-no	pighmeno	
–sour	**ksi**-ni	i krema ksini	η κρέμα ξινή
croissant	to kru-a-**san**	to kruasan	το κρουασάν
croquette	i kro-**ke**-ta	i kroketa	η κροκέττα
cucumber	to ang-**gu**-ri	to angguri	το αγγούρι
cumin	to **ki**-mi-no	to kimino	το κύμινο
cup	to fli-**dza**-ni	to flidzani	το φλιτζάνι
curd	to ti-**ro**-pigh-ma	to tiropighma	το τυρόπηγμα
cure, to	a-la-**ti**-zo	alatizo	αλατίζω
currants	i sta-**fi**-dhes	i stafidhes	οι σταφίδες
curry	to **ka**-ri	to kari	το κάρι
cutlery	ta ma-hye-ro-**pi**-ru-na	ta mahyeropiruna	τα μαχαιροπίρουνα
cutlets	ta pa-i-**dha**-kya	ta paidhakya	τα παϊδάκια
cuttlefish	oi su-**pyes**	i supyes	οι σουπιές

D

dandelion	to ta-ra-**ksa**-ko	to taraksako	το ταράξακο
dates	i hur-**ma**-dhes	i hurmadhes	οι χουρμάδες
delicatessen	to a-lan-do-po-**li**-o	to alandopolio	το αλλαντοπωλείο
dessert	to e-pi-**dhor**-pi-o	to epidhorpio	το επιδόρπιο
dill	o **a**-ni-thos	o anithos	ο άνιθος
dinner	to vra-dhi-**no**	to vradhino	το βραδινό
dittander	to **dhi**-kta-mo	to dhiktamo	το δίκταμο
dolmades	i dol-**ma**-dhes	i dolmadhes	οι ντολμάδες
dove, turtle	to tri-**gho**-ni	to trighoni	το τρυγόνι
dried	kse-**ros**	kseros	ξερός
drink	ta po-**to**	to poto	τα ποτό
duck	i **pa**-pya	i papya	η πάπια

E

eel	to **hye**-li	to hyeli	το χέλι
–moray	i **zmer**-na	i zmerna	η σμέρνα
eggplant	i me-li-**dza**-nes	i melidzanes	οι μελιτζάνες
eggs	ta a-**vgha**	ta avgha	τα αυγά
–fried	ti-gha-**ni**-ta	tighanita	τηγανητά
–hard-boiled	**skli**-ra	sklira	σκληρά
–poached	po-**se**	pose	ποσέ
–red-dyed	pa-sha-li-**na**	pashalina	Πασχαλινά
–soft-boiled	me-**la**-ta	melata	μελάτα
endive	to an-**di**-dhi	to andidhi	το αντίδι

F

fat, animal	zo-i-**ko li**-pos	zoiko lipos	ζωικό λίπος
fat, vegetable	i fi-**ti**-ni	i fitini	η φυτίνη
fennel	to **ma**-ra-tho	to maratho	το μάραθο
feta cheese	i **fe**-ta	i feta	η φέτα
figs	to **si**-ko	to siko	τα σύκο
fillet	to fi-**le**-to	to fileto	το φιλέτο
fillet, to	**ko**-vo se fi-**le**-to	kovo se fileto	κόβω σε φιλέτα
filo pastry	to **fi**-lo	to filo	το φύλλο
fish	to **psa**-ri	to psari	το ψάρι
–anchovy	o **gha**-vros	o ghavros	ο γαύρος
–blackfish	o ro-**fos**	o rofos	ο ροφός
–bogue	i **gho**-pa	i ghopa	γόπα
–bonito	i pa-la-**mi**-dha	i palamidha	η παλαμίδα
–cuttlefish	i su-**pyes**	i supyes	οι σουπιές
–dentex	i si-na-**ghri**-dha	i sinaghridha	η συναγρίδα
–dried	o ba-ka-**lya**-ros	o bakalyaros	ο μπακαλιάρος
salt cod			
–flat fish	i **ghlo**-sa	i ghlosa	η γλώσσα
–garfish	i zar-**gha**-na	i zarghana	η ζαργάνα
–gilt head	i tsi-**pu**-ra	i tsipura	η τσιπούρα
bream			
–grey mullet	o **ke**-fa-los	o kefalos	ο κέφαλος
–John Dory	to hri-**sto**-psa-ro	to hristopsaro	το χριστόψαρο
–mackerel	to sku-**mbri**	to skumbri	το σκουμπρί
–ray fish	to sa-**la**-hi	to salahi	το σαλάχι
–red mullet	ta bar-**bu**-nya	ta barbunya	τα μπαρμπούνια
–rockfish	to pe-**tro**-psa-ro	to petropsaro	το πετρόψαρο
–roe	to av-gho-**ta**-ra-ho	to avghotaraho	το αυγοτάραχο
–sardines	i sar-**dhe**-les	i sardheles	οι σαρδέλες
–scorpion	i skor-**pi**-na	i skorpina	η σκορπίνα
–sea bass	to la-**vra**-ki	to lavraki	το λαβράκι

–sea bream	to *fa-ghri*/li-*thri-ni*/ me-la-*nu*-ri	to faghri/lithrini/ melanuri	το φαγρί/λιθρίνι/ μελανούρι
–sea perch	i *per*-ka	i perka	η πέρκα
–skate	to sa-*la*-hi	to salahi	το σαλάχι
–snapper	i tsi-*pu*-ra	i tsipura	η τσιπούρα
–sparid fish	o si-na-*ghri*-dha	i sinaghridha	η συναγρίδα
–swordfish	o ksi-*fi*-as	o ksifias	ο ξιφίας
–trout	i pe-*stro*-fa	i pestrofa	η πέστροφα
–tuna	o *to*-nos	o tonos	ο τόνος
–tunny	i pa-la-*mi*-dha	i palamidha	η παλαμίδα
–turbot	to kal-*ka*-ni	to kalkani	το καλκάνι
–whitebait	i ma-*ri*-dhes	i maridhes	οι μαρίδες
flavour	i *yef*-si	i yefsi	η γεύση
flour	to a-*le*-vri	to alevri	το αλεύρι
–corn	a-ra-*vo*-si-tu	aravositu	αραβόσιτου
–plain	*ske*-to	sketo	σκέτο
–self-raising	a-ne-va-*to*	anevato	ανεβατό
–wholemeal	o-li-*kis* a-*le*-sis	olikis alesis	ολικής άλεσης
fork	to pi-*ru*-ni	to piruni	το πιρούνι
fresh	*fre*-skos	freskos	φρέσκος
fritters	i ti-*gha*-ni-tes	i tighanites	οι τηγανίτες
frog	o *va*-tra-hos	o vatrahos	ο βάτραχος
fruit	ta *fru*-ta	ta fruta	τα φρούτα
–cake	to ke-ik me *fru*-ta	to keik me fruta	το κέικ με φρούτα
–dried	a-po-ksi-ra-*me*-no	aploksirameno	αποξηραμένο
–juice	hyi-*mos*	ta fruta hyimos	τα φρούτα χυμός
–salad	i fru-to-sa-*la*-ta	i frutosalata	η φρουτοσαλάτα
–stewed	i kom-*po*-sta	i komposta	η κομπόστα
fry	ti-*gha*-ni-zo	tighanizo	τηγανίζω
–deep fry	me po-*li* la-*dhi*	tighanizo me poli ladhi	τηγανίζω με πολύ λάδι
–shallow fry	me *li*-gho la-*dhi*	tighanizo me ligho ladhi	τηγανίζω με λίγο λάδι
frying pan	to ti-*gha*-ni	to tighani	το τηγάνι

G

game	to ki-*ni*-yi	to kiniyi	το κυνήγι
garfish	i zar-*gha*-na	i zarghana	η ζαργάνα
garlic	to *skor*-dho	to skordho	το σκόρδο
–sauce	i skor-dha-*lya*	i skordhalya	η σκορδαλιά
gateau	i pa-sta/*tur*-ta	i pasta/turta	η πάστα/τούρτα
gelatine	i ze-la-*ti*-ni	i zelatini	η ζελατίνη
gherkin	to ang-gu-*ra*-ki tur-*si*	to angguraki tursi	το αγγουράκι τουρσί
giblets	ta en-*do*-sthi-a pu-*lyon*	ta endosthia pulyon	τα εντόσθια πουλιών

gin	to dzin	to dzin	το τζιν
ginger	i pi-pe-ro-ri-za	i piperoriza	η πιπερόριζα
goat	i ka-tsi-ka	i katsika	η κατσίκα
–kid	to ka-tsi-ka-ki	to katsikaki	το κατσικάκι
goose	i hyi-na	i hyina	η χήνα
grapefruit	ta gre-ip-frut	ta greipfrut	τα γκρέιπφρουτ
grapes	ta sta-fi-li-a	ta stafilia	τα σταφύλια
grate	tri-vo	trivo	τρίβω
grater	o tri-ftis	o triftis	ο τρίφτης
gravy	i sal-tsa a-po zo-mo kre-a-tos	i saltsa apo zomo kreatos	η σάλτσα από ζωμό κρέατος
grease	to li-pos	to lipos	το λίπος
Greek salad	i ho-ri-a-ti-ki sa-la-ta	i horiatiki salata	η χωριάτικη σαλάτα
Greek/ Turkish delight	to lu-ku-mi	to lukumi	το λουκούμι
greens, seasonal wild	(a-ghri-a) hor-ta	(aghria) horta	(άγρια) χόρτα
grill	i sha-ra	i shara	η σχάρα
grinder, coffee	o mi-los tu ka-fe	o milos tu kafe	ο μύλος του καφέ
grinder, salt & pepper	i a-la-tye-ra ke pi-pe-ri-e-ra	i alatyera ke piperiera	οι αλατιέρα και πιπεριέρα
grocery	to pan-do-po-li-o	to pandopolio	το παντοπωλείο
grouper	o ro-fos	o rofos	ο ροφός

H

ham	to zam-bon	to zambon	το ζαμπόν
hamburger	to bi-fte-ki	to bifteki	το μπιφτέκι
hare	o la-ghos	o laghos	ο λαγός
head, lamb's	to ke-fa-la-ki	to kefalaki	το κεφαλάκι
heart	i kar-dhya	i kardhya	η καρδιά
herbs	ta vo-ta-na	ta votana	τα βότανα
honey	to me-li	to meli	το μέλι

I

ice	o pa-ghos	o paghos	ο πάγος
ice cream	to pa-gho-to	to paghoto	το παγωτό
ingredient	to si-sta-ti-ko	to sistatiko	το συστατικό
innards	ta en-do-sthi-a	ta endosthia	τα εντόσθια
item (dishes on menu)	to i-dhos	to idhos	το είδος

J

jam	*i mar-me-la-dha*	i marmeladha	η μαρμελάδα
jelly	*to ze-le*	to zele	το ζελέ
John Dory fish	*to hri-sto-psa-ro*	to hristopsaro	το χριστόψαρο
juice	*o hyi-mos*	o hyimos	ο χυμός
–fruit	*ta fru-ta hyi-mos*	ta fruta hyimos	τα φρούτα χυμός
–orange	*por-to-ka-li*	portokali	πορτοκάλι
juicer	*o a-po-hyi-mo-tis*	o apohyimotis	ο αποχυμωτής

K

kettle/pot	*i hyi-tra*	i hyitra	η χύτρα
kidney	*to ne-fro*	to nefro	το νεφρό
kiosk	*to pe-ri-pte-ro*	to periptero	το περίπτερο
kitchen	*i ku-zi-na*	i kuzina	η κουζίνα
knife	*to ma-hye-ri*	to mahyeri	το μαχαίρι
–boning	*ya kse-ko-ka-li-zma*	ya ksekokalizma	για ξεκοκάλισμα
–bread	*pso-myu*	psomyu	ψωμιού
–butter	*vu-ti-ru*	vutiru	βουτύρου
–carving	*kre-a-tos*	kreatos	κρέατος
–serrated	*pri-o-no-to*	prionoto	πριονωτό
kumquat	*to kum-ku-at*	to kumkuat	το κουμκουάτ

L

ladle	*i ku-ta-la*	i kutala	η κουτάλα
lager	*i ksan-thi bi-ra*	i ksanthi bira	η ξανθή μπίρα
lamb	*to ar-ni*	to arni	το αρνί
–head	*to ke-fa-la-ki*	to kefalaki	το κεφαλάκι
–testicles	*ta a-me-le-ti-ta*	ta ameletita	τα αμελέτητα
–very young	*to ar-na-ki*	to arnaki	το αρνάκι
lard	*to lar-dhi*	to lardhi	το λαρδί
laurel leaf	*i dhaf-ni*	i dhafni	η δάφνη
leeks	*ta pra-sa*	ta prasa	τα πράσα
leg	*to bu-ti*	to buti	το μπούτι
legumes	*ta o-spri-a*	ta ospria	τα όσπρια
lemon	*to le-mo-ni*	to lemoni	το λεμόνι
lemonade	*i le-mo-na-dha*	i lemonadha	η λεμονάδα
lentils	*i fa-kes*	i fakes	οι φακές
lettuce	*to ma-ru-li*	to maruli	το μαρούλι
lime	*to ghli-ko-le-mo-no*	to ghlikolemono	το γλυκολέμονο
limpets (shellfish)	*i pe-ta-li-dhes*	i petalidhes	οι πεταλίδες
liqueur	*to li-ker*	to liker	το λικέρ
liquorice	*i ghli-ko-ri-za*	i ghlikoriza	η γλυκόριζα

liver	to si-**ko**-ti	to sikoti	το συκώτι
loaf	to kar-**ve**-li	to karveli	το καρβέλι
lobster	o a-**sta**-kos	o astakos	ο αστακός
local	to-**pi**-kos	topikos	τοπικός
loin	to fi-**le**-to	to fileto	το φιλέτο
loquat	to **mu**-zmu-la	to muzmulo	το μούσμουλα
lunch	to me-si-me-ri-**a**-no	to mesimeriano	το μεσημεριανό

M

macaroni	ta ma-ka-**ro**-nya	ta makaronya	τα μακαρόνια
mackerel	o ko-li-os	o kolios	ο κολιός
madeira	i ma-**de**-ra	i madera	η μαδέρα
mandarin	to man-da-**ri**-ni	to mandarini	το μανταρίνι
mango	to **man**-go	to mango	το μάγκο
marinade	i **sal**-tsa ma-ri-**na**-ta	i saltsa marinata	η σάλτσα μαρινάτα
marinate, to	ma-ri-**na**-ro	marinaro	μαρινάρω
marjoram	i man-dzu-**ra**-na	i mandzurana	η μαντζουράνα
market,	i a-**gho**-ra	i aghora	η αγορά
street	i **la**-ki a-**gho**-ra	i laiki aghora	η λαϊκή αγορά
marmalade	i mar-me-**la**-dha a-po	i marmeladha apo	η μαρμελάδα από
	e-spe-ri-dho-i-**dhi**	esperidhoidhi	εσπεριδοειδή
marrow	to ko-lo-**ki**-thi	to kolokithi	το κολοκύθι
marzipan	to za-ha-ro-**to** me	to zaharoto me	το ζαχαρωτό με
	a-**mi**-ghda-la	amighdhala	αμύγδαλα
mayonnaise	i ma-yo-**ne**-za	i mayoneza	η μαγιονέζα
meal	to **yev**-ma	to yevma	το γεύμα
meat	to **kre**-as	to kreas	το κρέας
medium	me-**tri**-a psi-**me**-nos	metria psimenos	μέτρια ψημένος
(cooked)			
melon	to pe-**po**-ni	to peponi	το πεπόνι
menu	o ka-**ta**-lo-ghos	o kataloghos	ο κατάλογος
–wine list	o ka-**ta**-lo-ghos	o kataloghos	ο κατάλογος
	kra-**syon**	krasyon	κρασιών
meringue	i ma-**reng**-ga	i marengga	η μαρέγγα
meze	o me-**ze**-dhes	o mezes	ο μεζέδες
milk	to **gha**-la	to ghala	το γάλα
–buttermilk	to vu-ti-ro-ga-lo	to vutirogalo	το βουτυρόγαλο
–condensed	sim-pi-kno-**me**-no	simpiknomeno	συμπυκνωμένο
(sweetened)	za-ha-**ru**-ho	zaharuho	ζαχαρούχο
–evaporated	e-va-po-**re**	evapore	εβαπορέ
–powdered	**sko**-ni	skoni	σκόνη
–skim	a-po-vu-ti-ro-**me**-no	apovutiromeno	αποβουτυρωμένο
–soy	**so**-yas	soyas	σόγιας
–thistle	o **tso**-hos	o tsohos	ο τσόχος
mill, salt &	i a-la-**tye**-ra ke	i alatyera ke	οι αλατιέρα και
pepper	pi-pe-**ri**-e-ra	piperiera	πιπεριέρα

millet	*to ke-hri*	to kehri	το κεχρί
mincemeat	*o ki-mas*	o kimas	ο κιμάς
–pie	*i ki-ma-dho-pi-ta*	i kimadhopita	η κιμαδόπιτα
mincer	*i mi-ha-ni kre-a-tos*	i mihani kreatos	η μηχανή κρέατος
mineral water	*to ne-ro me-ta-li-ko*	to nero metaliko	το νερό μεταλλικό
mint (spearmint)	*o dhyo-zmos*	o dhyozmos	ο δύοσμος
mix, to	*a-na-ka-te-vo*	anakatevo	ανακατεύω
mortar	*to ghu-dhi*	to ghudhi	το γουδί
muesli	*to mu-sli*	to musli	το μούσλι
mulberries	*ta mu-ra*	ta mura	τα μούρα
mullet, grey	*o ke-fa-los*	o kefalos	ο κέφαλος
mullet, red	*ta bar-bu-nya*	ta barbunya	τα μπαρμπούνια
mushrooms	*ta ma-ni-ta-ri-a*	ta manitaria	τα μανιτάρια
musaka	*o mu-sa-kas*	o musakas	ο μουσακάς
mussels	*ta mi-di-a*	ta midia	τα μύδια
must, grape	*to mu-sto*	to musto	το μούστο
mustard	*i mu-star-dha*	i mustardha	η μουστάρδα
mutton	*to pro-vi-o kre-as*	to provio kreas	το πρόβειο κρέας
Mythos (beer)	*i mi-thos*	i mithos	η Μύθος

N

napkin	*i pe-tse-ta*	i petseta	η πετσέτα
neck	*o le-mos*	o lemos	ο λαιμός
noodles, egg	*i hyi-lo-pi-tes*	i hyilopites	οι χυλοπίτες
noodles, vermicelli	*i fi-dhes*	i fidhes	οι φιδές
nougat	*a-mi-ghdha-lo-to ghli-ki-zma*	to amighdhaloto ghlikizma	το αμυγδαλωτό γλύκισμα
nutcracker	*o ka-ri-dho-thraf-stis*	o karidhothrafstis	ο καρυδοθραύστης
nutmeg	*to mo-sho-ka-ri-dho*	to moshokaridho	το μοσχοκάρυδο
nuts	*i kse-ri kar-pi*	i kseri karpi	οι ξηροί καρποί
–cashew	*to ka-syu*	to kasyu	το κάσιου
–chestnuts	*ta ka-sta-na*	ta kastana	τα κάστανα
–hazelnuts	*ta fun-du-kya*	ta fundukya	τα φουντούκια
–peanuts	*ta fi-sti-ki-a*	ta fistikia	τα φιστίκια
–pine nuts	*ta ku-ku-nar-ya*	ta kukunarya	τα κουκουνάρια
–pistachios	*e-yi-nis*	ta fistikia eyinis	τα φιστίκια Αιγίνης
nut seller	*o fi-sti-kas*	o fistikas	ο φιστικάς

O

oatmeal	*to pli-ghu-ri vro-mis*	to plighuri vromis	το πλιγούρι βρώμης
octopus	*to hta-po-dhi*	to htapodhi	το χταπόδι
offal	*ta en-do-sthi-a*	ta endosthia	τα εντόσθια

oil	to la-dhi	to ladhi	το λάδι
–olive	to e-le-o-la-dho	to eleoladho	το ελαιόλαδο
–peanut	to fi-sti-ke-le-o	to fistikeleo	το φιστικέλαιο
–sesame	to si-sa-me-le-o	to sisameleo	το σησαμέλαιο
–vegetable	to fi-ti-ko la-dhi	to fitiko ladhi	το φυτικό λάδι
okra	i bam-yes	i bamyes	οι μπάμιες
olives	i e-lyes	i elyes	οι ελιές
–black	ma-vres	mavres	μαύρες
–green	pra-si-nes	prasines	πράσινες
–oil	to e-le-o-la-dho	to eleoladho	το ελαιόλαδο
–paste	pel-te	pelte	πελτέ
–pickled	tur-si	tursi	τουρσί
omelette	i o-me-le-ta	i omeleta	η ομελέτα
onions	ta kre-mi-dhi-a	ta kremidhia	τα κρεμμύδια
–spring	to kre-mi-dha-ki	to kremidhaki	το κρεμμυδάκο
opener	to a-ni-hti-ri	to anihtiri	το ανοιχτήρι
orange	to por-to-ka-li	to portokali	το πορτοκάλι
–juice	o hyi-mos por-to-ka-li	o hyimos portokali	ο χυμός πορτοκάλι
oregano	i ri-gha-ni	i righani	η ρίγανη
organic	or-gha-ni-kos	orghanikos	οργανικός
ouzo	to u-zo	to ouzo	το ούζο
oven	o fur-nos	o furnos	ο φούρνος
oxtail	i u-ra vo-dyu	i ura vodyu	η ουρά βοδιού
oysters	ta stri-dhi-a	ta stridhia	τα στρείδια

P

pan, frying	to ti-gha-ni	to tighani	το τηγάνι
pancakes	i ti-gha-ni-tes	i tighanites	οι τηγανίτες
pancetta	i pan-tse-ta	i pantseta	η παντσέττα
paprika	i pa-pri-ka	i paprika	η πάπρικα
parmesan	i par-me-za-na	i parmezana	η παρμεζάνα
parsley	o ma-i-da-nos	o maidanos	ο μαϊντανός
partridge	i per-dhi-ka	i perdhika	η πέρδικα
pasta	ta zi-ma-ri-ka	ta zimarika	τα ζυμαρικά
pastrami	to ka-pni-sto vo-dhi-no kre-as	to kapnisto vodhino kreas	το καπνιστό βοδινό κρέας
pastry	i zi-mi	i zimi	η ζύμη
–filo	to fi-lo	to filo	το φύλλο
pastry (sweet)	to ghli-ki-zma	to ghlikizma	το γλύκισμα
patisserie	to za-ha-ro-pla-sti-o	to zaharoplastio	το ζαχαροπλαστείο
pea, yellow split	i fa-va	i fava	η φάβα
peach	to ro-dha-ki-no	to rodhakino	το ροδάκινο
peanuts	ta fi-sti-ki-a	ta fistikia	τα φιστίκια
pear	to a-hla-dhi	to ahladhi	το αχλάδι
–prickly	ta frang-go-si-ka	ta franggosika	τα φραγκόσυκα

pea	o a-ra-kas	o arakas	ο αρακάς
–black-eyed	ta lu-vya	ta luvya	τα λουβιά
–green	to bi-ze-li	to bizeli	το μπιζέλι
pecan	to pe-kan	to pekan	το πεκάν
peeler	to ka-tha-ri-sti-ri fli-u	to katharistiri fliu	το καθαριστήρι φλοιού
pepper (black)	to pi-pe-ri	to piperi	το πιπέρι
pepper	i pi-per-ya	i piperya	η πιπεριές
–red	i ko-ki-ni pi-per-ya	i kokini piperya	η κόκκινη πιπεριά
–yellow	i ki-tri-ni pi-per-ya	i kitrinpiperya	η κίτρινη πιπεριά
perch, sea	i per-ka	i perka	η πέρκα
pestle	to ghu-dho-hye-ri	to ghudhohyeri	το γουδοχέρι
pheasant	o fa-si-a-nos	o fasianos	ο φασιανός
pickle	to tur-si	to tursi	το τουρσί
pickled	tur-si	tursi	τουρσί
picnic	to pik-nik	to piknik	το πίκνικ
pie	i pi-ta	i pita	ι πίτα
–cheese	i ti-ro-pi-ta	i tiropita	η τυρόπιτα
–meat	i kre-a-to-pi-ta	i kreatopita	η κρεατόπιτα
–mincemeat	i ki-ma-dho-pi-ta	i kimadhopita	η κιμαδόπιτα
–seasonal greens	i hor-to-pi-ta	i hortopita	η χορτόπιτα
–spinach	i spa-na-ko-pi-ta	i spanakopita	η σπανακόπιτα
–zucchini	i ko-lo-ki-tho-pi-ta	i kolokithopita	η κολοκυθόπιτα
pig	to ghu-ru-ni	to ghuruni	το γουρούνι
–suckling	to ghu-ru-na-ki (tu gha-la-ktos)	to ghurunaki (tu ghalaktos)	το γουρουνάκι (του γάλακτος)
pigeon	to pe-ri-ste-ri	to peristeri	το περιστέρι
piglet	to ghu-ru-no-pu-lo	to ghurunopulo	το γουρουνόπουλο
pilaf	to pi-la-fi	to pilafi	το πιλάφι
pine nuts	ta ku-ku-nar-ya	ta kukunarya	τα κουκουνάρια
pineapple	o a-na-nas	o ananas	ο ανανάς
piquant	pi-kan-di-kos	pikandikos	πικάντικος
plate	to pya-to	to pyato	το πιάτο
plum, red	to dha-ma-ski-no	to dhamaskino	το δαμάσκηνο
plum, yellow	i ne-ra-mbu-la	i nerambula	η νεράμπουλα
poach	si-gho-vra-zo	sighovrazo	σιγοβράζω
pomegranate	to ro-dhi	to rodhi	το ρόδι
poppy	i pa-pa-ru-na	i paparuna	η παπαρούνα
pork	to hyi-ri-no	to hyirino	το χοιρινό
–chop	i hyi-ri-ni bri-zo-la	i hyirini brizola	η χοιρινή μπριζόλα
–roast	bu-ti psi-to	to hyirino buti psito	το χοιρινό μπούτι ψητό
leg of			
–salted	pa-sto	pasto	παστό
port	to por-to	to porto	το πόρτο

pot	i ka-tsa-ro-la	i katsarola	η κατσαρόλα
–cooking	i sta-mna	i stamna	η στάμνα
potatoes	i pa-ta-tes	i patates	οι πατάτες
–baked or roasted	sto fur-no	sto furno	στο φούρνο
–chips	ta tsips	ta tsips	τα τσιπς
–fried slices	ti-gha-ni-tes	tighanites	τηγανητές
–mashed	pu-re	pure	πουρέ
–salad	i pa-ta-to-sa-la-ta	i patatosalata	η πατατοσαλάτα
–sweet	i ghli-ko-pa-ta-ta	i ghlikopatata	η γλυκοπατάτα
poultry	ta pu-le-ri-ka	ta pulerika	τα πουλερικά
prawns	i gha-ri-dhes	i gharidhes	οι γαρίδες
preservative	to sin-di-ri-ti-ko	to sindiritiko	το συντηρητικό
pressure cooker	i hyi-tra ta-hyi-ti-tas	i hyitra tahyititas	η χύτρα ταχύτητας
price	i ti-mi	i timi	η τιμή
prune	to ksi-ro dha-ma-ski-no	to ksiro dhamaskino	το ξηρό δαμάσκηνο
pulses	ta o-spri-a	ta ospria	τα όσπρια
pumpkin	i ko-lo-ki-tha	i kolokitha	η κολοκύθα
puree	pu-re	pure	πουρέ
purslane	i ghli-stri-dha	i ghlistridha	η γλιστρίδα

Q

quail	to or-ti-ki	to ortiki	το ορτύκι
quantity	i po-so-ti-ta (to po-so)	i posotita (to poso)	η ποσότητα (το ποσό)
quince	to ki-dho-ni	to kidhoni	το κυδώνι

R

rabbit	to ku-ne-li	to kuneli	το κουνέλι
radish	to ra-pa-ni	to rapani	το ραπάνι
raisins	i sta-fi-dhes	i stafidhes	οι σταφίδες
raki (alcohol)	to ra-ki	to raki	το ρακί
rare (cooked)	li-gho psi-me-nos	ligho psimenos	λίγο ψημένος
raspberry	to va-to-mu-ro	to vatomuro	το βατόμουρο
ray fish	to sa-la-hi	to salahi	το σαλάχι
razor clams	i pi-nes	i pinnes	οι πίννες
receipt	i a-po-dhi-ksi	i apodhiksi	η απόδειξη
reservation	i kra-ti-si	i kratisi	η κράτηση
retsina	i re-tsi-na	i retsina	η ρετσίνα
rice	to ri-zi	to rizi	το ρύζι
–arborio	ar-bo-ri-o	arborio	αρμπόριο
–basmati	ba-zma-ti	bazmati	μπασμάτι

–brown	a-ka-**ter**-gha-sto	akaterghasto	ακατέργαστο
–glutinous	ko-**lo**-dhes	kolodhes	κολλώδες
–long-grain	ma-**kri**	makri	μακρύ
–short-grain	kon-**do**	kondo	κοντό
–wild	a-**ghri**-o	aghrio	άγριο
ripe	o-**ri**-mos	orimos	ώριμος
rissoles	i ke-**fte**-dhes	i keftedhes	οι κεφτέδες
roe, fish	to av-gho-**ta**-ra-ho	to avghotaraho	το αυγοτάραχο
rolling pin	o **pla**-stis zi-mis	o plastis zimis	ο πλάστης ζύμης
rooster	o **ko**-ko-ras	o kokoras	ο κόκορας
rosemary	to dhen-dro-**li**-va-no	to dhendrolivano	το δεντρολίβανο
rum	to **ru**-mi	to rumi	το ρούμι
rump	to **kon**-dra fi-le-to	to kondra fileto	το κόντρα φιλέτο
rusks	ta pa-ksi-**ma**-dya	ta paksimadya	τα παξιμάδια

S

saffron	to sa-**fran**	to safran	το σαφράν
sage	to fa-**sko**-mi-lo	to faskomilo	το φασκόμηλο
salad	i sa-**la**-ta	i salata	η σαλάτα
–fruit	i fru-to-sa-**la**-ta	i frutosalata	η φρουτοσαλάτα
–Greek	i ho-ri-a-**ti**-ki sa-la-ta	i horiatiki salata	η χωριάτικη σαλάτα
–potato	i pa-ta-to-sa-**la**-ta	i patatosalata	η πατατοσαλάτα
salami	to sa-**la**-mi	to salami	το σαλάμι
salmon	o so-**lo**-mos	o solomos	ο σολομός
salt	to a-**la**-ti	to alati	το αλάτι
sandwich, toasted	to tost	to tost	το τοστ
sardines	i sar-**dhe**-les	i sardheles	οι σαρδέλες
sauce	i **sal**-tsa	i saltsa	η σάλτσα
–bechamel	be-sa-**mel**	besamel	μπεσαμέλ
–garlic	i skor-dha-**lya**	i skordhalya	η σκορδαλιά
–gravy	a-**po** zo-**mo** kre-a-tos	apo zomo kreatos	από ζωμό κρέατος
–marinade	ma-ri-**na**-ta	marinata	μαρινάτα
–tartare	tar-**tar**	tartar	ταρτάρ
–tomato	do-**ma**-ta	domata	ντομάτα
–white	a-**spri**	aspri	άσπρη
saucepan	i ka-tsa-**ro**-la	i katsarola	η κατσαρόλα
saute	tsi-gha-ri-**stos**	tsigharistos	τσιγαριστός
savoury	to **thru**-mbi	to thrumbi	το θρούμπι
scales	i zi-**ghar**-ya	i zigharya	η ζυγαριά
scallop	to **kte**-ni (tha-la-si-no)	to kteni (thalasino)	το κτένι (θαλασσινό)
schnitzel	to **sni**-tsel	to snitsel	το σνίτσελ
scissors	to psa-**li**-dhi	to psalidhi	το ψαλίδι
sea anemone	i gha-**li**-pes	i ghalipes	οι γαλύπες
seafood	ta tha-la-**si**-na	ta thalasina	τα θαλασσινά
seasoning	ba-ha-ri-**ka**	ta baharika	τα μπαχαρικά

seed	spo-ros	sporos	σπόρος
–sunflower	o i-li-o-spo-ros	o iliosporos	ο ηλιόσπορος
semolina	i si-mi-ghdha-li	i simighdhali	η σμιγδάλι
serve	i me-ri-dha	i meridha	η μερίδα
service	e-ksi-pi-re-ti-si	i eksipiretisi	η εξυπηρέτηση
sesame seed	to su-sa-mi	to susami	το σουσάμι
shellfish	ta o-stra-ko-i-dhi	ta ostrakoidhi	τα οστρακοειδή
–lobster	o a-sta-kos	o astakos	ο αστακός
–mussels	ta mi-di-a	ta midia	τα μύδια
sherry	to se-ri	to seri	το σέρι
shop	to ma-ga-zi	to magazi	το μαγαζί
–cheese	to ti-ro-po-li-o	to tiropolio	το τυροπωλείο
–coffee	to ka-fe-ni-o	to kafenio	το καφενείο
–liquor	to i-no-po-li-o	to inopolio	το οινοπωλείο
shoulder of meat	i spa-la	i spala	η σπάλα
shrimps	i gha-ri-dhes	i gharidhes	οι γαρίδες
sieve	to ko-ski-no	to koskino	το κόσκινο
sifter	i a-la-tye-ra	i alatyera	η αλατιέρα
silverside	i spa-la mo-sha-ri-si-a	i spala mosharisia	η σπάλα μοσχαρίσια
simmer	si-gho-vra-zo	sighovrazo	σιγοβράζω
sirloin	to kon-dra fi-le-to	to kondra fileto	το κόντρα φιλέτο
skate fish	to sa-la-hi	to salahi	το σαλάχι
skewer	i su-vla	i suvla	η σούβλα
slice, to	ko-vo se fe-tes	kovo se fetes	κόβω σε φέτες
smoke, to	ka-pni-zo	kapnizo	καπνίζω
smoked	ka-pni-stos	kapnistos	καπνιστός
snack, mid-morning	to ko-la-tsyo	to kolatsyo	το κολατσιό
snacks	ta snaks	ta snaks	τα σνακς
snails	ta sa-ling-ga-ri-a	ta salinggaria	τα σαλιγκάρια
snapper	i tsi-pu-ra	i tsipura	η τσιπούρα
soda water	i so-dha	i sodha	η σόδα
soft drink	to a-na-psi-kti-ko	to anapsiktiko	το αναψυκτικό
–Coca-Cola	i ko-ka ko-la	i koka kola	η Κόκα Κόλα
–orange	i por-to-ka-la-dha	i portokaladha	η πορτοκαλάδα
sorbet	i gha-ni-ta	i ghanita	η γρανίτα
soup	i su-pa	i supa	η σούπα
sour	ksi-nos	ksinos	ξινός
sour cream	i kre-ma ksi-ni	i krema ksini	η κρέμα ξινή
souvlaki	to su-vla-ki	to souvlaki	το σουβλάκι
spaghetti	ta ma-ka-ro-nya	ta makaronya	τα μακαρόνια
spearmint (mint)	o dhyo-zmos	o dhyozmos	ο δυόσμος
spices	ba-ha-ri-ka	ta baharika	τα μπαχαρικά
spinach	to spa-na-ki	to spanaki	το σπανάκι

spirits, alcoholic	*ta i-no-pnev-ma-to-dhi*	ta inopnevmatodhi	τα οινοπνευματώδη
spit	*i su-vla*	i suvla	η σούβλα
spit-roasted	*sti su-vla*	sti suvla	στη σούβλα
spleen	*i spli-na*	i splina	η σπλήνα
spoon	*to ku-ta-li*	to kutali	το κουτάλι
–dessert	*tu ghli-ku*	tu ghliku	του γλυκού
–soup	*su-pas*	supas	σούπας
–teaspoon	*to ku-ta-la-ki*	to kutalaki	το κουταλάκι
spring onion	*to kre-mi-dha-ki fre-sko*	to kremidhaki fresko	το κρεμμυδάκι φρέσκο
squab	*ta pi-tsu-nya*	ta pitsunya	τα πιτσούνια
squash	*to ko-lo-ki-thi*	to kolokithi	το κολοκύθι
squid	*to ka-la-ma-ri*	to kalamari	το καλαμάρι
–baby	*ta ka-la-ma-ra-kya*	ta kalamarakya	τα καλαμαράκια
steak	*i bri-zo-la*	i brizola	η μπριζόλα
steam, to	*a-hni-zo*	ahnizo	αχνίζω
steamer	*i hyi-tra a-tmu*	i hyitra atmu	η χύτρα ατμού
steep	*mu-ske-vo*	muskevo	μουσκεύω
stinging nettles	*i tsu-kni-dhes*	i tsuknidhes	οι τσουκνίδες
stock	*to zu-mi*	to zumi	το ζουμί
–beef	*o zu-mos vo-dhi-nu*	o zumos vodhinu	ο ζουμός βοδινού
–chicken	*to ko-to-zu-mo*	to kotozumo	το κοτόζουμο
–fish	*to psa-ro-zu-mo*	to psarozumo	το ψαρόζουμο
–vegetable	*to la-ha-no-zu-mo*	to lahanozumo	το λαχανόζουμο
stone, sharpening	*i li-ma ya ma-hye-rya*	i lima ya mahyerya	η λίμα για μαχαίρια
straw	*to ka-la-ma-ki*	to kalamaki	το καλαμάκι
strawberry	*i fra-u-la*	i fraula	η φράουλα
stuffing	*to ye-mi-zma*	to yemizma	το γέμισμα
sturgeon	*i mu-ru-na*	i muruna	η μουρούνα
sugar	*i za-ha-ri*	i zahari	η ζάχαρη
–brown	*sku-ro-hro-mi*	skurohromi	σκουρόχρωμη
–demerara	*a-ro-ma-ti-ki sku-ro-hro-mi*	aromatiki skurohromi	αρωματική σκουρόχρωμη
–palm	*fi-ni-ko-za-ha-ri*	finikozahari	φοινικοζάχαρη
sun dried	*lya-stos*	lyastos	λιαστός
sunflower	*to i-li-e-le-o*	to ilileo	το ηλιέλαιο
–seed	*o i-li-o-spo-ros*	o iliosporos	ο ηλιόσπορος
swede	*i kram-vi*	i kramvi	η κράμβη
sweet	*to ghli-ko*	to ghliko	το γλυκό
sweet potato	*i ghli-ko-pa-ta-ta*	i ghlikopatata	η γλυκοπατάτα
swiss chard	*to se-sku-lo*	to seskulo	το σέσκουλο
swordfish	*o ksi-fi-as*	o ksifias	ο ξιφίας
syrup	*to si-ro-pi*	to siropi	το σιρόπι

231

T

table	*to tra-pe-zi*	to trapezi	το τραπέζι
tablecloth	*to tra-pe-zo-man-di-lo*	to trapezomandilo	το τραπεζόμαντιλο
tahini	*to ta-hi-ni*	to tahini	το ταχίνι
taramosalata	*i ta-ra-mo-sa-la-ta*	i taramosalata	η ταραμοσαλάτα
taro	*to ko-lo-ka-si*	to kolokasi	το κολοκάσι
tart	*i tar-ta*	i tarta	η τάρτα
tea	*to tsa-i*	to tsai	το τσάι
–chamomile	*ha-mo-mi-lo*	hamomilo	χαμόμηλο
–decaf- feinated	*ho-ris ka-fe-i-ni*	horis kafeini	χωρίς καφεΐνη
–green	*pra-si-no*	prasino	πράσινο
–peppermint	*men-ta*	menta	μέντα
–with lemon	*me le-mo-ni*	me lemoni	με λεμόνι
–with milk	*me gha-la*	me ghala	με γάλα
tequila	*i te-ki-la*	i tekila	η τεκίλα
thrush	*i tsi-hla*	i tsihla	η τσίχλα
thyme	*to thi-ma-ri*	to thimari	το θυμάρι
tip (service)	*to fi-lo-do-ri-ma/to pur-bu-ar*	to filodorima/ purbuar	το φιλοδώρημα/ το πουρμπουάρ
toast	*i fri-gha-nya*	i frighanya	η φρυγανιά
toaster	*i fri-gha-nye-ra*	i frighanyera	η φρυγανιέρα
tomato paste	*o do-ma-to-pel-tes*	o domatopeltes	ο ντοματομπελτές
tomato	*i do-ma-ta*	i domata	η ντομάτα
–sun-dried	*lya-sti*	lyasti	λιαστή
tongs	*i tsi-mbi-dha*	i tsimbidha	η τσιμπίδα
tongue	*i ghlo-sa*	i ghlosa	η γλώσσα
tonic water	*to to-nik*	to tonik	το τόνικ
toothpick	*i o-dhon-do-ghli-fi-dha*	i odhondoghlifidha	η οδοντογλυφίδα
topping	*i e-pi-ka-li-psi*	i epikalipsi	η επικάλυψη
total (of bill)	*to si-no-lo*	to sinolo	το σύνολο
tripe	*o pa-tsas*	o patsas	ο πατσάς
trotters	*ta po-dha-ra-kya*	ta podharakya	τα ποδαράκια
trout	*i pe-stro-fa*	i pestrofa	η πέστροφα
tuna	*o to-nos*	o tonos	ο τόνος
tunny fish	*i pa-la-mi-dha*	i palamidha	η παλαμίδα
turbot	*to kal-ka-ni*	to kalkani	το καλκάνι
turkey	*i gha-lo-pu-la*	i ghalopula	η γαλοπούλα
Turkish/ Greek delight	*to lu-ku-mi*	to lukumi	το λουκούμι
turnip	*to ghong-gi-li*	to ghonggili	η το γογγύλι

U

| urchins, sea | *a-hyi-ni* | i ahyini | οι αχινοί |

V

vanilla	*i va-ni-li-a*	i vanilia	η βανίλια
variety	*ta dhi-a-fo-ra*	ta dhiafora	τα διάφορα
veal	*to mo-sha-ri*	to moshari	το μοσχάρι
vegetables	*ta la-ha-ni-ka*	ta lahanika	τα λαχανικά
–sea	*tis tha-la-sas*	ta lahanika tis thalasas	τα λαχανικά της θάλασσας
–stuffed	*ye-mi-sta*	yemista	γεμιστά
vegetarian	*o hor-to-fa-ghos*	o hortofaghos	ο χορτοφάγος
venison	*to kre-as e-la-fyu*	to kreas elafyu	το κρέας ελαφιού
vetchling	*i pa-pu-les*	i papules	οι παπούλες
vinegar	*to ksi-dhi*	to ksidhi	το ξύδι
–cider	*a-po mi-lo*	apo milo	από μήλο
–malt	*a-po vi-ni*	apo vini	από βύνη
–rice	*a-po ri-zi*	apo rizi	από ρύζι
–wine	*a-po kra-si*	apo krasi	από κρασί
vodka	*i vot-ka*	i votka	η βότκα

W

walnuts	*ta ka-ri-dhi-a*	ta karidhia	τα καρύδια
water	*to ne-ro*	to nero	το νερό
–bottled	*em-fi-a-lo-me-no*	emfialomeno	εμφιαλωμένο
–flower	*to an-tho-ne-ro*	to anthonero	το ανθόνερο
–fresh	*fre-sko*	fresko	φρέσκο
–mineral	*me-ta-li-ko*	metaliko	μεταλλικό
–soda	*i so-dha*	i sodha	η σόδα
–tap	*tiz vri-sis*	tiz vrisis	της βρύσης
–tonic	*to to-nik*	to tonik	το τόνικ
watercress	*to ne-ro-kar-dha-mo*	to nerokardhamo	το νεροκάρδαμο
watermelon	*to kar-pu-zi*	to karpuzi	το καρπούζι
well done (cooked)	*ka-lo-psi-me-nos*	kalopsimenos	καλοψημένος
wheat	*to si-ta-ri*	to sitari	το σιτάρι
wheat germ	*o spo-ros star-yu*	o sporos staryu	ο σπόρος σταριού
whisk	*to sir-ma ya hti-pi-ma a-vgon*	to sirma ya htipima avgon	το σύρμα για χτύπημα αυγών
whisky	*to u-i-ski*	to uiski	το ουίσκυ
whitebait	*i ma-ri-dhes*	i maridhes	οι μαρίδες
wild	*a-ghri-os*	aghrios	άγριος
wild greens	*ta hor-ta*	ta horta	τα χόρτα
wine	*to kra-si*	to krasi	το κρασί
–draught	*hyi-ma*	hyima	χύμα
–list	*o ka-ta-lo-ghos kra-syon*	o kataloghos krasyon	ο κατάλογος κρασιών
–red	*ko-ki-no*	kokino	κόκκινο

–resinated red	*to ko-ki-ne-li*	to kokineli	το κοκκινέλι
–rosé	*ro-ze*	roze	ροζέ
–table	*dhe-me-sti-ha*	dhemestiha	Δεμέστιχα
–white	*a-spro/le-fkos*	to krasi aspro/ lefkos	το κρασί άσπρο/ λευκός
woodcock	*i be-ka-tsa*	i bekatsa	η μπεκάτσα

Y

yeast	*i ma-ya*	i maya	η μαγιά
yoghurt	*to ya-ur-ti*	to yaurti	το γιαούρτι
–cow's milk	*a-ye-la-dhos*	ayeladhos	αγελάδος
–fruit	*fru-ton*	fruton	φρούτων
–honey- topped	*me me-li*	me meli	με μέλι
–sheep's milk	*pro-vi-o*	provio	πρόβειο

Z

zest	*to ar-ti-ma yef-sis*	to artima yefsis	το άρτυμα γεύσης
zucchini	*ta ko-lo-ki-tha-kya*	ta kolokithakya	τα κολοκυθάκια
–flowers	*i ko-lo-ki-tho-an-thi*	i kolokithoanthi	οι κολοκυθόανθοι

Greek Culinary Dictionary

In Greek, the definite article is used with the names of people and places and when referring to specific things ('the book'), things as a class ('books'), and abstract ideas ('democracy'). Nouns belong to one of three genders – masculine, feminine, neuter. Each gender has its own article: o, i, to (o, η, το); the plurals are i, i, ta (οι, οι, τα).

Stress in Greek words is restricted to the last three syllables. The stressed vowel has an accent (′) written on it. Isolated verbs are given in their 'I cook/do cook/am cooking' form. Sub-groups of a word are preceded by a dash e.g., -yemistes for stuffed peppers. Articles are sometimes pronounced as a single word with their nouns.

A

i afelya η αφέλια
i a-fe-lya dish of thin pork strips marinated in dark red wine, fried in corn oil, rolled in crushed coriander seeds and fried in reduced marinade; dish of meat sauteed in oil then braised with potatoes and mushrooms in red wine and water

aghrafon Αγράφων
a-ghra-fon (*see* Cheese in Staples & Specialities)

aghria horta άγρια χόρτα
a-ghri-a hor-ta seasonal wild greens (*see also* **horta**)

aghria sparanggia άγρια σπαράγγια
a-ghri-a spa-rang-gi-a rake-thin tender wild asparagus, type of **horta**.

i aghries οι άγριες
angginares αγγινάρες
i a-ghri-es ang-gi-na-res small prickly artichokes. Peeled and eaten raw with salt and lemon juice.

aghrio hyrino άγριο χοιρινό
a-ghri-ó hy-ri-no boar

aghrio rizi άγριο ρύζι
a-ghri-ó ri-zi rice

aghrios άγριος
a-ghri-os wild

to ahladhi το αχλάδι
to a-hla-dhi pear

ahnizo αχνίζω
a-hni-zo to steam

i ahyini οι αχινοί
i a-hyi-ni sea urchins. Their sweet orange-coloured roe is dressed with lemon juice and oil.

–salata –σαλάτα
sa-la-ta sea urchin salad

–yemisti –γεμιστοί
ye-mi-sti sea urchin stuffed with rice, onions and ripe tomatoes (Spetses)

i ahyivadha η αχηβάδα
i a-hyi-va-dha clam

to aidhani aspro το αϊδάνι άσπρο
to ai-dha-ni as-pro white grape variety (*see* Grape Varieties in Drinks)

to akoskinisto το ακοσκίνιστο
to a-ko-ski-ni-sto whole wheat

–alevri –αλεύρι
a-le-vri whole wheat flour

ta alandika τα αλλαντικά
ta-lan-di-ka processed meats

to alandopolio το αλλαντοπωλείο
to a-lan-do-po-li-o delicatessen

to alati το αλάτι
to a-la-ti salt

alatizo αλατίζω
a-la-ti-zo to cure

i alatyera η αλατιέρα
i a-la-tye-ra sifter

i alatyera ke οι αλατιέρα και
piperiera πιπεριέρα
i a-la-tye-ra ke pi-pe-ri-e-ra salt & pepper mills

to alevri το αλεύρι
to a-le-vri flour

–anevato –ανεβατό
a-ne-va-to self-raising flour

–aravositu –αραβόσιτου
a-ra-vo-si-tu cornflour

–olikis alesis –ολικής άλεσης
o-li-kis a-le-sis whole meal flour

–sketo –σκέτο
ske-to plain flour

to alevrolemono το αλευρολέμονο
to a-le-vro-le-mo-no sauce of flour dissolved in water or stock and beaten with lemon juice. Used to flavour and thicken fish and vegetable stews.

i alfa η Άλφα
i al-fa Alpha (beer)

to alkool το αλκοόλ
to al-ko-ol alcohol

ta ambelofasula τα αμπελοφάσουλα
ta am-be-lo-fa-su-la green beans; also called **fasolakya**

ta ambelopulya τα αμπελοπούλια
ta am-be-lo-pu-lya tiny vineyard-dwelling birds preserved in vinegar and wine and eaten whole (Cyprus)

i amberoriza η αμπερόριζα
i am-be-ro-ri-za rose geranium. The leaves are used as an aromatic flavouring for cakes, pastries and **ghlika kutalyu**.

ta ameletita τα αμελέτητα
ta a-me-le-ti-ta lamb's testicles

ta amighdhala τα αμύγδαλα
ta-mi-ghdha-la almonds

ta amighdhalota τα αμυγδαλωτά
ta a-mi-ghdha-lo-ta pear-shaped almond shortbread sprinkled with icing sugar and chopped almonds

to amighdhaloto το αμυγδαλωτό
ghlikizma γλύκισμα
a-mi-ghdha-lo-to ghli-ki-zma nougat

to amstel το Άμστελ
to am-stel Amstel (beer)

anakatevo ανακατεύω
a-na-ka-te-vo to mix

i analates οι ανάλατες
thrumbes θρούμπες
i a-na-la-tes thrum-bes unsalted black olives

o ananas ο ανανάς
o a-na-nas pineapple

to anapsiktiko το αναψυκτικό
to a-na-psi-kti-ko soft drink

to andidhi το αντίδι
to an-di-dhi endive

i andzuya η αντσούγια
i an-dzu-ya salted anchovy

to aneri το ανερί
to a-ne-ri soft ricotta-like cheese made from goat's or sheep's milk (Cyprus)

i angginares οι αγγινάρες
i ang-gi-na-res globe artichokes

–alapolita –αλαπολίτα
a-la-po-li-ta 'Constantinople-style', earthy dish of artichokes, carrots and potatoes in dill-spiked chicken stock

–kaloghres –καλογρές
kal-o-ghres 'nuns', artichoke hearts braised in creamy onion broth (Crete)

–me kukya –με κουκιά
avgholemono αυγολέμονο
me ku-kya a-vgho-le-mo-no artichokes and broad beans simmered with oil, water, garlic and fennel leaves and thickened with egg and lemon sauce

to angguraki το αγγουράκι
tursi τουρσί
to ang-gu-ra-ki tur-si gherkin

to angguri το αγγούρι
to ang-gu-ri cucumber

i anggurodomata η αγγουροντομάτα
salata σαλάτα
i ang-gu-ro-do-ma-ta sa-la-ta cucumber slices, tomato wedges and parsley with oil, lemon juice, salt and pepper

i anggurosalata η αγγουροσαλάτα
i ang-gu-ro-sa-la-ta sliced cucumbers sprinkled with salt and served with oil and vinegar

to anihtiri το ανοιχτήρι
to a-ni-hti-ri bottle opener

–konservas –κονσέρβας
kon-ser-vas can opener

ta aniksyatika τα ανοιξιάτικα
ta a-ni-ksya-ti-ka spring greens (see also **horta**)

o anithos ο άνιθος
o a-ni-thos dill

to anthonero το ανθόνερο
to an-tho-ne-ro flower water (see also **neroli** and **rodhonero**)

o anthotiros ο ανθότυρος
o an-tho-ti-ros (see Cheese in Staples & Specialities)

236

i apodhiksi   η απόδειξη
i a-po-dhi-ksi receipt

o apohyimotis   ο αποχυμωτής
o a-po-hyi-mo-tis juicer

o arakas   ο αρακάς
o a-ra-kas fresh pea

–**ladheros**   –λαδερός
la-dhe-ros peas stewed with carrots, garlic bulbs and herbs in oil and paprika (Corfu)

to arnaki   το αρνάκι
to ar-na-ki milk-lamb, very young lamb

–**pashalino**   –Πασχαλινό
pa-sha-li-no milk-lamb slaughtered at Easter to make **arni sti suvla**. Its innards are used to make **mayiritsa**.

–**yemisto**   –γεμιστό
ye-mi-sto Easter dish of roast lamb stuffed with mincemeat, **sikotarya**, rice, onion, cinnamon and mint (Dodecanese)

to arni   το αρνί
to ar-ni lamb

–**eksohiko**   –εξοχικό
e-kso-hi-ko 'country-style', baked filo parcels of lamb, potato, feta and **kefalotiri**. Parchment paper or foil can be used in place of filo.

–**frikase me maruli**   –φρικασέ με μαρούλι
fri-ka-se me ma-ru-li lamb poached in its own stock with shredded lettuce, and finished with egg and lemon sauce. Can feature artichoke, celery or endive.

–**kefalaki righanato**   –κεφαλάκι ριγανατό
ke-fa-la-ki ri-gha-na-to lamb's head complete with tongue, cheek, brains and eyes. Generally roasted with olive oil, oregano, salt and pepper. Plays a starring role in **arni sti suvla**.

–**kleftiko**   –κλέφτικο
kle-fti-ko lamb in a clay pot (*see* the recipe)

–**kokinisto**   –κοκκινιστό
ko-ki-ni-sto lamb sauteed in oil or butter until browned then braised in white wine with onions and bay leaves

–**kokinisto me bamyes**   –κοκκινιστό με μπάμιες
ko-ki-ni-sto me ba-myes braised lamb and okra

–**ofto**   –οφτό
o-fto roast lamb on the spit (*see* the recipe)

–**palikari**   –παλικάρι
pa-li-ka-ri 'fearless lad' (*see* **arni kleftiko**)

–**psito**   –ψητό
psi-to (*see* **arni sto furno**)

–**sti suvla**   –στη σούβλα
sti su-vla spit-roast lamb basted with olive oil, lemon juice and garlic – often a bunch of oregano is used as the basting implement. A traditional Easter dish (*see also* **arnaki pashalino**).

–**sto furno**   –στο φούρνο
sto fur-no leg or shoulder of lamb plugged with garlic cloves, rubbed with salt and pepper and roasted. Generally lemon-sprinkled potatoes are baked with the lamb.

–**vrasto**   –βραστό
vra-sto slow-boiled mutton generally served with **pilafi** made from the mutton stock (Crete)

–**yahni**   –γιαχνί
ya-hni lamb stewed with tomatoes, onions, carrots and celery

–**yuvetsi me kritharaki**   –γιουβέτσι με κριθαράκι
yu-ve-tsi me kri-tha-ra-ki lamb baked with tomatoes and barley-shaped pasta in an earthenware pot (*see also* **yuvetsi**)

ta arnisia paidhakya   τα αρνίσια παϊδάκια
ta ar-ni-si-a pa-i-dha-kya marinated and chargrilled lamb cutlets

to artima yefsis   το άρτυμα γεύσης
to ar-ti-ma yef-sis zest

to artopiion   το αρτοποιείον
to ar-to-pi-i-on 'bread-makery', bakery

o artos   ο άρτος
o ar-tos (*see* **prosforo**)

to asirtiko   το ασύρτικο
to a-sir-ti-ko white grape variety (*see* Grape Varieties in Drinks)

DICTIONARY

to aspro lahano   το άσπρο λάχανο
to a-spro la-ha-no white cabbage

o astakos   ο αστακός
o a-sta-kos lobster, usually boiled or
chargrilled, split and dressed with **ladholemono** or **mayoneza.**

i atherina   η αθερίνα
i a-the-ri-na miniature whitebait *(see
also* **maridhes***)*

to athiri   το αθήρι
to a-thi-ri white grape variety *(see*
Grape Varieties in Drinks*)*

ta avgha   τα αυγά
ta a-vgha eggs

–horis alati   –χωρίς αλάτι
ho-ris a-la-ti without salt

–matya   –μάτια
ma-tya 'eyes' *(see* **avgha tighanita***)*

–me beikon   –με μπέικον
me be-i-kon eggs and bacon

–melata   –μελάτα
me-la-ta soft-boiled eggs

–me tiri   –με τυρί
me ti-ri eggs and cheese fried in butter

–pashalina   –Πασχαλινά
pa-sha-li-na red-dyed eggs prepared
at Easter

–pose   –ποσέ
po-se poached eggs

–sklira   –σκληρά
skli-ra hard-boiled eggs

–strapatsadha   –στραπατσάδα
stra-pa-tsa-dha scrambled eggs
with tomatoes

–tighanita   –τηγανητά
ti-gha-ni-ta fried eggs

–tighanita me   –τηγανητά με
pasturma   παστουρμά
ti-gha-ni-ta me pa-stur-ma fried eggs
and **pasturmas**

to avgholemono   το αυγολέμονο
       (σάλτσα)
to a-vgho-le-mo-no sauce made with
eggs, lemon juice and stock. A key
ingredient in many dishes. Also served
with poached fish and boiled or
steamed vegetables.

–supa   –σούπα
su-pa a zesty broth of chicken stock-
driven **avgholemono** plus a handful of
rice. An effective hangover cure.

to avghotaraho   το αυγοτάραχο
to av-gho-ta-ra-ho fish roe, rich, amber-
coloured appetiser made from grey
mullet roe that is salted, dried, coated
in beeswax then peeled and sliced *(see
also* **taramosalata***)*

to avokado   το αβοκάντο
to a-vo-ka-do avocado

to ayoryitiko   το αγιωργίτικο
to a-yor-yi-ti-ko red grape variety *(see*
Grape Varieties in Drinks*)*

B

to bahari   το μπαχάρι
to ba-ha-ri allspice

ta baharika   τα μπαχαρικά
ba-ha-ri-ka spices/seasoning

o bakalyaros   ο μπακαλιάρος
o ba-ka-lya-ros dried salt cod soaked for
several hours prior to cooking

–burdheto   μπουρδέτο
bur-dhe-to salt cod stew *(see the recipe)*

–kroketakya   –κροκετάκια
kro-ke-ta-kya salt cod mashed with
potato, butter and nutmeg, shaped into
little batons, rolled in breadcrumbs and
deep fried

–plaki   –πλακί
pla-ki salt cod simmered with onions,
potatoes, celery, carrots and garlic in a
tomato-based sauce

–tighanitos   –τηγανητός
ti-gha-ni-tos salt cod fried in crisp,
golden batter – traditionally accompanied with **skordhalya**

o baklavas   ο μπακλαβάς
o ba-kla-vas nut-filled layers of filo
bathed in honey syrup and cut into
diamond shapes

i bamyes   οι μπάμιες
i bam-yes okra

–ladheres   –λαδερές
la-dhe-res okra stewed in oil

–yahni　　　　　　　　–γιαχνί
ya-hni okra braised with pulped tomatoes and onions

i banana　　　　　　　η μπανάνα
i ba-na-na banana

ta barbunya　　　　τα μπαρμπούνια
ta bar-bu-nya small, sweet-fleshed red mullet

–psita ston anitho –ψητά στον άνιθο
psi-ta sto-na-ni-tho red mullet on a bed of dill (*see* the recipe)

–sti shara　　　　　　　–στη σκάρα
sti sha-ra red mullet basted with oil and lemon and chargrilled

–tighanita　　　　　　–τηγανητά
ti-gha-ni-ta red mullet rolled in seasoned flour and fried

to beikin　　　　　　　το μπέικιν
　pauder　　　　　　　πάουντερ
to be-i-kin pa-u-der baking powder

to beikon　　　　　　　το μπέικον
to be-i-kon bacon

i bekatsa　　　　　　η μπεκάτσα
i be-ka-tsa woodcock

–krasati　　　　　　　–κρασάτη
kra-sa-ti woodcock casserole with dry red wine, tomatoes and spices, served on fried bread

o bekri meze　　　ο μπεκρή μεζέ
o be-kri me-ze 'drunken meze', meat pieces cooked in tomato and red wine sauce

i besamel　　　　　η μπεσαμέλ
be-sa-mel bechamel sauce

to bifteki　　　　　το μπιφτέκι
to bi-fte-ki hamburger

–sti shara　　　　　　–στη σχάρα
sti sha-ra grilled homemade hamburger

–yemisto me tiri　–γεμιστό με τυρί
ye-mi-sto me ti-ri hamburger stuffed with cheese

i bira　　　　　　　　η μπίρα
i bi-ra beer

i biraria　　　　　η μπιραρία
i bi-ra-ri-a open-air eating place serving beer; smart bar specialising in boutique beers

ta biskota　　　　τα μπισκότα
ta bi-sko-ta biscuits/cookies
(*see also* **kulurakya**)

i biters　　　　　η μπίττερς
i bi-ters bitters

to bizeli　　　　　το μπιζέλι
to bi-ze-li green peas

i bizelosupa　　η μπιζελόσουπα
i bi-ze-lo-su-pa fragrant pea soup loaded with dill

to blender　　　　το μπλέντερ
to blen-der blender

i bobota　　　　　η μπομπότα
i bo-bo-ta sweet corn bread studded with raisins, walnuts, cloves and flavoured with cinnamon and orange juice. Often called 40 bobota – a reference to its role as a staple during WWII German Occupation. (Zakynthos)

i bolia　　　　　　η μπόλια
i bo-li-a lacy caul of fat encasing lamb's stomach

to bol ya　　　　το μπωλ για
　anamiksi ilikon ανάμειξη υλικών
to bol ya a-na-mi-ksi i-li-kon mixing bowl

to briami　　　　το μπριάμι
to bri-a-mi casserole of sliced potatoes, zucchini, capsicums, tomatoes and herbs; roast vegetables

to briki　　　　　το μπρίκι
to bri-ki long-handled metal pot used for making coffee. Broad at the base and tapering towards the top, which allows the coffee to boil quickly and form a heavy froth.

i brizoles　　　η οι μπριζόλες
i bri-zo-les chops/steaks

to brokolo　　　το μπρόκολο
to bro-ko-lo broccoli

i bughatsa　　　η μπουγάτσα
i bu-gha-tsa delicious creamy semolina pudding wrapped in a pastry envelope and baked

to bukali　　　το μπουκάλι
to bu-ka-li bottle

to burdheto　　το μπουρδέτο
to bur-dhe-to hot fish casserole spiked with paprika. Generally made with

white-fleshed fish (rockfish, red mullet, swordfish or scorpion fish), but there's also a feisty eel version.

ta burekakya　　　τα μπουρεκάκια
ta bu-re-ka-kya little **burekya** in cigar, cigarette and envelope shapes

ta burekya　　　τα μπουρέκια
ta bu-re-kya Turkish-influenced filo pies shaped into thin long rolls, batons and pin-wheels. Mainly savoury (cheese, minced meat or spinach) but sweet versions exist. Can be fried or baked; baked vegetable and **mizithra** terrine. (Crete)

–me aneri　　　–με ανερί
me a-ne-ri deep-fried, **aneri**-stuffed, sugar-dusted pastry pouches (Cyprus)

to buti　　　το μπούτι
to bu-ti leg

ta buzukya　　　τα μπουζούκια
ta bu-zu-kya 'the bouzouki joints' (*see* **nihterino kendro**)

D

i debina　　　η ντεμπίνα
i de-bi-na white grape variety (*see* Grape Varieties in Drinks)

i dhafni　　　η δάφνη
i dhaf-ni bay/laurel leaf

ta dhahtila　　　τα δάχτυλα
ta dha-hti-la 'fingers', pastries that are deep fried and nut-filled (Cyprus)

to dhamaskino　　　το δαμάσκηνο
to dha-ma-ski-no red plum

dhemestiha　　　Δεμέστιχα
dhe-me-sti-ha inexpensive table wine in both red and white varieties

to dhendrolivano　　　το δεντρολίβανο
to dhen-dro-li-va-no rosemary

ta dhiafora　　　τα διάφορα
ta dhi-a-fo-ra assortment/variety

to dhiktamo　　　το δίκταμο
to dhi-kta-mo 'burning bush', dittander, aromatic plant found in the mountains, mainly used for herbal teas. Now grown as a cultivated herb because too many collectors were falling down mountain ravines.

ta dhimitriaka　　　τα δημητριακά
ta dhi-mi-tri-a-ka cereal

i dhiples　　　οι δίπλες
i dhi-ples sweet pastry ribbons twirled into various spiraly shapes, deep fried and drizzled with warm honey and sesame seeds; also called **kserotighana**

i dhrili　　　οι δρύλοι
alevrolemono　　　αλευρολέμονο
i dhri-li a-le-vro-le-mo-no stalks of wild greens in lemony sauce

o dhyozmos　　　ο δυόσμος
o dhyo-zmos mint, Greek mint is spearmint

i dolmadhes　　　οι ντολμάδες
i dol-ma-dhes parcels of aromatic rice wrapped in fruit or vegetable leaves and cooked in water, oil and lemon juice. Classic dolmadhes are vine leaves stuffed with rice, tomato, onion, parsley, mint and fennel, served cold with a sprinkle of lemon juice. Vine leaves are the most common wrapping but fig, cabbage, lettuce, beetroot and **seskulo** leaves are also used.

–filyanes　　　–φυλλιανές
fi-lya-nes onion sleeves stuffed with minced veal, pork and rice. Christmas and New Year dish. (Lesvos)

–me avgholemono　　　–με αυγολέμονο
me a-vgho-le-mo-no dolmadhes made with rice, minced lamb, tomatoes, mint and cumin, served hot with **avgholemono**

–me kukya　　　–με κουκιά
me ku-kya dolmadhes made with boiled and sliced broad beans, **plighuri** and **pasturmas** and cooked on a bed of beef bones (Northern Greece)

–me lahanofila　　　–με λαχανόφυλλα
me la-ha-no-fi-la cabbage leaves stuffed with minced lamb, onion, tomato, rice, parsley and mint, served hot with **avgholemono**

–yalandzi　　　–γιαλαντζί
ya-lan-dzi 'fraud', meatless **dolmadhes** stuffed with rice, spring onions, mint, parsley and sometimes pine nuts and currants

–zmirneika –Σμυρνέικα
zmir-ne-i-ka dolmadhes stuffed with sauteed onions, rice, eggplant, oregano, dill, garlic and cooked in tomato broth

i domates οι ντομάτες
i do-ma-tes tomatoes

–lyastes –λιαστές
lya-stes sun-dried tomatoes

–yemistes –γεμιστές
ye-mi-stes large tomatoes stuffed with rice, tomato pulp, onion, garlic and herbs (*see also* yemista)

i domatokeftedhes οι ντομα τοκεφτέδες
i do-ma-to-ke-fte-dhes deep-fried toma-to rissoles

o domatopeltes ο ντοματομπελτές
o do-ma-to-pel-tes tomato paste

i domatosupa η ντοματόσουπα
i do-ma-to-su-pa soup made with toma-toes and sometimes a cup of pasta

to dzadziki το τζατζίκι
to dza-dzi-ki refreshing puree of grated cucumber, yoghurt and garlic (*see also* talaturi)

to dzin το τζιν
to dzin gin

E

i eksipiretisi η εξυπηρέτηση
i e-ksi-pi-re-ti-si service

to eleoladho το ελαιόλαδο
to e-le-o-la-dho olive oil

i eleopites οι ελαιόπιτες
e-le-o-pi-tes small olive and leek pies (Cyprus)

to eleopsomo το ελαιόψωμο
to e-le-o-pso-mo olive bread

to eleoti το ελαιότι
to e-le-o-ti light yeast bread baked with an embedded layer of chopped black olives and onions (Cyprus)

i elitses οι ελίτσες
i e-li-tses tiny sweet black olives

i elyes οι ελιές
i e-lyes olives

–amfisis –Αμφίσσης
am-fi-sis large blue-black olives with nutty flavour

–atalandis –Αταλάντης
a-ta-lan-dis big fruity greenish-purple or purple olives

–hamures –χαμούρες
ha-mu-res dried newly fallen olives

–harahtes –χαρακτές
ha-ra-htes scored olives

–ionion prasines –Ιονίων πράσινες
i-o-ni-on pra-si-nes mild green olives (Ionian Islands)

–kalamatas –Καλαμάτας
ka-la-ma-tas large black olives with pungent flavour. Olive oil is pressed from the smaller variety. The larger ones are used as table olives.

–mavres –μαύρες
ma-vres black olives

–nafpliu –Ναυπλίου
naf-pli-u nutty flavoured green olives (Nafplio)

–pastes –παστές
pa-stes dried salted olives

–pelte –πελτέ
pel-te olive paste

–prasines –πράσινες
pra-si-nes green olives

–tsakistes –τσακιστές
tsa-ki-stes cracked green olives that are marinated in oil, lemon and herbs

–tursi –τουρσί
tur-si pickled olives

ta endosthia τα εντόσθια
ta en-do-sthi-a offal/innards (*see also* sikotarya)

–pulyon –πουλιών
pu-lyon giblets

–pulyon kokinista –κοκκινιστά
pu-lyon ko-ki-ni-sta chicken giblets braised in rich gravy of tomato paste, wine vinegar, onion, brandy, garlic, oregano and parsley

to epidhorpio το επιδόρπιο
to e-pi-dhor-pi-o dessert

i epikalipsi η επικάλυψη
i e-pi-ka-li-psi topping

to esperidhoidhes το εσπεριδοειδές
to e-spe-ri-dho-i-dhes citrus

to estiatorio το εστιατόριο
to e-sti-a-to-ri-o restaurant

F

to faghri　　　　　　　　το φαγρί
to fa-ghri sea bream; also called **lithrini**
and **melanuri**

i fakes　　　　　　　　οι φακές
i fa-kes lentils

–me makaronya　　–με μακαρόνια
me ma-ka-ro-nya lentils simmered in
water and vinegar with mint, garlic and
homemade pearl pasta (Astypalea)

–supa　　　　　　　　–σούπα
su-pa lentil soup

i fanuropita　　η Φανουρόπιτα
i fa-nu-ro-pi-ta flat round cake spiced
with raisins, walnuts, tangerine rind,
brandy and cinnamon, sprinkled with
sesame seeds. Served on Saint
Fanourios Day.

o fasianos　　　　　ο φασιανός
o fa-si-a-nos pheasant

to faskomilo　　το φασκόμηλο
to fa-sko-mi-lo sage, used to make **tsai
tu vunu**

i fasoladha　　η φασολάδα
i fa-so-la-dha thick fragrant soup of
beans, tomatoes, tomato paste, carrots,
celery, garlic and parsley

ta fasolakya　　τα φασολάκια
ta fa-so-la-kya green beans; also called
ambelofasula

–ladhera　　　　　–λαδερά
la-dhe-ra green beans cooked in oil
with tomatoes and onions (and sometimes potatoes)

–salata　　　　　　–σαλάτα
sa-la-ta boiled fresh green beans with
ladholemono or **ladhoksidho**

ta fasolia　　　　τα φασόλια
ta fa-so-li-a dried beans, generally refers
to dried white haricot/lima beans

–maratho　　　　–μάραθο
ma-ra-tho dried beans browned in oil
and onions, simmered with tomato
pulp and fennel leaves

–salata　　　　　–σαλάτα
sa-la-ta bean salad

to fastfundadhiko το φαστφουντάδικο
to fast-fun-da-dhi-ko fast-food eatery

i fava　　　　　　　　η φάβα
i fa-va yellow split pea; smoky thick-
textured puree of split peas served with
raw onion rings and a drizzle of
olive oil

–pandremeni　　　　–παντρεμένη
pan-dre-me-ni 'married', leftover **fava**
recycled as a hot dish with the addition
of tomatoes and cumin

i feta　　　　　　　　η φέτα
i fe-ta white, crumbly, salty cheese
made from either sheep's milk or a mix
of sheep's and goat's milk

–i fetes psaryu me　　οι φέτες
domata ke　　　ψαριού με
stafidhes　　ντομάτα και σταφίδες
*i fe-tes psa-ryu me do-ma-ta ke sta-fi-
dhes* fish with tomato and cur-rants (*see*
the recipe)

–sharas　　　　　　–σχάρας
sha-ras grilled feta

i fidhes　　　　　　οι φιδές
i fi-dhes vermicelli noodles

to fileto　　　　　το φιλέτο
to fi-le-to fillet/steak/loin

to filo　　　　　　το φύλλο
to fi-lo flaky tissue-thin pastry used
extensively for pies and sweet pastries

to filodorima　　το φιλοδώρημα
to fi-lo-do-ri-ma tip (service)

ta finikia　　　τα φοινίκια
ta fi-ni-ki-a honey-dipped shortbread
sprinkled with cinnamon and marked
with a criss-cross design. Finikia
means, depending on the source, either
Venetian or Phoenician (whom it's said
introduced this biscuit to Greece); also
called **melomakarona**

ta firikia　　　τα φιρίκια
ta fi-ri-ki-a delicious small crisp apples
(Northern Greece)

–me amighdala　　–με αμύγδαλα
me a-mi-ghda-la **firikia** stuffed with
whole almonds and baked

–yemista　　　　　–γεμιστά
ye-mi-sta **firikia** stuffed with minced
veal, onions, coriander and cumin

o fistikas　　　　ο φιστικάς
o fi-sti-kas nut seller

to fistikeleo το φιστικέλαιο
to fi-sti-ke-le-o peanut oil

ta fistikia τα φιστίκια
ta fi-sti-ki-a peanuts

–eyinis –Αιγίνης
e-yi-nis pistachios

to fitiko ladhi το φυτικό λάδι
to fi-ti-ko la-dhi vegetable oil

i fitini η φυτίνη
i fi-ti-ni vegetable fat made from olive oil and sheep's butter

i flaunes οι φλαούνες
i fla-u-nes baked savoury tarts filled with **halumi**, **kefalotiri**, eggs, **masticha**, **mahlepi**, mint and raisins. Although an Easter speciality they are popular throughout the year. (Cyprus)

to flidzani το φλιτζάνι
to fli-dza-ni cup

florinis Φλωρίνης
flo-ri-nis see **piperyes florinis**

i formaela η φορμαέλλα Αράχωβας
arahovas parnasu Παρνασσού
i for-ma-e-la a-ra-ho-vas par-na-su (*see* Cheese in Staples & Specialities)

ta franggosika τα φραγκόσυκα
ta frang-go-si-ka prickly pear, peeled and eaten like a mango. Once a popular refreshment but now less so – maybe because the tiny thorns make your fingers itch like crazy.

o frapes ο φραπές
o fra-pes cold coffee shaken until it gets a big frothy head, served with ice

o frappe ο φραπέ
o fra-pe (*see* **frapes**)

i fraula η φράουλα
i fra-u-la strawberry

freskos φρέσκος
fre-skos fresh

ta frighadhelya τα φρυγαδέλια
ta fri-gha-dhe-lya little parcels of calf's or lamb's liver wrapped in lamb's caul and fried in oil and garlic or skewered and chargrilled (Northern Greece, Thessaly)

i frighanya η φρυγανιά
i fri-gha-nya toast; crisp baked bread slices

i frighanyera η φρυγανιέρα
i fri-gha-nye-ra toaster

frikase φρικασέ
fri-ka-se meat or vegetable stew thickened and flavoured with **avgholemono** or **alevrolemono**

ta fruta τα φρούτα
ta fru-ta fruit

–apoksirameno –αποξηραμένο
a-po-ksi-ra-me-no dried fruit

–hyimos –χυμός
hyi-mos fruit juice

–piatela –πιατέλα
pi-a-te-la seasonal fruit platter served at the end of a meal

i frutalya η φρουταλιά
i fru-ta-lya omelette-type dish consisting of eggs, potatoes, parsley and sliced smoked pork sausages (Andros)

i frutosalata η φρουτοσαλάτα
i fru-to-sa-la-ta fruit salad

ta fundukya τα φουντούκια
ta fun-du-kya hazelnuts

sto furno στο φούρνο
sto fur-no oven baked

o furnos ο φούρνος
o fur-nos oven/bakery

G

i gaidhurelya η γαϊδουρελιά
i ga-i-dhu-rel-ya 'donkey olive', named due to its large size

to ghala το γάλα
to gha-la milk

–apovutiromeno –αποβουτυρωμένο
a-po-vu-ti-ro-me-no skim milk

–evapore –εβαπορέ
e-va-po-re evaporated milk

–simpiknomeno –συμπυκνωμένο
zaharuho ζαχαρούχο
sim-pi-kno-me-no za-ha-ru-ho sweetened condensed milk

–skoni –σκόνη
sko-ni powdered milk

–soyas –σόγιας
so-yas soy milk

to ghalaktobureko το γαλακτομ
πούρεκο
to gha-la-kto-bu-re-ko baked custard-
cream filo pie sprinkled with a lemony
syrup, sliced into squares or diamonds

to ghalaktopolio το γαλακτοπωλείο
to gha-la-kto-po-li-o shop specialising in
dairy goods

i ghalipes οι γαλύπες
i gha-li-pes type of sea anemone; also
called **kolitsani**

–tighanites –τηγανητές
ti-gha-ni-tes lightly battered and
fried **ghalipes**

i ghalipokeftedhes οι γαλυποκεφτέδες
i gha-li-po-ke-fte-dhes delicately
flavoured **ghalipes** rissoles

i ghalopula η γαλοπούλα
i gha-lo-pu-la turkey

–yemisti –γεμιστή
ye-mi-sti roast turkey stuffed with
breadcrumbs, eggs, raisins, brandy,
herbs and spices. A Christmas dish that
is quickly replacing the traditional **ghurunaki sti suvla**.

to ghalotiri το γαλοτύρι
*to gha-lo-ti-ri see Cheese in Staples
& Specialities*

ta ghardumya τα γαρδούμια
ta ghar-du-mya small offal rolls (shaped
like tightly-coiled springs) made from
strips of lamb's stomach seasoned
with lemon juice and herbs, then
bound with intestines and roasted.
Sometimes chopped **sikotarya** is
added to the stuffing.

i gharidhes οι γαρίδες
i gha-ri-dhes prawns/shrimps

–saghanaki –σαγανάκι
sa-gha-na-ki prawns fried with tomatoes and red wine, topped with feta
and baked

–tighanites –τηγανητές
ti-gha-ni-tes fried prawns

–vrastes –βραστές
vra-stes boiled prawns accompanied
by **ladholemono**

–yuvetsaki –γιουβετσάκι
yu-ve-tsa-ki prawns with crushed
tomatoes, parsley, oregano and feta
chunks baked in earthenware pots (*see
also* **yuvetsi**)

i gharidhosalata η γαριδοσαλάτα
i gha-ri-dho-sa-la-ta prawn salad

ta gharifala τα γαρίφαλα
ta gha-ri-fa-la cloves

i ghastra η γάστρα
i gha-stra distinctive kind of meat cookery sometimes translated as charcoal
baking. Also name of cooking pot.

o ghavros ο γαύρος
o gha-vros fresh anchovy

ta ghlika τα γλυκά
kutalyu κουταλιού
ta ghli-ka ku-ta-lyu 'spoon sweets',
homemade preserved fruits served in
small bowls with a teaspoon for eating –
always accompanied by a glass of water

to ghlikaniso το γλυκάνισο
to ghli-ka-ni-so aniseed

ta ghlika tapsyu τα γλυκά ταψιού
ta ghli-ka ta-psyu cakes and pies and
pan sweets made with filo

to ghlikizma το γλύκισμα
to ghli-ki-zma sweet pastry, cake

to ghliko το γλυκό
to ghli-ko sweet

i ghlikokolokitha η γλυκοκολοκύθα
i ghli-ko-ko-lo-ki-tha pumpkin; also
called **kolokitha**

to ghlikolemono το γλυκολέμονο
to ghli-ko-le-mo-no lime

i ghlikopatata η γλυκοπατάτα
i ghli-ko-pa-ta-ta sweet potato

i ghlikoriza η γλυκόριζα
i ghli-ko-ri-za liquorice

i ghlistridha η γλιστρίδα
i ghli-stri-dha purslane, small-leafed
plant with lemony flavour and crisp
texture used mainly in salad

–me kaparofila –με καππαρόφυλλα
salata σαλάτα
me ka-pa-ro-fi-la sa-la-ta purslane
leaves, sliced tomatoes, black olives and
caper leaves with oil and lemon dressing

–me yaurti   **–με γιαούρτι**
me ya-ur-ti chopped purslane beaten with strained yoghurt, garlic, lemon, salt and oil (Crete)

i ghlosa   **η γλώσσα**
i ghlo-sa tongue; name for any flat fish

–mosharisia   **–μοσχαρίσια**
krasati   **κρασάτη**
mo-sha-ri-si-a kra-sa-ti boiled veal tongue sliced and fried in butter then poached in its own stock with white wine, celery and garlic

to ghonggili   **η το γογγύλι**
to ghong-gi-li turnip

i ghopa   **γόπα**
i gho-pa bogue, type of fish

i ghranita   **η γρανίτα**
i ghra-ni-ta sorbet

i ghravyera   **η γραβιέρα**
i ghra-vye-ra (*see* Cheese in Staples & Specialities)

to ghudhi   **το γουδί**
to ghu-dhi mortar

to ghudhohyeri   **το γουδοχέρι**
to ghu-dho-hye-ri pestle

to ghurunaki   **το γουρουνάκι**
(tu ghalaktos)   **(του γάλακτος)**
to ghu-ru-na-ki (tu gha-la-ktos) suckling pig (*see also* **ghurunopulo**)

–sti suvla   **–στη σούβλα**
sti su-vla whole suckling pig rubbed inside and out with lemon, salt and oregano and spit-roasted until tender. During festivals the piglet is stuffed with veal liver, rice, apples and raisins.

–yemisto me feta   **–γεμιστό με φέτα**
ye-mi-sto me fe-ta suckling pig seasoned with salt, pepper, oregano and oil, stuffed with feta and roasted

to ghuruni   **το γουρούνι**
to ghu-ru-ni pig

to ghurunopulo   **το γουρουνόπουλο**
to ghu-ru-no-pu-lo piglet

ta greipfrut   **τα γκρέιπφρουτ**
ta gre-ip-frut grapefruit

H

to halorini   **το χαλορίνι**
to ha-lo-ri-ni soft pouch-shaped cheese filled with crushed coriander (Cyprus)

to halumi   **το χαλούμι**
to ha-lu-mi firm, white, sheep's milk cheese with elastic texture and salty taste. Often flavoured with mint. Used mainly for pies, breads and **saghanaki**. (Cyprus)

i halumopites   **οι χαλουμόπιτες**
i ha-lu-mo-pi-tes savoury cake made with **halumi**, eggs, mint, sultanas and **masticha** (Cyprus)

to halumopsomo   **το χαλουμόψωμο**
to ha-lu-mo-pso-mo bread baked with chunks of **halumi** (Cyprus)

o halvas   **ο χαλβάς**
o hal-vas rich creamy sweet of Turkish origin made from sesame seeds and honey. Sold in blocks the size of house bricks. Flavoured with pistachio, **masticha**, chocolate, almonds or vanilla.

–simighdhalenios   **–σιμιγδαλένιος**
si-mi-ghdha-le-ni-os moist, slightly sticky cake of semolina and honey, cooked in a saucepan, poured into a cake mould and decorated with almonds and cinnamon

halvas tiz rinas   **–της Ρίνας**
tiz ri-nas baked semolina and almond cake served hot with sugar syrup. Named after the cake's creator.

to hamomili   **το χαμομήλι**
to ha-mo-mi-li chamomile, used to make **tsai tu vunu**

to hampsopilafi   **το χαμψοπίλαφι**
to ham-pso-pi-la-fi anchovy and onion **pilafi** seasoned with oregano

ta hampsya   **τα χαμψιά**
ta ham-psya fresh anchovy; also called **ghavros**

sto harti   **στο χαρτί**
sto har-ti method of baking meat and vegetables in parchment or grease-proof paper

i hasapotaverna   **η χασαποταβέρνα**
i ha-sa-po-ta-ver-na basic restaurant attached to a butcher in a market

to havyari   **το χαβιάρι**
to ha-vya-ri caviar

i hohlii οι χοχλιοί
oi ho-hli-i snails (see also **salinggaria**)

–buburisti –μπουμπουριστοί
bu-bu-ri-sti 'upside-down', live snails deep fried and doused with vinegar and rosemary. Always given a smack on their bottoms with a fork for easier shell-extraction.

to hondros το χόντρος
to hon-dros hand-milled wheat used in soups, **dolmadhes**, snail dishes and vegetable and meat stews (see also **ksinohondros**)

i horiatiki η χωριάτικη
salata σαλάτα
i ho-ri-a-ti-ki sa-la-ta 'village salad', salad of tomatoes, cucumber, olives and feta and perhaps lettuce and sweet peppers. Known everywhere as Greek salad.

horiatikos χωριάτικος
ho-ri-a-ti-kos village/country style

ta horta τα χόρτα
ta hor-ta wild or cultivated greens used in salads, or boiled and served hot with an oil and lemon dressing. Also a favourite for filling pies and adding to casseroles. Popular horta include wild asparagus, amaranth, purslane, stinging nettle, chicory, dandelion, milk thistle and wild silverbeet.

–tsighari –τσιγάρι
tsi-gha-ri lightly fried wild greens; also called **tsighari**

o hortofaghos ο χορτοφάγος
o hor-to-fa-ghos vegetarian

i hortopita η χορτόπιτα
i hor-to-pi-ta pies made from **horta** seasonal greens

i hortosalata η χορτοσαλάτα
i hor-to-sa-la-ta warm salad of greens dressed with salt, oil and lemon

i hortosupa η χορτόσουπα
i hor-to-su-pa vegetable soup

to hristopsaro το χριστόψαρο
to hri-sto-psa-ro John Dory

to hristopsomo το χριστόψωμο
to hri-sto-pso-mo sweet yeast Christmas bread baked in the shape of a cross;
circular loaf with a large X (first letter of the Greek spelling of Christ) etched in the dough

to htapodhi το χταπόδι
to hta-po-dhi octopus

–keftedhes –κεφτέδες
ke-fte-dhes rissoles of minced octopus, onion, mint and **kefalotiri**

–krasato –κρασάτο
kra-sa-to octopus prepared then cooked in red wine sauce

–lyasto –λιαστό
lya-sto sun-dried, chargrilled octopus sprinkled with oil and lemon juice

–me makaroni kofto –με μακαρόνι
κοφτό *me ma-ka-ro-ni ko-fto* casserole of thick-cut octopus, tomatoes, tomato puree, short macaroni and red wine

–sta karvuna –στα κάρβουνα
sta kar-vu-na grilled octopus (see the recipe)

–stifadho –στιφάδο
sti-fa-dho octopus ragout spiced with bay leaves and garlic (see also **stifadho**)

–tursi –τουρσί
tur-si pickled octopus

–vrasto –βραστό
vra-sto boiled octopus coated with oil and lemon sauce

i hurmadhes οι χουρμάδες
i hur-ma-dhes dates

to hyeli το χέλι
to hye-li eel

–plaki –πλακί
pla-ki eel baked with tomatoes, onions, potatoes and herbs (Corfu)

ta hyili tis τα χείλη της
hanumisas χανούμισσας
ta hyi-li tis ha-nu-mi-sas 'the Turkish lady's lips', crunchy honey cakes (Rhodes)

i hyilofta η χυλόφτα
i hyi-lo-fta curly macaroni served with hot butter and grated **kefalotiri**. Sometimes melted **mizithra** is poured over hyilofta. (Crete)

i hyilopites οι χυλοπίτες
i hyi-lo-pi-tes egg noodles often added to dishes to soak up juices

–me kima —με κιμά
me ki-ma boiled noodles with mince-meat and onion sauce

hyima χύμα
hyi-ma bulk or loose produce; draught wine served in carafes at restaurants and tavernas

o hyimos ο χυμός
o hyi-mos juice

–portokali —πορτοκάλι
por-to-ka-li orange juice

i hyina η χήνα
i hyi-na goose

i hyirines οι χοιρινές
brizoles μπριζόλες
i hyi-ri-nes bri-zo-les pork chops

–krasates —κρασάτες
kra-sa-tes pork chops simmered in red wine

–sti shara —στη σχάρα
sti sha-ra pork chops chargrilled with salt, pepper and lemon juice

–tighanites —τηγανητές
ti-gha-ni-tes fried pork chops

to hyirino το χοιρινό
to hyi-ri-no pork

–buti psito —μπούτι ψητό
bu-ti psi-to crispy, roast leg of pork

–me kidhonya —με κυδώνια
me ki-dho-nya pork and quinces simmered in red wine spiced with orange peel and cinnamon

–me prasa —με πράσα
me pra-sa pork and leek casserole

–me selino —με σέλινο
avgolemono αυγολέμονο
me se-li-no a-vgo-le-mo-no pork and celery in egg and lemon sauce. Celeriac or endive can be substituted for the celery.

–pasto —παστό
pa-sto salted pork

to hyiromeri το χοιρομέρι
to hyi-ro-me-r cured leg of ham similar to prosciutto (Cyprus, Zakynthos)

i hyitra η χύτρα
i hyi-tra pot/kettle

–atmu —ατμού
a-tmu steamer

–tahyititas —ταχύτητας
ta-hyi-ti-tas pressure cooker

I

to idhos το είδος
to i-dhos item (often referring to dishes on restaurant menu)

to ilieleo το ηλιέλαιο
to i-li-e-le-o sunflower

o iliosporos ο ηλιόσπορος
o i-li-o-spo-ros black sunflower seed

to imam baildi το ιμάμ–μπαϊλντί
to i-mam ba-il-di fragrant oil-doused Turkish-inspired dish of eggplant split lengthways stuffed with eggplant pulp, tomato, garlic, onion, parsley and then baked

ta inopnevmatodhi τα οινοπνευ-
ματώδη *ta i-no-pnev-ma-to-dhi* alcoholic spirits

to inopolio το οινοπωλείο
to i-no-po-li-o liquor shop

K

to kafenion το καφενείο
to ka-fe-ni-o coffee shop, also serves **ouzo** and **mezedhakya**

o kafes ο καφές
o ka-fes coffee

–elinikos —ελληνικός
e-li-ni-kos freshly brewed Greek coffee

–ghlikos —γλυκός
ghli-kos sweet coffee

–metrios —μέτριος
me-tri-os medium-strength coffee with a little sugar

–pola varis —πολλά βαρύς
po-la va-ris strong coffee

–sketos —σκέτος
ske-tos sugarless coffee

–varighlikos —βαρύγλυκος
va-ri-ghli-kos strong and sweet coffee

i kafeteria η καφετερία
i ka-fe-te-ri-a cafeteria

to kaimaki το καϊμάκι
to ka-i-ma-ki froth that forms on top of Greek coffee while it brews. A full creamy layer is the sign of a really good coffee.

–pighmeno —πηγμένο
pigh-me-no clotted cream

to kakao το κακάο
to ka-ka-o cocoa

i kakavya η κακαβιά
i ka-ka-vya fish soup made from saltwater fish. Named after the pot with three legs used for in-boat cooking. Rumoured to have inspired French bouillabaisse.

to kalamaki το καλαμάκι
to ka-la-ma-ki straw

ta kalamarakya τα καλαμαράκια
ta ka-la-ma-ra-kya baby squid

to kalamari το καλαμάρι
to ka-la-ma-ri squid

–levrianna –Λεβριανά
le-vri-an-na squid stewed with green olives, tomatoes, onions and parsley in dry red wine

–me rizi –με ρύζι
me ri-zi fried squid with onions simmered with water, crushed tomatoes, rice and cinnamon

–tighanito –τηγανητό
ti-gha-ni-to squid cut in rings or strips, lightly battered and fried

–yemisto –γεμιστό
ye-mi-sto whole squid stuffed with rice, chopped and sauteed squid's tentacles, spring onions, dill, parsley and baked in lemony broth

to kalambokalevro το καλαμπο
κάλευρο
to ka-la-mbo-ka-le-vro cornflour

to kalamboki το καλαμπόκι
to ka-la-mbo-ki sweet corn

to kalathaki το καλαθάκι
to ka-la-tha-ki (see Cheese in Staples & Specialities)

ta kalitsunya τα καλιτσούνια
ta ka-li-tsu-nya small cheese pies made with mizithra

to kalkani το καλκάνι
to kal-ka-ni turbot

kalopsimenos καλοψημένος
ka-lo-psi-me-nos well done (cooked)

i kanela η κανέλα
i ka-ne-la cinnamon

i kantina η καντίνα
i kan-ti-na canteen, mobile food van

o kapamas ο καπαμάς
o ka-pa-mas method of stewing meat with tomatoes, wine, cinnamon and sometimes red capsicum and cloves

i kapari η κάππαρη
i ka-pa-ri caper, usually pickled and eaten as an appetiser. Also picked fresh, boiled and dressed with chopped raw onion, vinegar and oil.

ta kaparofila τα καππαρόφυλλα
ta ka-pa-ro-fi-la tender young caper leaves used in salads and casseroles, or pickled and dressed with olive oil and black pepper (Santorini)

kapnistos καπνιστός
ka-pni-stos smoked

kapnizo καπνίζω
ka-pni-zo to smoke

to kaponi το καπόνι
to ka-po-ni capon

o kapros ο κάπρος
o ka-pros wild boar

i karafa η καράφα
i ka-ra-fa carafe

i karamela η καραμέλα
i ka-ra-me-la candy/caramel

i karaoli οι καραόλοι
i ka-ra-o-li see **salinggaria**

i karavidha η καραβίδα
i ka-ra-vi-dha crayfish

i karavoli οι καραβόλοι
i ka-ra-vo-li see **salinggaria**

to kardhamo το κάρδαμο
to kar-dha-mo cardamom

i kardhya η καρδιά
i kar-dhya heart

to kari το κάρι
to ka-ri curry

i karidha η καρύδα
i ka-ri-dha coconut

ta karidhia τα καρύδια
ta ka-ri-dhi-a walnuts

–yemista –γεμιστά
ye-mi-sta walnuts impregnated with roasted almonds (and sometimes cloves) and preserved in syrup (Cyprus)

i karidhopita η καρυδόπιτα
i ka-ri-dho-pi-ta rich moist walnut cake

okaridhothrafstis ο καρυδοθραύστης
*o ka-ri-dho-**thraf**-stis* nutcracker

ta karikevmata τα καρυκεύματα
*ta ka-ri-**kev**-ma-ta* condiments

to karoto το καρότο
*to ka-**ro**-to* carrot

to karpuzi το καρπούζι
*to kar-**pu**-zi* watermelon

to karveli το καρβέλι
*to kar-**ve**-li* loaf

sta karvuna στα κάρβουνα
*sta kar-**vu**-na* chargrilled/barbecued

to kaseri το κασέρι
*to ka-**se**-ri* (see Cheese in Staples & Specialities)

ta kastana τα κάστανα
*ta ka-**sta**-na* chestnuts. Autumn snack-food roasted on portable braziers by street vendors. Also added to stuffing.

to kasyu το κάσιου
to ka-syu cashews

to kataifi το καταΐφι
to ka-ta-i-fi 'angel hair' pastry; syrupy nest-like nut-filled rolls created from this pastry

to katakathi το κατακάθι
*to ka-ta-**ka**-thi* sludge-like sediment left at the bottom of cups after drinking Greek coffee. Fortune-tellers read destinies from katakathi.

o kataloghos ο κατάλογος
*o ka-**ta**-lo-ghos* menu

–krasyon –κρασιών
*kra-**syon*** wine list

to katharistiri fliu το καθαριστήρι φλοιού
*to ka-tha-ri-**sti**-ri fli-u* peeler

i katsarola η κατσαρόλα
*i ka-tsa-**ro**-la* pot/saucepan

katsarolas κατσαρόλας
*ka-tsa-**ro**-las* method of casseroling or pot-roasting meat

i katsika η κατσίκα
*i ka-**tsi**-ka* goat

to katsikaki το κατσικάκι
*to ka-tsi-**ka**-ki* goat, kid

–patudho –πατούδο
*pa-**tu**-dho* roast kid stuffed with liver, rice, breadcrumbs, feta and raisins or **kefalotiri**, bacon, rice and dill (Cyclades)

–psito –ψητό
*psi-**to*** roast kid, sometimes served with a spicy red wine sauce

–yuvetsi –γιουβέτσι
*yu-**ve**-tsi* kid-on-the-bone baked with **kritharaki**, pulped tomatoes, tomato paste and oregano (see also **yuvetsi**)

to kavuri το καβούρι
*to ka-**vu**-ri* crab

–vrasto –βραστό
*vra-**sto*** crab boiled and dressed with **ladholemono**

to kefalaki το κεφαλάκι
*to ke-fa-**la**-ki* head, usually refers specifically to lamb's head (see also **arni kefalaki righanato**)

i kefaloghraviera η κεφαλογραβιέρα
i ke-fa-lo-ghra-vi-e-ra (see Cheese in Staples & Specialities)

o kefalos ο κέφαλος
*o **ke**-fa-los* grey mullet

to kefalotiri το κεφαλοτύρι
*to ke-fa-lo-**ti**-ri* (see Cheese in Staples & Specialities)

ta keftedhakya τα κεφτεδάκια
*ta ke-fte-**dha**-kya* miniature meat rissoles served at parties

i keftedhes οι κεφτέδες
*i ke-**fte**-dhes* small tasty rissoles, often made with minced lamb, pork or veal, onion, egg and herbs (and sometimes **ouzo** as a moistener), shaped into flattened balls and fried. Other rissole varieties include **kolokithokeftedhes**, **patates keftedhes**, **ghalipokeftedhes**, **psaro-keftedhes**, **revithokeftedhes** and **domatokeftedhes**

–sti shara –στη σχάρα
*sti **sha**-ra* chargrilled meat rissoles

to kehri το κεχρί
*to **ke**-hri* millet

to keik το κέικ
*to **ke**-ik* cake

–me fruta —με φρούτα
me fru-ta fruit cake

to kerasi το κεράσι
to ke-ra-si cherry

to kidhoni το κυδώνι
to ki-dho-ni quince

–beltes —μπελτές
bel-tes quince jelly

–ghliko —γλυκό
ghli-ko quince preserve flavoured with **amberoriza**, type of **ghlika kutalyu**

–sto furno —στο φούρνο
sto fur-no quince dabbed with butter and baked in a water and sugar solution until liquid has caramelised

–thalasino —θαλασσινό
tha-la-si-no cockle

–yemisto —γεμιστό
ye-mi-sto large quince stuffed with minced beef, rice, onions, raisins, cloves and nutmeg

to kidhonopasto το κυδωνόπαστο
to ki-dho-no-pa-sto dark-red quince paste dried until firm, cut in small diamonds and dusted with sugar. They are sometimes decorated with blanched almonds.

o kihori ο κιχώρι
o ki-ho-ri chicory, which is also known as **radhiki**

i kimadhopita η κιμαδόπιτα
i ki-ma-dho-pi-ta mincemeat pie

o kimas ο κιμάς
o ki-mas mincemeat; sauce made from mincemeat, onions, pulped tomatoes, tomato paste (and sometimes red wine) served with macaroni, spaghetti or rice

to kimino το κύμινο
to ki-mi-no cumin

to kiniyi το κυνήγι
to ki-ni-yi game

to kipelo το κύπελλο
to ki-pe-lo bowl

to kirio fayito το κύριο φαγητό
to ki-ri-o fa-yi-to main course

i kitrinpiperya η κίτρινη πιπεριά
i ki-tri-ni pi-per-ya yellow capsicum (pepper)

i klimatarya η κληματαριά
i kli-ma-tar-ya grapevine arbour that provides a shady place for great eating and drinking

to klimatofilo το κληματόφυλλο
to kli-ma-to-fi-lo vine leaf

to kofisi το κοφίσι
to ko-fi-si pie made from boiled and shredded dried fish mixed with onion, garlic, rice and tomatoes (Kefallonia)

i koka kola η Κόκα Κόλα
i ko-ka ko-la Coca-Cola

i koki kafe οι κόκκοι καφέ
i ko-ki ka-fe coffee beans

to kokineli το κοκκινέλι
to ko-ki-ne-li red resinated wine

i kokini piperya η κόκκινη πιπεριά
i ko-ki-ni pi-per-ya red capsicum (pepper)

kokinistos κοκκινιστός
ko-ki-ni-stos 'reddened', refers to sauteing meat until it browns; method of simmering meat, chicken or rice with tomatoes

to kokino fasoli το κόκκινο φασόλι
to ko-ki-no fa-so-li red kidney bean

–lahano —λάχανο
la-ha-no red cabbage

to kokinopipero το κοκκινοπίπερο
to ko-ki-no-pi-pe-ro cayenne

o kokoras ο κόκορας
o ko-ko-ras rooster

–krasatos —κρασάτος
kra-sa-tos lightly floured rooster fried with onions and spices then cooked in red wine sauce

to kokoretsi το κοκορέτσι
to ko-ko-re-tsi coarsely chopped lamb offal wrapped in lamb's intestines, flavoured with oregano and lemon juice and grilled until succulent on the inside and crunchy on the outside. Served in slices.

to kokorozumo το κοκορόζουμο
to ko-ko-ro-zu-mo lemony rooster broth used as a post-party pick-me-up (Cyclades)

to **kokteil** το κοκτέιλ
to ko-kte-il cocktail

to **kolatsyo** το κολατσιό
to ko-la-tsyo mid-morning snack

o **kolios** ο κολιός
o ko-li-os mackerel; also called **skumbri**

–**ladhorighani** –λαδορίγανη
la-dho-ri-gha-ni mackerel baked with oil, lemon, oregano, garlic and parsley

i **kolitsani** οι κολιτσάνοι
i ko-li-tsa-ni type of sea anemone; also called **ghalipes**

i **koliva** η κόλυβα
i ko-li-va traditional commemorative sweet dish eaten after the death of a family member and on the anniversary of their death. Bags of soft-boiled wheat kernels mixed with dried fruit, pomegranate seeds, sugar and nuts.

to **kolokasi** το κολοκάσι
to ko-lo-ka-si taro (Cyprus)

i **koloketa** η κολοκέτα
i ko-lo-ke-ta pastries stuffed with red pumpkin, raisins and cracked wheat (Cyprus)

i **kolokitha** η κολοκύθα
i ko-lo-ki-tha pumpkin (see also **ghlikokolokitha** and **kolokithi**)

ta **kolokithakya** τα κολοκυθάκια
ta ko-lo-ki-tha-kya zucchini

–**me avgha** –με αυγά
me a-vgha zucchini and egg omelette

–**tighanita** –τηγανητά
ti-gha-ni-ta thick zucchini rounds or strips battered and deep fried, squeezed with lemon and served with **skordhalya**.

–**vrasta** –βραστά
vra-sta boiled baby zucchini with oil and lemon dressing

to **kolokithi** το κολοκύθι
to ko-lo-ki-thi marrow/squash/pumpkin

i **kolokithoanthi** οι κολοκυθόανθοι
i ko-lo-ki-tho-an-thi zucchini flowers

–**tighaniti** –τηγανητοί
ti-gha-ni-ti zucchini flowers lightly battered and fried; zucchini flower and cheese fritters (Andros)

–**yemisti** –γεμιστοί
ye-mi-sti fat, golden, zucchini flower **dolmadhes** stuffed with rice, tomato and parsley and simmered until tender

i **kolo-k-** οι κολο-κ-
ithokeftedhes υθοκεφτέδες
i ko-lo-ki-tho-ke-fte-dhes pale green rissoles of pureed zucchini, parsley, onion, mint and garlic.

i **kolok-** οι κολοκ-
ithokorfadhes υθοκορφάδες
i ko-lo-ki-tho-kor-fa-dhes (see **kolok-ithoanthi yemisti**)

i **kolokithopita** η κολοκυθόπιτα
i ko-lo-ki-tho-pi-ta zucchini pie

to **kolyandros** το κόλιαντρος
to ko-lyan-dros coriander

i **komandaria** η Κομμανταρία
i ko-man-da-ri-a heavy dessert wine originally made during the Crusades by the Knights of the Order of St John (Cyprus)

i **komposta** η κομπόστα
i kom-po-sta stewed fruit; compote

to **kondosuvli** το κοντοσούβλι
to kon-do-su-vli spit-roast pieces of lamb or pork seasoned with onions, oregano, salt and pepper

i **kondra fileto** το κόντρα φιλέτο
to kon-dra fi-le-to rump/sirloin

i **konserva** η κονσέρβα
i kon-ser-va can

i **konservolya** η κονσερβολιά
i kon-ser-vo-lya common variety of olive, from the central mainland

to **konsome** το κονσομέ
to kon-so-me consomme

to **konyak** το κονιάκ
to kon-yak brandy/cognac

i **kopanisti** η κοπανιστή
i ko-pa-ni-sti (see Cheese in Staples & Specialities)

to **kornbeif** το κορνμπέιφ
to korn-be-if corn beef

i **koroneiki** η κορωναίικη
i ko-ro-ne-i-ki a smaller, oil-bearing variety of kalamata olive

to koskino το κόσκινο
to ko-ski-no sieve

i kotoleta η κοτολέτα
i ko-to-le-ta
cutlet; also called **paidhakya**

i kotopita η κοτόπιτα
i ko-to-pi-ta chicken filo pastry

to kotopulo το κοτόπουλο
to ko-to-pu-lo chicken

–hylopites –χυλοπίτες
hyi-lo-pi-tes whole chicken and noodles simmered in tomato, onion and cinnamon broth until liquid is absorbed

–lemonato –λεμονάτο
le-mo-na-to roast chicken basted with butter and lemon juice

–me bamyes –με μπάμιες
me ba-myes chicken and okra braised in tomato and onion gravy

–sti shara –στη σχάρα
sti sha-ra grilled chicken

i kotosupa η κοτόσουπα
i ko-to-su-pa soup made from boiled whole chicken, (when thickened with rice and **avgholemono** it becomes **avgholemono supa**). Generally the fowl is served alongside or after the soup.

to kotozumo το κοτόζουμο
to ko-to-zu-mo chicken stock

to kotsifali το κοτσιφάλι
to ko-tsi-fa-li red grape variety (*see* Grape Varieties in Drinks)

kovo se fetes κόβω σε φέτες
ko-vo se fe-tes to slice

kovo se fileto κόβω σε φιλέτο
ko-vo se fi-le-to to fillet

i kramvi η κράμβη
i kram-vi swede

to krasato το κρασάτο
to kra-sa-to red grape variety (*see* Grape Varieties in Drinks)

krasatos κρασάτος
kra-sa-tos cooked in wine

to krasi το κρασί
to kra-si wine

–aspro –άσπρο
a-spro white wine; also **krasi lefko**

–kokino –κόκκινο
ko-ki-no red wine

–lefko –λευκό
le-fko white wine; also called **krasi aspro**

–roze –ροζέ
ro-ze rosé wine

–vareli –βαρέλι
va-re-li barrel wine

i kratisi η κράτηση
i kra-ti-si reservation

to kreas το κρέας
to kre-as meat

–elafyu –ελαφιού
e-la-fyu venison

–sti stamna –στη στάμνα
sti sta-mna meat cooked in a pot

–sto furno me patates –στο φούρνο με πατάτες
sto fur-no me pa-ta-tes roast meat with potatoes

ta kreatika τα κρεατικά
ta kre-a-ti-ka meat dishes, mostly stewed or roasted

i kreatopita η κρεατόπιτα
i kre-a-to-pi-ta meat pie made with a filling of lamb or veal, tomato and cinnamon

–kefalonitiki –Κεφαλλονίτικη
ke-fa-lo-ni-ti-ki pie of cubed lamb, goat, beef and/or pork cooked with onions, eggs, rice, potatoes, tomatoes, garlic and cinnamon (Kefallonia)

–tis kritis (kritiki kreatopita) –της Κρήτης (Κρητική κρεατότουρτα)
tis kri-tis (kri-ti-ki kre-a-to-pi-ta) pie of alternating layers of cubed lamb (or goat) and **mizithra** covered in butter and **staka**. Baked in shortcrust pastry. (Crete)

i kreatosupa η κρεατόσουπα
i kre-a-to-su-pa nourishing broth made from boiled meat – sometimes thickened with rice and **avgholemono**

i krema η κρέμα
i kre-ma cream

–ksini –ξινή
ksi-ni sour cream

–patiseri –πατισσερί
pa-ti-se-ri sweet custard cream for filling pastries

–santiyi –σαντιγή
san-ti-yi whipped cream

to kremidhaki το κρεμμυδάκι
to kre-mi-dha-ki small onion, shallot

–fresko –φρέσκο
fre-sko spring onion

–tursi –τουρσί
tur-si pickling onion

ta kremidhia τα κρεμμύδια
ta kre-mi-dhi-a onions

i kremidhopita η κρεμμυδόπιτα
i kre-mi-dho-pi-ta pie with a filling of **mizithra**, grated onion, eggs and dill (Mykonos)

i kreperi η κρεπερί
i kre-pe-ri eatery selling crepes

to kritharaki το κριθαράκι
to kri-tha-ra-ki tiny spindle-shaped barley pasta used for pasta dishes, soups and **yuvetsi**

–me vutiro ke tiri –με βούτυρο και τυρί
me vu-ti-ro ke ti-ri tiny pasta boiled in stock or water and baked with brown butter, **mizithra**, lemon juice and herbs

to krithari το κριθάρι
to kri-tha-ri barley

to kritharokuluri το κριθαροκουλούρι
to kri-tha-ro-ku-lu-ri barley rolls/rusks (see also **paksimadya**)

o kritikos dakos ο Κρητικός ντάκος
o kri-ti-kos da-kos (see **paksimadya**)

i kroketa η κροκέττα
i kro-ke-ta croquette

to kruasan το κρουασάν
to kru-a-san croissant

i ksanthi bira η ξανθή μπίρα
i ksan-thi bi-ra lager

i kseri karpi οι ξηροί καρποί
i kse-ri kar-pi nuts

kseros ξερός
kse-ros dried

ta kserotighana τα ξεροτήγανα
ta kse-ro-ti-gha-na see **dhiples**

to ksidhi το ξύδι
to ksi-dhi vinegar

–apo krasi –από κρασί
a-po kra-si wine vinegar

–apo milo –από μήλο
a-po mi-lo cider vinegar

–apo rizi –από ρύζι
a-po ri-zi rice vinegar

–apo vini –από βύνη
a-po vi-ni malt vinegar

o ksifias ο ξιφίας
o ksi-fi-as swordfish

–suvlaki –σουβλάκι
su-vla-ki swordfish nuggets drizzled with oil, lemon juice, oregano, salt and pepper, threaded onto wooden skewers with tomato and capsicum pieces, and chargrilled

i ksilini spatula η ξύλινη σπάτουλα
i ksi-li-ni spa-tu-la wooden spatula

ksinohondros ξινόχοντρος
ksi-no-hon-dros ground wheat cooked in sour milk and dried

to ksinomavro το ξινόμαυρο
to ksi-no-ma-vro red grape variety (see Grape Varieties in Drinks)

i ksinomizithra η ξινομυζήθρα
i ksi-no-mi-zi-thra savoury **mizithra**

ksinos ξινός
ksi-nos sour

to ksiro dhamaskino το ξηρό δαμάσκηνο *to ksi-ro dha-ma-ski-no* prune

i ksobliastres οι ξομπλιάστρες
i kso-bli-a-stres village women who specialise in the decorating of special festival breads (see also **psomya me anaghlifes diakozmisis**)

to kteni (thalasino) το κτένι (θαλασσινό) *to kte-ni (tha-la-si-no)* scallop

to kufeto το κουφέτο
to ku-fe-to sugared almonds presented at weddings and christenings – a symbol of good fortune and fertility. Legend says if you put two almonds under your pillow you'll dream of who you'll marry. Almond praline shared by bride and groom at wedding ceremony. (Santorini)

ta kukunarya τα κουκουνάρια
ta ku-ku-nar-ya pine nuts

i kukuvaya η κουκουβάγια
i ku-ku-va-ya rusk salad; also called
paksimadya salata

ta kukya τα κουκιά
ta ku-kya broad beans

–ksera vrasta –ξερά βραστά
kse-ra vra-sta broad beans boiled in
water and lemon juice and served with
oil, dill and onion rings

–me –με
aghriangginares αγριαγκινάρες
me a-ghri-ang-gi-na-res broad beans
with artichokes *(see the recipe)*

to kulukopsomo το κουλουκόψωμο
to ku-lu-ko-pso-mo open rusk sandwich
(see also **paksimadya me domates
ke feta)**

ta kulurakya τα κουλουράκια
ta ku-lu-ra-kya cookies/biscuits/buns

–me petimezi –με πετιμέζι
me pe-ti-me-zi sweet buns made with
petimezi, cinnamon and spices

to kuluri το κουλούρι
to ku-lu-ri crisp sesame-coated bread
rings sold on streets and outside church
after Sunday mass; generic name for
circular rolls, buns and biscuits

ta kuluria τα κουλούρια
astipalitika αστυπαλίτικα
ta ku-lu-ri-a a-sti-pa-li-ti-ka the saffron
biscuits of Astypalea *(see* the recipe)

to kumkuat το κουμκουάτ
to kum-ku-at kumquat

–liker –λικέρ
li-ker kumquat liqueur (Corfu)

to kuneli το κουνέλι
to ku-ne-li rabbit

–krasato –κρασάτο
kra-sa-to rabbit casserole with red wine,
garlic and bay leaves

–me karidhi –με καρύδι
me ka-ri-dhi rabbit marinated in wine,
spices, celeriac, carrots and garlic, fried
and simmered in white wine infused
with coarsely ground walnuts

–me yaurti –με γιαούρτι
me ya-ur-ti rabbit marinated in lemon
juice and black pepper then baked with
a creamy egg and yoghurt sauce

–stifadho –στιφάδο
sti-fa-dho rabbit ragout spiced with
cloves, cinnamon, and cumin *(see also*
stifadho)

to kunupidhi το κουνουπίδι
to ku-nu-pi-dhi cauliflower

–tighanito –τηγανητό
ti-gha-ni-to lightly battered and
fried cauliflower

–tursi –τουρσί
tur-si pickled cauliflower

ta kupepia τα κουπέπια
ta ku-pe-pya **dolmadhes** made with
minced lamb and veal and served hot
with **avgholemono** sauce (Cyprus)

i kupes οι κούπες
i ku-pes deep-fried, cigar-shaped
purghuri pastries filled with mincemeat, onion and spices (Cyprus)

i kurambyedhes οι κουραμπιέδες
i ku-ra-mbye-dhes buttery almond
shortbread blanketed with icing sugar

to kurkuti το κουρκούτι
to kur-ku-ti batter

i kutala η κουτάλα
i ku-ta-la ladle

to kutalaki το κουταλάκι
to ku-ta-la-ki teaspoon

to kutali το κουτάλι
to ku-ta-li spoon

–supas –σούπας
su-pas soup spoon

–tu ghliku –του γλυκού
tu ghli-ku dessert spoon

tu kutyu του κουτιού
tu ku-tyu canned

to kuver το κουβέρ
to ku-ver cover charge

i kuzina η κουζίνα
i ku-zi-na kitchen

L

ta ladhadhika τα λαδάδικα
ta la-dha-dhi-ka popular eateries that
specialise in oil-based vegetable dishes
and casseroles

ladheros λαδερός
la-dhe-ros cooked in oil

to ladhi το λάδι
to la-dhi oil, nearly always referring to **eleoladho**

to ladhoksidho το λαδόξιδο
to la-dho-ksi-dho vinaigrette made with oil, vinegar, parsley, salt and pepper

to ladholemono το λαδολέμονο
to la-dho-le-mo-no thick dressing of oil beaten with lemon juice, salt and pepper

to ladhorighano το λαδορίγανο
to la-dho-ri-gha-no method of cooking with oil and oregano

to ladhotiri το λαδοτύρι
to la-dho-ti-ri (see Cheese in Staples & Specialities)

i laghana η λαγάνα
i la-gha-na long, flat oval loaf sprinkled with sesame seeds baked on the first day of the Lenten fast

o laghos ο λαγός
o la-ghos hare

–stifadho –στιφάδο
sti-fa-dho hare ragout spiced with cumin and cloves, sometimes cooked in its own blood but more usually marinated in vinegar prior to cooking (see also **stifadho**)

to laghoto το λαγωτό
to la-gho-to kefallonian ragout of hare (see the recipe)

ta lahana τα λάχανα
ta la-ha-na seasonal wild greens (see also **horta**)

–me lardhi –με λαρδί
me lar-dhi casserole of seasonal greens and fatty bacon (Mykonos)

ta lahanika τα λαχανικά
ta la-ha-ni-ka vegetables

–tis thalasas –της θάλασσας
tis tha-la-sas sea vegetables

to lahano το λάχανο
to la-ha-no cabbage

–kokinisto –κοκκινιστό
ko-ki-ni-sto cabbage stewed with tomatoes, onions, parsley, dill and paprika (Corfu)

–me kima –με κιμά
me ki-ma cabbage braised with onions, mincemeat and tomatoes, and finished with fresh butter (Chios)

i lahanodolmadhes οι λάχανο-ν τολμάδες
i la-ha-no-dol-ma-dhes (see **dolmadhes me lahanika**)

i lahanosalata η λάχανοσαλάτα
i la-ha-no-sa-la-ta shredded white cabbage sprinkled with oil, lemon juice and salt

to lahanozumo το λαχανόζουμο
to la-ha-no-zu-mo vegetable stock

i laiki aghora η λαϊκή αγορά
i la-i-ki a-gho-ra an open-air produce market

i lakerdha η λακέρδα
i la-ker-dha pickled bonito/tuna

to lardhi το λαρδί
to lar-dhi lard

to lavraki το λαβράκι
to la-vra-ki sea bass

–sto alati –στο αλάτι
sto a-la-ti whole sea bass buried in salt and baked. The salt-encrusted skin is slit and the flesh is eaten from the bone with a dressing of oil and lemon juice.

lefkos λευκός
le-fkos white (see also **krasi**)

i lemonadha η λεμονάδα
i le-mo-na-dha lemonade

lemonatos λεμονάτος
le-mo-na-tos method of cooking with oil and lemon juice

to lemoni το λεμόνι
to le-mo-ni lemon

o lemos ο λαιμός
o le-mos neck

ligho psimenos λίγο ψημένος
li-gho psi-me-nos rare (cooked)

to liker το λικέρ
to li-ker liqueur

o likurinos ο λικουρίνος
o li-ku-ri-nos smoked grey mullet (Northern Greece)

i lima ya mahyerya η λίμα για μαχαίρια
i li-ma ya ma-hye-rya sharpening stone

to lipos το λίπος
to li-pos grease

to lithrini το λιθρίνι
to li-thri-ni sea bream; also called **melanuri** and **faghri**

o logharyazmos ο λογαριασμός
o lo-ghar-yaz-mos bill

ta lukanika τα λουκάνικα
ta lu-ka-ni-ka pork sausages seasoned with coriander, orange peel and garlic; generic terminology for sausages and frankfurters

i lukanopites οι λουκανόπιτες
i lu-ka-no-pi-tes filo-wrapped sausages

i lukumadhes οι λουκουμάδες
i lu-ku-ma-dhes rosette-shaped, light-as-air doughnuts served hot with honey and cinnamon

to lukumadhiko το λουκουμάδικο
to lu-ku-ma-dhi-ko shop that sells **lukumadhes**

to lukumi το λουκούμι
to lu-ku-mi Turkish delight. Most Turkish delight comes from Syros where they say Turks pinched the idea.

ta lukumya τα λουκούμια
ta lu-ku-mya wedding shortbread (Cyprus)

i lundza η λούντζα
i lun-dza spicy ham made from cured smoked pork fillet (Cyprus, Cyclades)

–me halumi –με χαλούμι
me ha-lu-mi grilled ham topped with melted **halumi** (Cyprus)

ta luvya τα λουβιά
ta lu-vya black-eyed peas; also called **mavromatika fasolya**

–me lahana –με λάχανα
me la-ha-na warm salad of black-eyed peas and seasonal greens with oil and lemon dressing (Cyprus)

o luzes ο λούζες
o lu-zes salted fillet of pork stuffed into thick pig's intestine and sun-dried (Mykonos)

lyastos λιαστός
lya-stos sun dried

to lyatiko το λιάτικο
to lya-ti-ko red grape variety (*see* Grape Varieties in Drinks)

M

i madera η μαδέρα
i ma-de-ra madeira

to mahalepi το μαχαλεπί
to ma-ha-le-pi creamy custard pudding swimming in rose-water syrup (Cyprus)

to mahlepi το μαχλέπι
to ma-hle-pi pungent bitter-sweet black cherry pips used for spicing breads and stuffings

to mahyeri το μαχαίρι
to ma-hye-ri knife

–kreatos –κρέατος
kre-a-tos carving knife

–prionoto –πριονωτό
pri-o-no-to serrated knife

–kreatos –κρέατος
kre-a-tos carving knife

–prionoto –πριονωτό
pri-o-no-to serrated knife

–psomyu –ψωμιού
pso-myu bread knife

–vutiru –βουτύρου
vu-ti-ru butter knife

–ya ksekokalizma –για ξεκοκάλισμα
ya kse-ko-ka-li-zma boning/paring knife

ta mahyeropiruna τα μαχαιροπίρουνα
ta ma-hye-ro-pi-ru-na cutlery

o maidanos ο μαϊντανός
o ma-i-da-nos parsley

i makaronadha η μακαρονάδα
i ma-ka-ro-na-dha generic term for spaghetti dish

ta makaronya τα μακαρόνια
ta ma-ka-ro-nya spaghetti/macaroni

–me kima –με κιμά
me ki-ma **makaronya** with a sauce of mincemeat, tomatoes, onions and red wine

–me saltsa –με σάλτσα
me sal-tsa **makaronya** with tomato, onion and oregano sauce

–me vutiro –με βούτυρο
ke tiri και τυρί
me vu-ti-ro ke ti-ri **makaronya** with butter sauce and grated cheese

–sto furno –στο φούρνο
sto fur-no **makaronya** baked in cheese and butter sauce

to mandarini το μανταρίνι
to man-da-ri-ni mandarin

i mandhilarya η μανδηλαριά
i man-dhi-lar-ya red grape variety (*see* Grape Varieties in Drinks)

to mandi το μαντί
to man-di small pasta pockets filled with mincemeat, cooked in meat broth seasoned with capsicum and served with a yoghurt and garlic sauce. Traditionally cooked in a buttered **tapsi**. (Northern Greece)

i mandzurana η μαντζουράνα
i man-dzu-ra-na marjoram

to mango το μάνγκο
to man-go mango

ta manitaria τα μανιτάρια
ta ma-ni-ta-ri-a mushrooms

–marinata –μαρινάτα
ma-ri-na-ta marinated mushrooms

–tighanita –τηγανητά
ti-gha-ni-ta fried mushrooms

to manuri το μανούρι
to ma-nu-ri (*see* Cheese in Staples & Specialities)

to maratho· το μάραθο
to ma-ra-tho fennel

–me uzo supa –με ούζο σούπα
me u-zo su-pa ouzo & fennel soup (*see* the recipe)

i marengga η μαρέγγα
i ma-reng-ga meringue

i maridha η μαρίδα
pikandiki πικάντικη
i ma-ri-dha pi-kan-di-ki whitebait, tomato and mint fritters (Rhodes)

i maridhes οι μαρίδες
i ma-ri-dhes whitebait

–lyastes –λιαστές
lya-stes whitebait seasoned with oregano and strung out to dry then chargrilled and served with oil and lemon juice

–tighanites –τηγανητές
ti-gha-ni-tes whitebait rolled in flour and deep fried until crisp, served with lemon wedges

marinaro μαρινάρω
ma-ri-na-ro to marinate

marinatos μαρινάτος
ma-ri-na-tos method of marinating meat or fish prior to cooking

i marmeladha η μαρμελάδα
i mar-me-la-dha jam/conserve

–apo –από
esperidhoidhi εσπεριδοειδή
a-po e-spe-ri-dho-i-dhi marmalade

to maruli το μαρούλι
to ma-ru-li lettuce

–salata –σαλάτα
sa-la-ta lettuce salad

i masticha η μαστίχα
i ma-sti-ha mastic; pale gold, semi-translucent crystallised resin from the mastic bush. Eaten as chewing gum and used as a flavouring for desserts, breads and sweets. (Chios)

i mavrodhafni η Μαυροδάφνη
i ma-vro-dhaf-ni sweet dessert wine with intense purple colour; red grape variety (*see* Grape Varieties in Drinks)

ta mavromatika τα μαυρομάτικα
fasolya φασόλια
ta ma-vro-ma-ti-ka fa-so-lya black-eyed peas; also called **luvya**

–me horta –με χόρτα
me hor-ta black-eyed peas stewed with seasonal greens, onions, tomatoes, parsley, mint and garlic (Crete)

i maya η μαγιά
i ma-ya yeast

o mayiras ο μάγειρας
o ma-yi-ras chef

i mayiritsa η μαγειρίτσα
i ma-yi-ri-tsa lamb's offal soup thickened with rice and **avgholemono**. Similar to **patsas**. Eaten to celebrate the end of Lent.

i mayoneza η μαγιονέζα
i ma-yo-ne-za mayonnaise

me με
me with

i megharitiki η μεγαρίτικη
i me-gha-ri-ti-ki olive grown in Attica, near Athens, named after the city of Megara

to melanuri το μελανούρι
to me-la-nu-ri sea bream; also called **lithrini** and **faghri**

to meli το μέλι
to me-li honey

–me ksirus karpus –με ξηρούς καρπούς
me ksi-rus kar-pus toothsome concoction of honey poured over shelled walnuts and/or almonds offered as a welcome treat for visitors, eaten by bridal couple at weddings; also jars of honey embedded with nuts.

i melidzanes οι μελιτζάνες
i me-li-dza-nes eggplant

–sto furno –στο φούρνο
sto fur-no sliced eggplant fried with potatoes, and baked with tomatoes, cumin, parsley and feta

–tighanites –τηγανητές
ti-gha-ni-tes (*see* **kolokithakya tighanita**)

i melidzanosalata η μελιτζανοσαλάτα
i me-li-dza-no-sa-la-ta smoky puree of grilled mashed eggplant, onion, garlic, oil and lemon

to melitini το μελιτίνι
to me-li-ti-ni golden pastry tarts filled with fresh **tirovolya**, eggs, sugar and masticha. Traditionally eaten at Easter.

to melomakarono το μελομακάρονο
to me-lo-ma-ka-ro-no (*see* **finikia**)

i melopita η μελόπιτα
i me-lo-pi-ta cheesecake made with **mizithra** and clear honey in a short-crust pastry

i meridha η μερίδα
i me-ri-dha serve

to mesimeriano το μεσημεριανό
to me-si-me-ri-a-no lunch

metaksa Μεταξά
me-ta-ksa Greek brandy, comes in 3-, 5- and 7-star varieties

to metaliko nero το μεταλλικό νερό
to me-ta-li-ko ne-ro mineral water

metria psimenos μέτρια ψημένος
me-tri-a psi-me-nos medium (cooked)

to metsovone kapnisto το Μετσοβόνε καπνιστό *to me-tso-vo-ne ka-pni-sto* (*see* Cheese in Staples & Specialities)

to mezedhaki το μεζεδάκι
to me-ze-dha-ki tasty morsels served with **ouzo**. Favourites include olives, salted cucumber slices, feta, salted anchovies, **tsiros** and **keftedhakya**.

i mezedhes οι μεζέδες
i me-ze-dhes (*see* **mezes**)

to mezedhopolio το μεζεδοπωλείο
to me-ze-dho-po-li-o restaurant specialising in **mezedhes**

o mezes ο μεζές
o me-zes 'small dish', customary way of eating at tavernas and **mezedhopolio** where a range of dishes are shared by guests/friends

ta midia τα μύδια
ta mi-di-a mussels

–krasata –κρασάτα
kra-sa-ta mussels poached with finely shredded carrots, leeks and onions in white wine

–tighanita –τηγανητά
ti-gha-ni-ta mussels shucked, lightly battered, fried in hot oil and served with a garlic yoghurt sauce

–yemista –γεμιστά
ye-mi-sta mussels stuffed with rice, onions and parsley, and slow-simmered in fish stock, tomato puree and white wine. Sometimes pine nuts and currants are added to the stuffing.

i mihani kreatos η μηχανή κρέατος
i mi-ha-ni kre-a-tos mincer

o militis inos ο μηλίτης οίνος
o mi-li-tis i-nos cider

to milo το μήλο
to mi-lo apple

ta milopitakya τα μηλοπιτάκια
ta mi-lo-pi-ta-kya crescent-shaped, sugar-dusted apple and walnut pies

o milos tu kafe ο μύλος του καφέ
o mi-los tu ka-fe coffee grinder

i mithos η Μύθος
i mi-thos Mythos (beer)

i mizithra η μυζήθρα
i mi-zi-thra soft mild ricotta-like cheese made from sheep's or goat's milk. Can be sweet or savoury. Distinguished by woven markings made by the wicker baskets in which the cheese sets.

i mizithropites οι μυζηθρόπιτες
i mi-zi-thro-pi-tes delicate deep-fried pies made with **mizithra** (Crete)

i monemvasya η μονεμβασιά
i mo-nem-vas-ya white grape variety (*see* Grape Varieties in Drinks)

to moshari το μοσχάρι
to mo-sha-ri veal (more often than not tender yearling beef)

–katsarolas me araka –κατσαρόλας με αρακά
ka-tsa-ro-las me a-ra-ka veal stewed with fresh peas in white wine and thyme

–kokinisto me makaronya –κοκκινιστό με μακαρόνια
ko-ki-ni-sto me ma-ka-ro-nya veal stewed with small crushed tomatoes and served with spaghetti and grated **kefalotiri**

–psito –ψητό
psi-to boned and rolled leg of veal rubbed with lemon juice, pepper and salt and pot-roasted with onion, tomatoes and wine

–stifadho –στιφάδο
sti-fa-dho veal ragout with garlic, peppercorns and bay leaves

to moshato το μοσχάτο
to mo-sha-to white grape variety (*see* Grape Varieties in Drinks)

–aleksandhrias –Αλεξανδρίας
to mo-sha-to a-le-ksan-dhri-as white grape variety (*see* Grape Varieties in Drinks)

to moshokaridho το μοσχοκάρυδο
to mo-sho-ka-ri-dho nutmeg

o moussakas ο μουσακά
o mu-sa-kas (*see* musakas)

ta mukendra τα μουκέντρα
ta mu-ken-dra stewed lentils and rice garnished with fried onion rings and wrinkled black olives (Cyprus)

ta mura τα μούρα
ta mu-ra mulberries; generic term for berries

i muruna η μουρούνα
i mu-ru-na sturgeon

o musakas ο μουσακάς
o mu-sa-kas thick-sliced eggplant and mincemeat (usually a mix of lamb and veal sauteed with tomatoes, white wine and onions) arranged in layers, topped with bechamel and baked. Potato or grated **kefalotiri** layers can be added, or zucchini can be substituted for the eggplant.

–me angginares –με αγγινάρες
me ang-gi-na-res alternating layers of minced veal and artichoke hearts

muskevo μουσκεύω
mu-ske-vo steep

to musli το μούσλι
to mu-sli muesli

i mustalevria η μουσταλευριά
i mu-sta-le-vri-a dark gelatinous pudding made from boiled grape must thickened with flour, poured onto plates and sprinkled with cinnamon, sesame seeds and crushed nuts

i mustardha η μουστάρδα
i mu-star-dha mustard

to musto το μούστο
to mu-sto grape must collected from crushed wine grapes during the harvest

–kulura –κουλούρα
ku-lu-ra hard, turban-shaped grape must buns

to muzmulo το μούσμουλα
to mu-zmu-la loquat

ta myala τα μυαλά
ta mya-la brains

–arnisia   –αρνίσια
ladholemono   λαδολέμονο
ar-ni-si-a la-dho-le-mo-no lamb's brains poached in water and vinegar, seasoned with black pepper and served with oil and lemon sauce

–tighanita   –τηγανητά
ti-gha-ni-ta fried brains

N

to nefro   το νεφρό
to ne-fro kidney

i negoska   η νεγκόσκα
i ne-go-ska red grape variety (*see* Grape Varieties in Drinks)

i nerambules   οι νεράμπουλες
i ne-ra-mbu-les yellow plums

to nerandzaki   το νεραντζάκι
ghliko   γλυκό
to ne-ran-dza-ki ghli-ko preserved small bitter green oranges, type of **ghlika kutalyu**

i nerati   η νεράτη
i ne-ra-ti variety of **tiropita** consisting of a scoop of **mizithra** nestled in a ball of dough, pressed into an oiled pan and fried (Crete)

to nero   το νερό
to ne-ro water

–emfialomeno   –εμφιαλωμένο
em-fi-a-lo-me-no bottled water

–fresko   –φρέσκο
fre-sko fresh water

–horis anthrakiko –χωρίς ανθρακικό
ho-ris an-thra-ki-ko still water

–metaliko   –μεταλλικό
me-ta-li-ko mineral water

–tiz vrisis   –της βρύσης
tiz vri-sis tap

to nerokardhamo   το νεροκάρδαμο
to ne-ro-kar-dha-mo watercress

to neroli   το νερόλι
to ne-ro-li essential oil distilled from orange blossoms

–nero   –νερό
ne-ro fragrant orange flower water collected from the distillation of **neroli**. Used in cakes, pastries and sweets.

o nes kafes   ο Νες Καφές
o nes ka-fes instant coffee

to nihaki   το νυχάκι
to ni-ha-ki kalamata table olive from the Peloponnese regions of Messenia and Laconia

to nihterino   το νυχτερινό
kendro   κέντρο
to ni-hte-ri-no ken-dro restaurant where Greeks have a night out: dine, smash plates and dance to live music

ta nistisima   τα νηστήσιμα
ta ni-sti-si-ma Lenten fasting food, meat, dairy products and sea creatures which bleed are taboo although cephalopods like octopus and crustaceans are acceptable

to numbulo   το νουμπουλό
to num-bu-lo bacon-flavoured sausage (Corfu)

O

i odhondoghlifidha η οδοντογλυφίδα
i o-dhon-do-ghli-fi-dha toothpick

i ofti salata   η οφτή σαλάτα
i o-fti sa-la-ta grilled salad of potatoes, onions and **stafidholyes** foil-wrapped and chargrilled (Crete)

ofto   οφτό
o-fto method of spit-roasting meat over charcoal pits – once practised by mountain shepherds and resistance-fighters but rarely seen today (Crete)

i omadyes   οι ομαδιές
i o-ma-dyes fragrant offal sausage made from pig's intestine stuffed with chopped pig's innards, rice, walnuts, pistachios, raisins, cinnamon and orange peel. A Christmas dish dating back to Byzantine days. (Crete)

i omeleta   η ομελέτα
i o-me-le-ta omelette

ta orektika   τα ορεκτικά
ta o-re-kti-ka appetisers

orghanikos   οργανικός
or-gha-ni-kos organic

orimos   ώριμος
o-ri-mos ripe

to ortiki   το ορτύκι
  to or-ti-ki quail
–sti shara   –στη κάρα
  sti sha-ra chargrilled marinated quail
ta ospria   τα όσπρια
  ta o-spri-a legumes/pulses
ta ostrakoidhi   τα οστρακοειδή
  ta o-stra-ko-i-dhi shellfish
ouzeri   ουζερί
  u-ze-ri bar or taverna which serves
  ouzo and **mezedhakya**
to ouzo   το ούζο
  to u-zo clear spirit distilled from grape
  seeds, stems and skins with a strong
  aniseed flavour. Taken neat or with ice.

P

o paghos   ο πάγος
  o pa-ghos ice
to paghoto   το παγωτό
  to pa-gho-to ice cream
ta paidhakia   τα παϊδάκια
  ta pa-i-dha-kya chops/cutlets
ta paksimadya   τα παξιμάδια
  ta pa-ksi-ma-dya hard rusks (traditionally double-baked for winter storage)
  eaten slightly moistened with water at
  meal times. Nowadays both wheat and
  barley varieties are common unlike earlier years when barley was the staple.
  Currently enjoying a renaissance.
–me domates   –με ντομάτες
  ke feta   και φέτα
  me do-ma-tes ke fe-ta paksimadya moistened with water or tomato juice and
  topped with sliced tomatoes, feta,
  oregano, oil, salt and pepper. Very
  popular snack or light lunch; also called
  kulukopsomo
–salata   –σαλάτα
  sa-la-ta paksimadya broken into pieces,
  moistened with water and sprinkled
  with diced tomatoes, crumbled **feta** or
  ksinomizithra, oregano, oil, salt and
  pepper; also called **kukuvaya**

i palamidha   η παλαμίδα
  i pa-la-mi-dha bonito; tunny fish (a
  variety of tuna)
–psiti me horta   –ψητή με χόρτα
  psi-ti me hor-ta marinated bonito
  steaks seared with bay leaves, paprika
  and chopped greens, and finished with
  a garlic and vinegar sauce
ta palikaria   τα παλικάρια
  ta pa-li-ka-ri-a mix of legumes and
  grains boiled and tossed with oil,
  onions and dill
to pandopolio   το παντοπωλείο
  to pan-do-po-li-o grocery
pandremeni   παντρεμένοι
  pan-dre-me-ni beans that have been
  'married' with other foods. It might be
  wed to rice, betrothed to meat, conjoined with tomatoes.
to pandzari   το παντζάρι
  to pan-dza-ri beetroot
–salata   –σαλάτα
  sa-la-ta boiled thickly sliced beetroot
  (or when available baby beets with leafy
  green tops) dressed with vinaigrette
  and served with **skordhalya**
pane   πανέ
  pa-ne crumbed and fried
i pantseta   η παντσέττα
  i pan-tse-ta pancetta
–yemisti sto   –γεμιστή στο
  furno   φούρνο
  ye-mi-sti sto fur-no Italian-inspired dish
  of pig's stomach stuffed with **kefalotiri**
  or **parmesan**, garlic, onions and
  oregano, basted with oil, wine and
  lemon juice and baked with potatoes
  (Zakynthos)
i paparuna   η παπαρούνα
  i pa-pa-ru-na poppy
i paprika   η πάπρικα
  i pa-pri-ka paprika
i papules   οι παπούλες
  i pa-pu-les vetchling, semi-bitter salad
  green with spindly antenna-tipped
  leaves often eaten raw with oil and
  vinegar dressing

to paputsaki το παπουτσάκι
to pa-pu-tsa-ki 'little shoe', baby egg-plant split lengthwise, stuffed with wine-simmered minced lamb and parsley (and sometimes crushed tomato), topped with bechamel sauce and baked. Often the mince mixture includes cinnamon and nutmeg.

i papya η πάπια
i pa-pya duck

–me saltsa rodhyu –με σάλτσα ροδιού
me sal-tsa ro-dhyu fried duck breasts served with sauce made from pomegranate seeds, lemon juice, duck stock and walnuts (Northern Greece)

–salmi –σαλμί
sal-mi whole duck seared in oil, then jointed and cooked in its own juices, wine, orange juice and onions

i paradhosiaki psarotaverna η παρα δοσιακή ψαροταβέρνα
i pa-ra-dho-si-a-ki psa-ro-ta-ver-na tavernas serving fish

i parmezana η παρμεζάνα
i par-me-za-na parmesan

o pasatembos ο πασατέμπος
o pa-sa-te-mbos 'pass the time', roasted pumpkin seeds sold as a snack

i pasta η πάστα
i pa-sta gateau

to pasteli το παστέλι
to pa-ste-li sweet honey and sesame seed wafers. On Andros they're studded with chopped walnuts and scented with orange flower water.

i pastitsadha η παστιτσάδα
i pa-sti-tsa-dha pot-roasted veal with tomato, red wine, cloves, cinnamon and paprika. Thick spaghetti or macaroni is cooked with the meat to absorb the flavours. Sometimes served as a split meal with the pasta as an entree. (Corfu)

to pastitsio το παστίτσιο
to pa-sti-tsi-o layers of buttery macaroni and seasoned minced lamb topped with white sauce and grated **kefalotiri**, and baked.

pastos παστός
pa-stos salted and dried

o pasturmas ο παστουρμάς
o pa-stur-mas spicy dried ox meat salted and spiced with garlic and pepper. Looks like slab bacon. Originally imported from Turkey where it was made with lean camel meat.

i patates οι πατάτες
i pa-ta-tes potatoes

–keftedhes –κεφτέδες
ke-fte-dhes fried potato, feta and parsley rissoles

–lemonates –λεμονάτες
le-mo-na-tes potatoes roasted with oil, lemon juice, oregano, salt and pepper

–pure –πουρέ
pu-re mashed

–sto furno –στο φούρνο
sto fur-no potatoes baked or roasted with oil, salt and oregano

–tighanites –τηγανητές
ti-gha-ni-tes fried potato slices

–yahni –γιαχνί
ya-hni potatoes fried and stewed with tomatoes, onions and oregano

i patatosalata η πατατοσαλάτα
i pa-ta-to-sa-la-ta potato salad

i patatu η πατατού
i pa-ta-tu baked mashed potato pie (Cyclades)

to patsadhiko το πατσάδικο
to pa-tsa-dhi-ko shop specialising in tripe soup (Northern Greece)

o patsas ο πατσάς
o pa-tsas tripe; rich-textured and surprisingly delicate-flavoured soup made with the stomach of a young lamb (and often the trotters) finished with **avgholemono**

patudha πατούδα
pa-tu-dha half-moon pastries filled with walnuts, almonds and cinnamon, and baked. Sprinkled with orange flower water and dredged in icing sugar. (Crete)

to peinirli   το πεϊνιρλί
to pe-i-nir-li boat-shaped, savoury pastries with a variety of fillings such as mincemeat, feta, ham and egg, and **pasturmas**

to pekan   το πεκάν
to pe-kan pecan

to peponi   το πεπόνι
to pe-po-ni melon/canteloupe

i perdhikes   οι πέρδικες
i per-dhi-kes partridges

—me elyes   —με ελιές
ke selino   και σέλινο
me e-lyes ke se-li-no partridges browned in butter, and simmered in their own juices with green olives, sliced celery and tomatoes

—yemistes   —γεμιστές
ye-mi-stes roasted partridges stuffed with a mixture of rice, tomatoes, parsley, grated **kefaloghraviera**, salt, pepper and lemon juice (Lefkada)

to periptero   το περίπτερο
to pe-ri-pte-ro kiosk

to peristeri   το περιστέρι
to pe-ri-ste-ri pigeon

i perka   η πέρκα
i per-ka sea perch

i pestrofa   η πέστροφα
i pe-stro-fa trout

i petalidhes   οι πεταλίδες
i pe-ta-li-dhes limpets

—me thalasinus   —με θαλασσινούς
hohlius   χοχλιούς
me tha-la-si-nus ho-hli-us limpets and sea snails fresh from the rocks shaken with salt, lemon juice and oregano in an oiled pan, then stewed with ripe tomatoes, onions and black pepper (Lesvos)

to petimezi   το πετιμέζι
to pe-ti-me-zi syrup made from unfermented grape juice. Used to flavour rolls, cakes and sweets. When mixed with cold water makes a refreshing drink.

to petropsaro   το πετρόψαρο
to pe-tro-psa-ro rockfish

i petseta   η πετσέτα
i pe-tse-ta napkin

pikandikos   πικάντικος
pi-kan-di-kos piquant/savoury

i pikilia   η ποικιλία
i pi-ki-li-a assortment/variety

to piknik   το πίκνικ
to pik-nik picnic

pikros   πικρός
pi-kros bitter

to pilafi   το πιλάφι
to pi-la-fi rice and stock simmered in a covered pan until all the liquid is absorbed – most often cooked to a firm-textured creamy consistency. Served plain to complement boiled meat or chicken which provide the cooking stock for the rice.

—me domates   —με ντομάτες
me do-ma-tes pilafi with the addition of tomatoes, meat stock, garlic, parsley, salt and pepper

—me gharidhes   —με γαρίδες
me gha-ri-dhes pilafi with prawns, onions and oregano

—me midhya   —με μύδια
me mi-dhya pilafi with fresh mussels, onions and white wine

—me perdhikia   —με περδίκια
me per-dhi-ki-a pilafi with partridge, tomato, onion and cloves (Kefallonia)

i pinnes   οι πίνες
i pi-nes razor clams

to piperi   το πιπέρι
to pi-per-i black pepper

i piperoriza   η πιπερόριζα
i pi-pe-ro-ri-za ginger

i piperyes   οι πιπεριές
i pi-per-yes peppers/capsicums

—florinis   —Φλωρίνης
flo-ri-nis big bright red capsicums from Florina

—kafteres   —καυτερές
ka-fte-res fiery, long and lean green or red capsicums

—ladhoksidho   —λαδόξιδο
la-dho-ksi-dho capsicums roasted and then skinned and drizzled with oil and vinegar

–me tiri   –με τυρί
me ti-ri slender pale green capsicums stuffed with **ghalotiri** or **manuri** and baked or fried

–tighanites   –τηγανητές
ti-gha-ni-tes capsicums fried and dressed with salt and vinegar

–tursi   –τουρσί
tur-si pickled capsicums

to piroski   το πιροσκί
to pi-ro-ski deep-fried, dough-wrapped sausage roll

to piruni   το πιρούνι
to pi-ru-ni fork

i pita   η πίτα
i pi-ta pie, large pies and flans cut into squares, wedges or diamonds and smaller triangular or crescent-shaped pies. Filo is the most common pastry used but there are also dishes that use shortcrust or puff pastry. **Tiropita**, **spanakopita**, and **kreatopita** are popular versions. Flat doughy circular bread seared on grill until golden. Mainly used for wrapping **suvlaki** and **yiros**.

ta pitsunya   τα πιτσούνια
ta pi-tsu-nya squab; love-bird; any tiny bird used for cooking

–krasata   –κρασάτα
kra-sa-ta baby squabs doused in red wine, tomato pulp, cinnamon and cloves and braised

–me kukunarya   –με κουκουναριά
me ku-ku-na-rya squab that has been rubbed with salt, pepper and nutmeg, braised with oil, oregano and pine nuts, ignited with brandy, splashed with **retsina** and dressed with a garlic cream sauce (Northern Greece)

–me kukya   –με κουκιά
me ku-kya stewed squab and fresh broad beans cooked in chicken stock, white wine, dill, garlic and lots of black pepper

to pituro   το πίτουρο
to pi-tu-ro bran

plaki   πλακί
pla-ki method of baking or braising with tomatoes, onion, garlic and parsley. May also include carrots, celery, peppers or leek.

o plastis zimis   ο πλάστης ζύμης
o pla-stis zi-mis rolling pin

to plighuri   το πλιγούρι
to pli-ghu-ri cracked wheat, burghul; also called **purghuri**

–vromis   –βρώμης
vro-mis oatmeal

ta podharakya   τα ποδαράκια
ta po-dha-ra-kya trotters

–arnisia   –αρνίσια
ar-ni-si-a thick sticky fricassee made from boiled lamb's trotters browned in butter and garlic and roasted, then cooked in own stock and finished with egg and lemon sauce. Served on slices of fried bread.

to porto   το πόρτο
to por-to port

i portokaladha   η πορτοκαλάδα
i por-to-ka-la-dha orange soft drink

to portokali   το πορτοκάλι
to por-to-ka-li orange

–ghliko   –γλυκό
ghli-ko preserved orange segments; the preserved orange peel rolls from thick-skinned oranges, type of **ghlika kutalyu**

i posotita   η ποσότητα
(to poso)   (το ποσό)
i po-so-ti-ta (to po-so) amount/quantity, often refers to the number of dishes ordered at a taverna

to poto   το ποτό
to po-to drinks; the word **potas** on a menu usually means spirits

ta prasa   τα πράσα
ta pra-sa leeks

–alevrolemono   –αλευρολέμονο
a-lev-ro-le-mo-no braised leeks in lemony sauce

–me dhamaskina   –με δαμάσκηνα
me dha-ma-ski-na leeks and prunes sprinkled with cinnamon and nutmeg and sauteed with chopped tomatoes and baby onions

–me rizi   –με ρύζι
me ri-zi leeks and celery simmered with rice, water and crushed tomatoes

ta prasakia   τα πρασάκια
me patates   με πατάτες
ta pra-sa-ki-a me pa-ta-tes sweet young leeks and sliced potatoes braised or baked in butter with water or chicken stock, onions, oregano and parsley

i prasopita   η πρασόπιτα
i pra-so-pi-ta pie made with braised leeks, feta, **mizithra** and skim milk (Western Greece)

to proino   το πρωινό
to pro-i-no breakfast

to prosforo   το πρόσφορο
to pros-fo-ro a flat, circular church-offering bread stamped with a sacred seal before baking

to proto pyato   το πρώτο πιάτο
to pro-to pya-to first course

to provio kreas   το πρόβειο κρέας
to pro-vi-o kre-as mutton

to psalidhi   το ψαλίδι
to psa-li-dhi scissors

to psari   το ψάρι
to psa-ri fish

–marinato   –μαρινάτο
ma-ri-na-to small whole fish coated with seasoned flour, fried until golden and finished in the pan with a piquant sauce of garlic, rosemary and vinegar; also called **psari savori**

–plaki   –πλακί
pla-ki whole fish basted with oil, lemon and parsley, and baked on a bed of chopped tomatoes and onions.

–savori   –σαβόρι
sa-vo-ri see **psari marinato**

–spetsioto   –Σπετσιώτο
spe-tsi-o-to fragrant whole fish or fish steaks baked with peeled and chopped tomatoes, garlic, toasted bread crumbs and white wine (Spetses)

–sti shara   –στη σχάρα
sti sha-ra whole fish chargrilled and dressed with oil and lemon juice

–sto furno   –στο φούρνο
ladhorighani   λαδορίγανη
sto fur-no la-dho-ri-gha-ni sliced fish and narrow potato wedges sprinkled with salt, pepper and oregano, baked in a broth of oil, water and lemon juice

–tighanito   –τηγανητό
ti-gha-ni-to battered and fried fish

–vrasto me   –βραστό με
lahanika   λαχανικά
vra-sto me la-ha-ni-ka whole fish poached with potatoes, baby onions, zucchini, carrots and celery. The broth is often strained, thickened with **avgholemono** and served with (or before) the fish and vegetables.

i psarokeftedhes   οι ψαροκεφτέδες
i psa-ro-ke-fte-dhes fried fish rissoles

to psaronefri   το ψαρονέφρι
to psa-ro-ne-fri superior quality pork fillet steak

i psarosupa   η ψαρόσουπα
i psa-ro-su-pa fish soup thickened with rice and **avgholemono**

i psarotaverna   η ψαροταβέρνα
i psa-ro-ta-ver-na a taverna that specialises in fish

to psarozumo   το ψαρόζουμο
to psa-ro-zu-mo fish stock

psino   ψήνω
psi-no bake

–stin katsarola   –στην κατσαρόλα
stin ka-tsa-ro-la braise

i psistarya   η ψησταριά
i psi-star-ya eatery specialising in char-grilled or spit-roasted meats

psitos   ψητός
psi-tos method of roasting chicken, meat and fish. Also an all-purpose term for grilling, baking and barbecuing.

to psomi   το ψωμί
to pso-mi bread

ta psomya me   τα ψωμιά με
anaghlifes   ανάγλυφες
diakozmisis   διακοσμήσεις
ta pso-mya me a-na-ghli-fes di-a-ko-zmi-sis breads (usually made with doughs of different colours) with

intricate inlaid decorations prepared for festivals, baptisms, weddings and engagements (*see also* **ksobliastres**)

ta pulerika τα πουλερικά
ta pu-le-ri-ka poultry

to puli το πουλί
to pu-li bird

pupe πούπαι
pu-pe blood sausage (Thessaly)

i purandza η πουράντζα
i pu-ran-dza borage

to purbuar το πουρμπουάρ
to pur-bu-ar tip (service)

pure πουρέ
pu-re puree

to purghuri το πουργούρι
to pur-ghu-ri cracked wheat, burghul (Cyprus)

–pilafi –πιλάφι
pi-la-fi cracked wheat, fried onions and vermicelli simmered in chicken stock until liquid is absorbed

to pyato το πιάτο
to pya-to plate

R

to radhiki το ραδίκι
to ra-dhi-ki chicory; term used for common varieties of **horta**

–salata –σαλάτα
sa-la-ta spring salad of young dandelion leaves splashed with oil and lemon

ta rafiolia τα ραφιόλια
ta ra-fi-o-li-a sweet half-moon filo pastries stuffed with **mizithra**, eggs, cinnamon, orange rind and **ouzo** (Cyclades)

to raki το ρακί
to ra-ki fiery village spirit made from grape waste like **ouzo** but without the aniseed taste. High in alcohol. Also known as **tsipuro** and **tsikudya**.

to rapani το ραπάνι
to ra-pa-ni radish

i ravioles οι ραβιόλες
i ra-vi-o-les pasta envelopes stuffed with a mixture of **halumi**, **aneri** and mint. Served with melted butter and grated cheese. (Cyprus)

to rebetiko το ρεμπέτικο
to re-be-ti-ko Greek rhythm & blues

i rengga η ρέγγα
i reng-ga smoked herrings, eaten plain or grilled with oil and lemon

to resi το ρέσσι
to re-si **pilafi** made with burghul and lamb (including the tail) and served at weddings (Cyprus)

i retsina η ρετσίνα
i re-tsi-na pine-resinated wine. Its clean sharp flavour and woody aftertaste is an acquired taste – so much so that it inspires a love-hate relationship in non-Greeks. Often served chilled. Usually pale gold in colour, but also comes in red and rosé varieties.

to revani το ρεβανί
to re-va-ni very sweet semolina sponge, flavoured with vanilla and orange juice and smothered with honey syrup

ta revithia τα ρεβίθια
ta re-vi-thi-a chickpeas

–alevrolemono –αλευρολέμονο
a-le-vro-le-mo-no chickpeas simmered in a rich lemony broth

–sto furno –στο φούρνο
sto fur-no casserole of chickpeas, onions, garlic and bay leaves. Favourite fasting food during Lent. On the Cyclades the dish is slow-baked in a clay pot with a dough-sealed lid.

–supa –σούπα
su-pa chickpea soup

i revithokeftedhes οι ρεβιθοκεφτέδες
i re-vi-tho-ke-fte-dhes rissoles of mashed chickpeas, potatoes, onion, parsley and black pepper

righanatos ριγανάτος
ri-gha-na-tos seasoned with oregano, salt and pepper

i righani η ρίγανη
i ri-gha-ni Greek oregano, famous for its pungency. The dried heads are used as well as the leaves.

i rizada η ριζάδα
i ri-za-da thick soup made with rice, stock and either shellfish or tiny game birds (Corfu)

to rizi το ρύζι
to ri-zi rice

–aghrio –άγριο
a-ghri-o wild rice

–akaterghasto –ακατέργαστο
a-ka-ter-gha-sto brown rice

–arborio –αρμπόριο
ar-bo-ri-o arborio rice

–bazmati –μπασμάτι
ba-zma-ti basmati rice

–kolodhes –κολλώδες
ko-lo-dhes glutinous rice

–kondo –κοντό
kon-do short-grain rice

–makri –μακρύ
ma-kri long-grain rice

to rizoghalo το ρυζόγαλο
to ri-zo-gha-lo creamy vanilla-flavoured rice pudding sprinkled with cinnamon and served cold

i robola η ρομπόλα
i ro-bo-la white grape variety (*see* Grape Varieties in Drinks)

to rodhakino το ροδάκινο
to ro-dha-ki-no peach

to rodhi το ρόδι
to ro-dhi pomegranate. The ruby-coloured seeds are offered to guests (eaten from a glass bowl with a silver spoon, type of **ghlika kutalyu**). Also used to flavour sweets, syrups, cakes and salads.

o rodhitis ο ροδίτης
o ro-dhi-tis white grape variety (*see* Grape Varieties in Drinks)

to rodhonero το ροδόνερο
to ro-dho-ne-ro fragrant rose flower water used to flavour cakes, pies and **ghlika kutalyu**

o rofos ο ροφός
o ro-fos grouper/blackfish

to rolo apo kima το ρολό από κιμά
to ro-lo a-po ki-ma baked mincemeat roll with hard-boiled eggs cuddled in the middle

to rumi το ρούμι
to ru-mi rum

S

to safran το σαφράν
to sa-fran saffron

to saghanaki το σαγανάκι
to sa-gha-na-ki shallow two-handled frying pan principally used for cooking **mezedhes**; method of frying food in this pan; popular name for **tiri saghanaki**

to salahi το σαλάχι
to sa-la-hi ray fish, skate

–salata –σαλάτα
sa-la-ta salad of chopped, boiled ray fish, onions and parsley dressed with **ladholemono**

to salami το σαλάμι
to sa-la-mi salami

i salata η σαλάτα
i sa-la-ta salad

–me kafteres piperyes –με καυτερές πιπεριές
me ka-fte-res pi-per-yes fiery capsicum dip made with slender red capsicum seared until soft, skinned and mashed with oil, lemon juice and cumin

i salatiera η σαλατιέρα
i sa-la-ti-e-ra salad bowl

ta salinggaria τα σαλιγκάρια
ta sa-ling-ga-ri-a snails. Collected fresh from the mountains and kept alive in thyme-filled crocks. Slightly chewy and gamey tasting. Always cooked in the shell and eaten with a fork. Once disparaged as 'poor man's food' snails are now considered a delicacy; also called **karavoli** and **hohlii**

–frikase –φρικασέ
fri-ka-se large snails sauteed in oil and stewed with zucchini, onions, fresh dill and finished with **avgholemono**

–me saltsa –με σάλτσα
me sal-tsa snails cooked with crushed tomatoes, tomato paste, onions and oregano

–simbetheryo –συμπεθεριό
sim-be-the-ryo 'in-laws', snails cooked with sliced eggplant, tomato pulp and **ksinohondros**

–sta karvuna —στα κάρβουνα
sta kar-vu-na live snails chargrilled and doused with **ladholemono** and bay leaves (Cyclades)

–stifadho —στιφάδο
sti-fa-dho snail ragout with bay leaves (Crete) *(see also* stifadho*)*

to salmi το σαλμί
to sal-mi method of casseroling with red wine, vegetables and herbs

i saltsa η σάλτσα
i sal-tsa sauce; generic term for tomato sauce

–apo zomo —από ζωμό
kreatos κρέατος
a-po zo-mo kre-a-tos gravy

–aspri —άσπρη
a-spri 'white sauce', bechamel sauce with the addition of eggs and sometimes grated hard cheese. Used mainly with **pastitsio** and **musaka**.

–aspri ksini —άσπρη ξινή
a-spri ksi-ni 'sharp white sauce', made with butter, flour, meat stock, eggs and lemon. Poured hot over **dolmadhes** and stuffed vegetables.

–avgholemono —αυγολέμονο
a-vgho-le-mo-no (see avgholemono*)*

–besamel —μπεσαμέλ
be-sa-mel bechamel sauce

–domata —ντομάτα
do-ma-ta tomato sauce. Includes bay leaves, finely chopped onion, and sometimes basil, parsley or garlic.

–domata me kima –ντομάτα με κιμά
do-ma-ta me ki-ma tomato and mince-meat sauce

–marinata —μαρινάτα
ma-ri-na-ta marinade

–mustardha —μουστάρδα
mu-star-dha mustard and garlic beaten with lemon juice

–tartar —ταρτάρ
tar-tar tartare sauce

i samos η Σάμος
i sa-mos rich golden dessert wine (Samos)

i sampanya η σαμπάνια
i sam-pa-nya champagne

to sanidhi ya το σανίδι για
temahizmo/ τεμαχισμό/
kopsimo κόψιμο
to sa-ni-dhi ya te-ma-hi-zmo/ko-psi-mo chopping board

ta sarakostiana τα σαρακοστιανά
ta sa-ra-ko-sti-a-na (see nistisima*)*

i sardheles οι σαρδέλες
i sar-dhe-les sardines

–pastes —παστές
pa-stes salted sardines

–sto furno —στο φούρνο
sto fur-no sardines baked with oil, lemon, garlic and oregano

o sarmas ο σαρμάς
o sar-mas pie-like offal dish made with **sikotarya** that's fried, simmered with rice and arranged on slices of lamb's fat in a roasting pan. Covered with lamb's caul and roasted. (Northern Greece)

to savatyano το σαββατιανό
to sa-va-tya-no white grape variety *(see* Grape Varieties in Drinks)

ta seftalya τα σεφταλιά
ta se-fta-lya rissoles of minced pork, onion, parsley, toasted rusk crumbs, black pepper, mint and cinnamon wrapped in sheep's caul and chargrilled (Cyprus)

to selino το σέλινο
to se-li-no celery

i selinoriza η σελινόριζα
i se-li-no-ri-za celeriac

–me avgholemono –με αυγολέμονο
me a-vgho-le-mo-no a creamy dish of celeriac braised in chicken stock and finished with egg and lemon sauce

–me prasa –με πράσα
me pra-sa braised celeriac wedges and leek strips thickened with **alevrolemono**

i selinosalata η σελινοσαλάτα
i se-li-no-sa-la-ta parsley salad *(see* the recipe)

to seri το σέρι
to se-ri sherry

to seskulo το σέσκουλο
se-sku-lo swiss chard, type of **horta**

–me kima –με κιμά
me ki-ma silverbeet sauteed with chopped onion in butter and cooked with minced lamb, rice, dill, lemon juice and salt

to seskulorizo το σεσκουλόρυζο
to se-sku-lo-ri-zo (see **spanakorizo**)

i sfakianopites οι σφακιανόπιτες
i sfa-ki-a-no-pi-tes cheese pies consisting of balls of **mizithra** wrapped in dough and rolled flat, then fried and served with a dollop of honey

i sfiridha η σφυρίδα
i sfi-ri-dha member of grouper family

to sfunggato το σφουγγάτο
to sfung-ga-to Spanish-style omelette made with more vegetables than eggs. Can include zucchini, eggplant, cauliflower, artichoke, okra and asparagus. Can be fried or baked; baked mincemeat and zucchini omelette. (Rhodes)

i shara η σχάρα
i sha-ra grill

sti shara στη σχάρα
sti sha-ra method of chargrilling meat and fish

sighovrazo σιγοβράζω
si-gho-vra-zo simmer/poach

to siko τα σύκο
to si-ko fig

apostolyatiko –αποστολιάτικο
a-po-sto-lya-ti-ko early green fig

–ghliko –γλυκό
ghli-ko green fig preserve, type of **ghlika kutalyu**

–sto furno –στο φούρνο
sto fur-no figs baked in a syrup of honey, vanilla, orange juice and orange flower water, served with **mizithra**. Sometimes sweet wine is substituted for orange juice.

i sikopita η συκόπιτα
i si-ko-pi-ta fig cake (Corfu)

to sikopsomo το συκόψωμο
to si-ko-pso-mo heavy aromatic fig cake. Dried green figs minced and mixed

with **ouzo**, must and white pepper, shaped into balls, flattened, dried and wrapped in vine leaves tied with raffia.

i sikotarya η συκωταριά
i si-ko-tar-ya mix of lamb's innards: liver, heart, stomach and pancreas

to sikoti το συκώτι
to si-ko-ti liver

–krasata –κρασάτα
kra-sa-ta chopped liver marinated in red wine, lightly coated in flour and sauteed in oil, oregano (or rosemary) and the wine marinade

–ladhorighani –λαδορίγανη
la-dho-ri-gha-ni grilled liver with oil, lemon and oregano

–marinata –μαρινάτα
ma-ri-na-ta thinly sliced livers fried and finished with vinegar, white wine and rosemary

–me kremidhakya –με κρεμμυδάκια
me kre-mi-dha-kya livers sliced and fried with spring onions and whole cloves and finished in a reduced sauce of white wine and tomato juice

i simighdhali η σιμιγδάλι
i si-mi-ghdha-li semolina

i sinaghridha η συναγρίδα
i si-na-ghri-dha dentex; sparid fish

to sindiritiko το συντηρητικό
to sin-di-ri-ti-ko preservative

to sinolo το σύνολο
to si-no-lo total (of bill)

to sirma ya το σύρμα για
htipima avgon χτύπημα αυγών
to sir-ma ya hti-pi-ma a-vgon whisk

to siropi το σιρόπι
to si-ro-pi syrup

to sisameleo το σησαμέλαιο
to si-sa-me-le-o sesame oil

to sistatiko το συστατικό
to si-sta-ti-ko ingredient

to sitari το σιτάρι
to si-ta-ri wheat

i skaltsotseta η σκαλτσοτσέτα
i skal-tso-tse-ta paper-thin slices of fillet steak spread with a mixture of grated **kefalotiri**, feta, chopped tomatoes,

parsley, crushed garlic and rusk crumbs, then rolled, skewered with toothpicks and simmered in oil, water and tomatoes

to sketo alevri το σκέτο αλεύρι
to ske-to a-le-vri plain flour

i skordhalya η σκορδαλιά
i skor-dha-lya garlic sauce
(see the recipe)

to skordho το σκόρδο
to skor-dho garlic

–**stumbi** –στούμπι
stu-mbi vinegar bottled with a garlic bulb. It is used for dressing vegetable dishes and salads. (Ionian Islands)

–**tsigharista** –τσιγαριστά
tsi-gha-ri-sta fried whole garlic bulbs; peeled and sliced garlic cloves fried and simmered in white wine, tomato paste, salt and pepper (Ithaca)

i skorpina η σκορπίνα
i skor-pi-na scorpion fish

to skumbri το σκουμπρί
to sku-mbri mackerel; also called **kolios**

–**se klimatofila** –σε κληματόφυλλα
se kli-ma-to-fi-la mackerel in vine leaves
(see the recipe)

ta snaks τα σνακς
ta snaks snacks (see also **mezedhakya**)

to snitsel το σνίτσελ
to sni-tsel schnitzel

i sodha η σόδα
i so-dha soda water

to sofrito το σοφρίτο
to so-fri-to fried veal slices braised in a sauce of crushed garlic, wine vinegar, parsley, mint and brandy. Sometimes fried potatoes are added. (Corfu)

i sokolata η σοκολάτα
i so-ko-la-ta chocolate

–**ghala** –γάλα
gha-la hot chocolate

o solomos ο σολομός
o so-lo-mos salmon

to souvlaki το σουβλάκι
to su-vla-ki (see suvlaki)

i spala η σπάλα
i spa-la shoulder of meat

–**mosharisia** –μοσχαρίσια
mo-sha-ri-si-a silverside

to spanaki το σπανάκι
to spa-na-ki spinach

i spanakopita η σπανακόπιτα
i spa-na-ko-pi-ta spinach filo pie, can include feta and/or **kefalotiri**, eggs and herbs

to spanakorizo το σπανακόρυζο
to spa-na-ko-ri-zo sauteed spinach, rice, spring onions and dill simmered in water until liquid is absorbed. Served with black pepper and lemon juice. Can be prepared with leeks, silverbeet and cabbage.

ta sparaggia τα σπαράγγια
ta spa-rang-gi-a asparagus

to spedzofai το σπετζοφάι
to spe-dzo-fa-i sliced pork sausages stewed with sweet green peppers, eggplant, tomatoes and oregano

i splina η σπλήνα
i spli-na spleen

–**yemisti** –γεμιστή
ye-mi-sti calf's spleen stuffed with chopped sauteed liver, onion, garlic and herbs then roasted

ta splinandera τα σπληνάντερα
ta spli-nan-de-ra spit-roast sausage made from sheep's or goat's intestine stuffed with sliced spleen and garlic (and sometimes chopped **sikotarya**)

o sporos staryu ο σπόρος σταριού
o spo-ros star-yu wheat germ

i stafidhes οι σταφίδες
i sta-fi-dhes raisins/currants

i stafidholyes οι σταφιδολιές
i sta-fi-dho-lyes type of olive that is harvested then sundried until wrinkled. Then they are lightly salted and packed, or immersed in oil.

ta stafidota τα σταφιδωτά
ta sta-fi-do-ta oval shortbread biscuits with chewy raisin centres

ta stafilia τα σταφύλια
ta sta-fi-li-a grapes

i staka οι στάκα
i sta-ka creamy, tasty butter made fresh goat's or sheep's milk. Used to flavour pies, **yemista** and **pilafi**.

–me avgha –με αυγά
me a-vgha omelette-type dish consisting of **staka** beaten with eggs (Crete)

i stamna η στάμνα
i sta-mna cooking pot

sti stamna στη στάμνα
sti sta-mna old-fashioned method of cooking meat, potatoes and herbs in an amphora-like pot sealed with wet clay and baked in charcoal embers

to stifadho το στιφάδο
to sti-fa-dho meat, game or seafood cooked in a sauce of tomatoes, tomato puree, tomato paste, vinegar, red wine, spices and a signature smothering of whole tiny onions. Cooked until the sauce is thick and jammy and the meat succulent. More ragout than stew, more religious than culinary experience. (see also **kuneli stifadho**, **laghos stifadho**, **htapodhi stifadho**, **moshari stifadho** and **salinggaria stifadho**)

to stithos το στήθος
to sti-thos breast

ta straghalya τα στραγάλια
ta stra-gha-lya roasted chickpeas for snacking

i strapatsadha η στραπατσάδα
i stra-pa-tsa-dha see **avgha strapatsadha**

ta stridhia τα στρείδια
ta stri-dhi-a oysters

ta sudzukakya τα σουτζουκάκια
ta su-dzu-ka-kya zeppelin-shaped, cumin-spiked rissoles of minced lamb, veal or pork braised in a very spicy tomato gravy

to sudzuki το σουτζούκι
to su-dzu-ki chewy sweets which look like short knobbly lengths of purple bamboo. Made by dipping strings of almonds into hot thick **petimezi** syrup (a bit like making candles) and hanging them to dry in the sun.

to sughli το σούγλι
to su-ghli salted and sun-dried baby bogue fish coated in a thin batter and fried (Cyclades)

i supa η σούπα
i su-pa soup

–ksidhati –σούπα ξιδάτη
ksi-dha-ti sour soup of lentils, spring onions, garlic, parsley and vinegar

–me tsuknidhes –με τσουκνίδες
me tsu-kni-dhes electric-green soup of stinging nettles and diced potatoes cooked in chicken stock and thickened with milk

i supyes οι σουπιές
oi su-pyes cuttlefish

–krasates –κρασάτες
kra-sa-tes cuttlefish cooked in wine

–me saltsa melanis –με σάλτσα μελάνης
me sal-tsa me-la-nis cuttlefish cooked in a rich sauce made from its own black ink and wine (Crete)

–me spanaki –με σπανάκι
me spa-na-ki cuttlefish cooked with spinach, onions, dill and mint. Local varieties of **horta** can also be used instead of spinach. Sometimes the ink sac is removed, or pierced and emptied into the pan which results in a dark sauce with a strong flavour.

to susami το σουσάμι
to su-sa-mi sesame seed

i suvla η σούβλα
i su-vla spit/skewer; method of chargrilling skewered meat or fish

sti suvla στη σούβλα
sti su-vla spit-roasted

to suvladzidhiko το σουβλατζίδικο
to su-vla-dzi-dhi-ko shop which sells take-away **suvlaki** on wooden skewers or wrapped in **pita** cones with onions, tomatoes and yoghurt sauce or **tzadziki**

to suvlaki το σουβλάκι
to su-vla-ki skewer; tender chunks of seasoned or marinated meat (or fish) skewered and chargrilled

–me pita –με πίτα
me pi-ta suvlaki with pita

T

to tahini   το ταχίνι
to ta-hi-ni paste using sesame seeds

i   tahinosupa   η ταχινόσουπα
i ta-hi-no-su-pa creamy lemony soup made from sesame paste – a favourite during Lent

to talaturi   το ταλαττούρι
to ta-la-tu-ri **tzadziki** flavoured with mint (Cyprus)

to tapsi   το ταψί
to ta-psi large round aluminium pan used for baking

to taraksako   το ταράξακο
to ta-ra-ksa-ko dandelion

o taramas   ο ταραμάς
o ta-ra-mas salted pressed roe of the grey mullet or cod

i taramosalata   η ταραμοσαλάτα
i ta-ra-mo-sa-la-ta thick pink creamy puree of **taramas**, bread crumbs, oil and lemon juice. Sometimes mashed potato is substituted for breadcrumbs – a practice frowned upon by experts. Extremely rich and addictive.

i tarta   η τάρτα
i tar-ta tart

o tavas   ο ταβάς
o ta-vas casserole of beef or lamb, fried onions, diced tomatoes, oil, vinegar, cinnamon, salt and pepper

i taverna   η ταβέρνα
i ta-ver-na taverna

i tekila   η τεκίλα
i te-ki-la tequila

o telemes   ο τελεμές
o te-le-mes heavily salted feta-style cheese

ta thalasina   τα θαλασσινά
ta tha-la-si-na seafood

–tu eyeu   –του Αιγαίου
tu e-ye-u paella-style rice dish cooked with prawns, mussels, squid, cuttlefish and baby octopus (Hydra)

to thimari   το θυμάρι
to thi-ma-ri thyme

i thrumbes   οι θρούμπες
i thru-mbes ripe black olives

to thrumbi   το θρούμπι
to thru-mbi savoury

to tighani   το τηγάνι
to ti-gha-ni frying pan

i tighanites   οι τηγανίτες
i ti-gha-ni-tes pancakes/fritters

tighanitos   τηγανητός
ti-gha-ni-tos fried

tighanizo   τηγανίζω
ti-gha-ni-zo fry

–me ligho ladhi   –με λίγο λάδι
me li-gho la-dhi shallow fry

–me poli ladhi   –με πολύ λάδι
me po-li la-dhi deep fry

to tighanopsomo   το τηγανόψωμο
to ti-gha-no-pso-mo fried tomato and spring onion pan bread (Santorini)

to tilio   το τίλιο
to ti-li-o infusion of lime leaves

i timi   η τιμή
i ti-mi price

to tiri   το τυρί
to ti-ri cheese

–ble   –μπλε
ble blue cheese

–imiskliro   –ημίσκληρο
i-mi-skli-ro semi-firm cheese

–katsikisio   –κατσικίσιο
ka-tsi-ki-si-o goat's cheese

–kremodhes   –κρεμώδες
kre-mo-dhes cream cheese

–malaki mizithra –μαλακή μυζήθρα
ma-la-ki mi-zi-thra cottage cheese

–malako   –μαλακό
ma-la-ko soft cheese

–saghanaki   –σαγανάκι
sa-gha-na-ki sharp, hard cheese cut into flat wedges or squares and fried until crispy on the outside and soft in the centre – served with a squeeze of lemon juice. Cheeses with high melting points (**kefaloghraviera**, **halumi** and **kefalotiri**) are used for this dish.

–skliro   –σκληρό
skli-ro hard cheese

i tirokafteri η τυροκαυτερή
i ti-ro-ka-fte-ri puree of feta beaten
with oil and lemon juice and spiced
with oregano and red **piperyes kafteres**

to tiropighma το τυρόπηγμα
to ti-ro-pigh-ma curd

i tiropita η τυρόπιτα
i ti-ro-pi-ta cheese pies, the classic mixture is feta and **kefalotiri** bound with
egg and parsley, wrapped in flaky filo
pastry and baked

to tiropolio το τυροπωλείο
to ti-ro-po-li-o cheese shop

i tirosalata η τυροσαλάτα
i ti-ro-sa-la-ta (*see* **tirokafteri**)

i tirovolya η τυροβολιά
i ti-ro-vo-lya (*see* Cheese in Staples
& Specialities)

ti soras της ώρας
ti-so-ras dishes cooked to order, such as
steaks or chops

to kapnisto το καπνιστό
vodhino kreas βοδινό κρέας
to ka-pni-sto vo-dhi-no kre-as pastrami

to tsureki το τσουρέκι
to tsu-re-ki braided Easter yeast bread
spiced with lemon rind, allspice and
mahlepi and sprinkled with almonds
and crushed **masticha**. During baking
Avgha pashalina are always nestled
into the crust.

to tonik το τόνικ
to to-nik tonic water

o tonos ο τόνος
o to-nos tuna

–salata –σαλάτα
sa-la-ta tuna salad

topikos τοπικός
to-pi-kos local

to tost το τοστ
to tost toasted sandwich

o trahanas ο τραχανάς
o tra-ha-nas granulated pasta used as a
base for winter soups. Traditionally
made from wheat boiled with sour
milk, dried and stored in sacks. Now
produced commercially with semolina

and sour milk. Often prepared porridge style with butter and water for
early morning breakfasts and late night
suppers. (*see also* **trahanosupa**)

i trahanosupa η τραχανόσουπα
i tra-ha-no-su-pa thick gruel of **trahanas** cooked in chicken broth with
butter, lemon juice and perhaps a tum-
bler of red wine

to trapezi το τραπέζι
to tra-pe-zi table

to trapezomandilo το τραπεζόμαντιλο
to tra-pe-zo-man-di-lo tablecloth

to triandafilo το τριαντάφυλλο
ghliko γλυκό
to tri-an-da-fi-lo ghli-ko delicate soft
jam made from dark red rose petals

o triftis ο τρίφτης
o tri-ftis grater

to trighoni το τρυγόνι
to tri-gho-ni turtle dove

trivo τρίβω
tri-vo grate

to tsai το τσάι
to tsa-i tea

–hamomilo –χαμόμηλο
ha-mo-mi-lo chamomile tea

–horis kafeini –χωρίς καφεΐνη
ho-ris ka-fe-i-ni decaffeinated tea

–me ghala –με γάλα
me gha-la tea with milk

–me lemoni –με λεμόνι
me le-mo-ni tea with lemon

–menta –μέντα
men-ta peppermint tea

–prasino –πράσινο
pra-si-no green tea

–tu vunu –του βουνού
tu vu-nu tea made from field and
mountain herbs often sweetened with
honey. Favourites are **dhiktamo**, lime,
sage, thyme and aniseed.

to tsaiv το τσάιβ
to tsa-iv chive

tsighari τσιγάρι
tsi-gha-ri (*see* **horta tsighari**)

tsigharistos τσιγαριστός
tsi-gha-ri-stos saute

i tsihla   η τσίχλα
i tsi-hla thrush; chewing gum

i tsikudya   η τσικουδιά
i tsi-ku-dya (see **raki**)

i tsimbidha   η τσιμπίδα
i tsi-mbi-dha tongs

ta tsips   τα τσιπς
ta tsips potato chips

i tsipura   η τσιπούρα
i tsi-pu-ra gilt head bream, snapper

to tsipuro   το τσίπουρο
to tsi-pu-ro (see **raki**)

o tsiros   ο τσίρος
o tsi-ros small dried mackerel, generally served chargrilled with oil and vinegar.

o tsohos   ο τσόχος
o tso-hos milk thistle, mild sweet-tasting green used in warm salads, pies and stews, type of **horta**

i tsuknidhes   οι τσουκνίδες
i tsu-kni-dhes stinging nettles, type of **horta**. Used in soups and warm salads, and delicious sauteed. Gloves are worn while collecting them but they lose their sting when cooked.

to tulumotiri   το τουλουμοτύρι
to tu-lu-mo-ti-ri (see **Cheese in Staples & Specialities**)

to tursi   το τουρσί
to tur-si pickle; pickled

i turta   η τούρτα
i tur-ta cake/tart/gateau

to tzatziki   το τζατζίκι
to dza-dzi-ki refreshing puree of grated cucumber, yoghurt and garlic (see also **talaturi**)

U

to uiski   το ουίσκυ
to u-i-ski whisky

i ura vodyu   η ουρά βοδιού
i u-ra vo-dyu oxtail

V

o vakalaos   ο βακαλάος
o va-ka-la-os (see **bakalyaros**)

i vanilia   η βανίλια
i va-ni-li-a vanilla

o vasilikos   ο βασιλικός
o va-si-li-kos Greek basil, used rarely in cooking. Main role is that of decorative 'watch-dog' herb flourishing in pots on doorsteps and window sills to safeguard against the 'evil eye'.

i vasilopita   η βασιλόπιτα
i va-si-lo-pi-ta New Year loaf decorated with white almonds in the numerals of the incoming year. Whoever finds the coin in the bread gets lucky for the next year. Named after the patron saint of New Year, St Basil.

to vatomuro   το βατόμουρο
to va-to-mu-ro blackberry/raspberry

ta vatrahopodhara   τα βατραχοπόδαρα
tighanita   τηγανητά
ta va-tra-ho-po-dha-ra ti-gha-ni-ta fried frog's legs (Western Greece)

o vatrahos   ο βάτραχος
o va-tra-hos frog

ta verikoka   τα βερίκοκα
ta ve-ri-ko-ka apricots

i visinadha   η βυσσινάδα
i vi-si-na-dha syrup of morello cherries. Mixed with cold water for summertime cordials.

to visino   το βύσσινο
to vi-si-no morello, sour black cherry

–ghliko   –γλυκό
ghli-ko morello cherry preserve, type of **ghlika kutalyu**

to vitam   το βιτάμ
to vi-tam a brand of olive oil margarine

to vlito   το βλίτο
to vli-to 'love lies bleeding', amaranth, a type of **horta**. A sweet nutty flavour and soft texture make it popular for warm salads. Grows on mountain slopes throughout late summer and early autumn. When in flower sprouts gigantic claret-red feathery stalks.

to vodhino   το βοδινό
to vo-dhi-no beef

–kapama   –καπαμά
ka-pa-ma beef stew with tomatoes, onions, garlic, red wine, cinnamon and cloves. Often served with spaghetti or fried potatoes.

—me lahanika   —με λαχανικά
me la-ha-ni-ka beef cut into walnut-sized pieces and braised with onions, carrots, potatoes, celery and leeks

i volvi   οι βολβοί
i vol-vi bulbs of the grape hyacinth

—vrasti   —βραστοί
vra-sti boiled and dressed with dill vinaigrette, and often accompanied by **skordhalya**

ta votana   τα βότανα
ta vo-ta-na herbs

i votka   η βότκα
i vot-ka vodka

to vradhino   το βραδινό
to vra-dhi-no dinner

vrastos/vrazmenos   βραστός/
                             βρασμένος
vra-stos/vra-zme-nos boiled

vrazo   βράζω
vra-zo boil

i vruva   η βρούβα
i vru-va charlock, field green with sharp peppery taste, type of **horta**

to vutiro   το βούτυρο
to vu-ti-ro butter

to vutirogalo   το βουτυρόγαλο
to vu-ti-ro-ga-lo buttermilk

Y

yahni   γιαχνί
ya-hni method of stewing food with tomatoes and onions

i yalisteres   οι γυαλιστερές
i ya-li-ste-res shellfish eaten alive with a squeeze of lemon juice (Dodecanese Islands)

to yaurti   το γιαούρτι
to ya-ur-ti yoghurt. Greek yoghurt is thick and heavy with a tangy bite. Can be made from sheep's, goat's or cow's milk. Used for making sweets, pureed salads and sauces. In Cyprus and Northern Greece it is often served plain with **pilafi** and fried vegetables.

—ayeladhos   —αγελάδος
a-ye-la-dhos cow's milk yoghurt

—fruton   —φρούτων
fru-ton fruit yoghurt

—me meli   —με μέλι
me me-li honey-topped yoghurt, popular breakfast food for tourists

—provio   —πρόβειο
pro-vi-o made from sheep's milk

i yaurtoghlu   η γιαουρτογλού
i ya-ur-to-ghlu pita cooked with finely sliced grilled meat, topped with a yoghurt sauce

i yaurtopita   η γιαουρτόπιτα
ya-ur-to-pi-ta light moist cake made with yoghurt, sugar, lemon rind and lots of eggs

—tiz dhramas   της Δράμας
tiz-dhra-mas yoghurt pie with vine leaves (*see* the recipe)

i yefsi   η γεύση
i yef-si flavour

ta yemista   τα γεμιστά
ta ye-mi-sta stuffed vegetables. You can find capsicums, tomatoes, zucchini, eggplant, artichokes, potatoes or onions stuffed with an aromatic filling of rice, fresh tomato pulp, finely chopped onion, grated hard cheese and herbs such as dill, mint and parsley. Sometimes the stuffing also includes mincemeat.

yemistos   γεμιστός
ye-mi-stos method of stuffing meat, fish or vegetables prior to cooking

to yemizma   το γέμισμα
to ye-mi-zma stuffing

to yevma   το γεύμα
to yev-ma meal

i yidha vrasti   η γίδα βραστή
i yi-dha vra-sti aromatic/fragrant dish of boiled goat

i yighandes   οι γίγαντες
i yi-ghan-des 'giants', enormous creamy coloured haricot beans

o yiros   ο γύρος
o yi-ros 'to spin', Greek version of doner kebab. Lengths of seasoned lamb packed onto a spit and rotisseried upright. Carved for meat platters or served in pita bread with tomatoes, onions and **tzadziki**.

i yorti η γιορτή
i yor-ti festive porridge consisting of small pieces of pork and goat boiled with corn and topped with melted butter, cinnamon and black pepper (Samos)

ta yuvarlakya τα γιουβαρλάκια
ta yu-var-la-kya egg-shaped rissoles of minced beef or lamb, rice, onion and parsley simmered in a light stock and finished with egg and lemon sauce

to yuvetsi το γιουβέτσι
to yu-ve-tsi casserole of meat, fish or other seafood with crushed tomatoes and **kritharaki**. Traditionally baked in a clay pot from which the dish takes its name.

–me thalasina –με θαλασσινά
me tha-la-si-na casserole of mussels, prawns, squid, clams, **kritharaki**, tomatoes, tomato paste, onions and chicken stock (Ionian Islands)

i yuzlemedhes οι γιουσλεμέδες
oi yuz-le-me-dhes golden crescent-shaped pies filled with a mixture of beaten eggs and **kefalotiri**, deep fried and served hot with a sprinkling of grated cheese (Lesvos)

Z

i zahari η ζάχαρη
i za-ha-ri sugar

–ahni –άχνη
a-hni icing/caster sugar

–aromatiki –αρωματική
skurohromi σκουρόχρωμη
a-ro-ma-ti-ki sku-ro-hro-mi demerara sugar

–finikozahari –φοινικοζάχαρη
fi-ni-ko-za-ha-ri palm sugar

–skurohromi –σκουρόχρωμη
sku-ro-hro-mi brown sugar

to zaharoplastio το ζαχαροπλαστείο
to za-ha-ro-pla-sti-o patisserie or sweet shop

ta zaharopulya τα ζαχαροπούλια
ta za-ha-ro-pu-lya marzipan sweets in the shape of birds, flowers, fruits and pyramids (Lesvos)

to zaharoto το ζαχαρωτό
me amighdhala με αμύγδαλα
to za-ha-ro-to me a-mi-ghdha-la marzipan

to zambon το ζαμπόν
to zam-bon ham

i zarghana η ζαργάνα
i zar-gha-na garfish

i zelatini η ζελατίνη
i ze-la-ti-ni gelatine

to zele το ζελέ
to ze-le jelly

i zigharya η ζυγαριά
i zi-ghar-ya scales

ta zimarika τα ζυμαρικά
ta zi-ma-ri-ka pasta

i zimi η ζύμη
i zi-mi pastry

–me yaurti –με γιαούρτι
me ya-ur-ti baked pasta dish consisting of homemade macaroni, strained yoghurt and onions (Kos)

i zmerna η σμέρνα
i zmer-na moray eel

o zomos ο ζωμός
o zo-mos broth

to zumi το ζουμί
to zu-mi stock

o zumos vodhinu ο ζουμός βοδινού
o zu-mos vo-dhi-nu beef stock

i zvinggi οι σβίγγοι
i zving-gi deep-fried puffy sweet fritters served with honey, cinnamon and cognac syrup

Recommended Reading

Habegger, O'Reilly & Alexander *Travelers' Tales Greece* Traveler's Tales (2002)

Andrew Dalby *Siren Feasts* Routledge (1997)

Diana Louise & June Marinos *Prospero's Kitchen* M. Evans and Company (1995)

Nikos and Maria Psilakis *Olive Oil* Karmanor

Website

Matt Barrett's website: **http://www.greecetravel.com**

The Lonely Planet Story

Lonely Planet published its first book in 1973 in response to the numerous 'How did you do it?' questions Maureen and Tony Wheeler were asked after driving, bussing, hitching, sailing and railing their way from England to Australia. Written at a kitchen table and hand collated, trimmed and stapled, Across Asia on the Cheap became an instant local bestseller.

Eighteen months in South-East Asia resulted in their second guide, South-East Asia on a Shoestring, which they put together in a backstreet Chinese hotel in Singapore in 1975. The 'yellow bible', as it quickly became known to backpackers around the world, soon became the guide to the region. It has sold well over ¾ million copies and is now in its 10th edition, still retaining its familiar yellow cover.

Today there are over 400 titles, including travel guides, walking guides, language kits & phrasebooks, travel atlases & maps, diving guides, restaurant guides, first time travel guides, condensed guides, illustrated pictorials and travel literature. The company is the largest independent travel publisher in the world.

The emphasis continues to be on travel for independent travellers. Tony and Maureen still travel for several months of each year and play an active part in the writing, updating and quality control of Lonely Planet's guides.

They have been joined by over 120 authors and over 400 staff at our offices in Melbourne (Australia), Oakland (USA), London (UK) and Paris (France). Travellers themselves also make a valuable contribution to the guides through the feedback we receive in thousands of letters each year and on our web site.

The people at Lonely Planet strongly believe that travellers can make a positive contribution to the countries they visit, both through their appreciation of the countries' culture, wildlife and natural features, and through the money they spend. In addition, the company makes a direct contribution to the countries and regions it covers. Since 1986 a percentage of the income from each book has been donated to ventures such as famine relief in Africa; aid projects in India; agricultural projects in Central America; Greenpeace's efforts to halt French nuclear testing in the Pacific.

Lonely Planet Offices

Australia
90 Maribyrnong Street Footscray, Victoria, 3011
☎ 03 8379 8000
fax 03 8379 8111
email: talk2us@lonelyplanet.com.au

USA
150 Linden St, Oakland, CA 94607
☎ 510 893 8555 TOLL FREE: 800 275 8555
fax 510 893 8572
email: info@lonelyplanet.com

UK
10a Spring Place, London NW5 3BH
☎ 020 7428 4800
fax 020 7428 4828
email: go@lonelyplanet.co.uk

France
1 rue du Dahomey, 75011 Paris
☎ 01 55 25 33 00
fax 01 55 25 33 01
email: bip@lonelyplanet.fr